Immigration Consequences
of a Criminal Conviction in North Carolina

2017

Sejal Zota
John Rubin

UNC | SCHOOL OF GOVERNMENT

This manual is part of the North Carolina Indigent Defense Manual Series. Production of the series is made possible by funding from the North Carolina Office of Indigent Defense Services. John Rubin is series editor.

The School of Government at the University of North Carolina at Chapel Hill works to improve the lives of North Carolinians by engaging in practical scholarship that helps public officials and citizens understand and improve state and local government. Established in 1931 as the Institute of Government, the School provides educational, advisory, and research services for state and local governments. The School of Government is also home to a nationally ranked Master of Public Administration program, the North Carolina Judicial College, and specialized centers focused on community and economic development, information technology, and environmental finance.

As the largest university-based local government training, advisory, and research organization in the United States, the School of Government offers up to 200 courses, webinars, and specialized conferences for more than 12,000 public officials each year. In addition, faculty members annually publish approximately 50 books, manuals, reports, articles, bulletins, and other print and online content related to state and local government. The School also produces the *Daily Bulletin Online* each day the General Assembly is in session, reporting on activities for members of the legislature and others who need to follow the course of legislation.

Operating support for the School of Government's programs and activities comes from many sources, including state appropriations, local government membership dues, private contributions, publication sales, course fees, and service contracts.

Visit sog.unc.edu or call 919.966.5381 for more information on the School's courses, publications, programs, and services.

© 2017
School of Government
The University of North Carolina at Chapel Hill

First edition 2007. Second edition 2017.

Printed in the United States of America

21 20 19 18 17   1 2 3 4 5

ISBN 978-1-56011-912-8

Contents

Preface   **v**

About the Series and Authors   **vi**

Chapter 1
Obligations of Defense Counsel   **1-1**

1.1	Purpose of Manual	1-2
1.2	Obligations of Defense Counsel	1-2
1.3	How to Meet Your Obligations	1-7
1.4	Important Terminology Used in this Manual	1-8

Chapter 2
Determining Your Client's Citizenship and Immigration Status   **2-1**

2.1	Determining Whether Your Client is a U.S. Citizen	2-2
2.2	Determining Your Noncitizen Client's Particular Immigration Status	2-4
2.3	Additional Interview Objectives for a Noncitizen Client	2-8
2.4	Sample Questions to Identify Client's Immigration Status and Eligibility for Relief	2-10
	Appendix 2-1: Sample Images of Immigration Documents	2-12
	Appendix 2-2: Sample Intake Form	2-18

Chapter 3
Criminal Grounds of Removal and Other Immigration Consequences   **3-1**

3.1	Removal Defined	3-2
3.2	Deportability vs. Inadmissibility	3-2
3.3	Determining Whether a State Offense Triggers Removal	3-5
3.4	Crime-Related Grounds of Deportability	3-8
3.5	Crime-Related Grounds of Inadmissibility	3-23
3.6	Criminal Bars to Naturalization	3-26
3.7	Criminal Bars to Deferred Action for Childhood Arrivals	3-27

Chapter 4
Conviction and Sentence for Immigration Purposes   **4-1**

4.1	Conviction for Immigration Purposes	4-2
4.2	Effect of North Carolina Dispositions	4-3
4.3	Sentence to a Term of Imprisonment	4-8

Each chapter contains a detailed table of contents.

Chapter 5
Determining Possible Immigration Consequences Based on Your Client's Immigration Status ... 5-1
5.1 Lawful Permanent Resident ... 5-2
5.2 Refugee (who has not yet obtained LPR status) ... 5-6
5.3 Person Granted Asylum (who has not yet obtained LPR status) ... 5-9
5.4 Nonimmigrant Visa Holder ... 5-11
5.5 Noncitizens with Temporary Protected Status ... 5-14
5.6 Noncitizens without Immigration Status ... 5-14
5.7 Summary of Priorities in Representing Noncitizen Clients by Status ... 5-20

Chapter 6
Options for Minimizing Adverse Immigration Consequences ... 6-1
6.1 General Rules ... 6-2
6.2 Cases Involving Aggravated Felonies ... 6-4
6.3 Cases Involving Drugs ... 6-8
6.4 Cases Involving Crimes Involving Moral Turpitude ... 6-12
6.5 Cases Involving Firearms ... 6-13
6.6 Cases Involving Domestic Violence ... 6-15
6.7 Cases Involving Child Abuse ... 6-16

Chapter 7
Procedures Related to Removal ... 7-1
7.1 Summary of Procedures Related to Removal ... 7-1
7.2 Identification of In-Custody Persons Subject to Removal ... 7-2
7.3 Immigration Detainer ... 7-3
7.4 What Happens after Your Client is Released into the Custody of ICE ... 7-5

Chapter 8
State Post-Conviction Relief ... 8-1
8.1 Authority for State Post-Conviction Relief ... 8-1
8.2 Challenges under *Padilla v. Kentucky* ... 8-2
8.3 Judge's Failure to Provide Immigration Advisement ... 8-5
8.4 Other Errors ... 8-6
8.5 Immigration Effect of Motion for Appropriate Relief ... 8-7

Appendix A
Selected Immigration Consequences of North Carolina Offenses ... A-1

Appendix B
Relevant Immigration Decisions ... B-1

Preface

We are excited to issue the 2017 edition of our manual, specific to North Carolina law and practice, on the immigration consequences of convictions in North Carolina. Our goal has been to develop a clear, usable resource for attorneys representing noncitizen defendants in criminal cases. We also hope the manual will be a useful resource for others who need to understand this challenging area of law.

It is critical for criminal defense attorneys to have an understanding of this area when representing noncitizen clients. For years, national practice standards have recognized criminal defense counsel's role in advising noncitizen defendants about the immigration consequences of a criminal conviction. Now such advice is constitutionally required by the U.S. Supreme Court's landmark decision in *Padilla v. Kentucky*, 559 U.S. 356 (2010). A failure to give competent advice to clients about the immigration consequences of a criminal conviction may constitute ineffective assistance of counsel. This manual is intended to help criminal defense counsel navigate this highly technical area of law and live up to their constitutional obligation.

This manual would not have been possible without the support and assistance of several people. Thanks go to the members of the Advisory Committee for the first edition of this manual, who volunteered their time to review each chapter and offered their insights into the intersection of immigration and criminal law. Thanks must also go to Dan Kesselbrenner of the National Immigration Project of the National Lawyers Guild for supporting this project and for sharing his vast knowledge of this area time and time again. We also want to acknowledge Manny Vargas and the Immigrant Defense Project of the New York State Defenders Association for their immigration consequences manual, *Representing Immigrant Defendants in New York*, which served as a guide for us in developing this manual.

Special recognition goes to the Office of Indigent Defense Services, the School of Government, and the School's Indigent Defense Education Group for their support of this manual. Their collaboration on this and other education projects has enhanced the resources available to indigent defense attorneys and has improved the service that indigent defenders are able to provide to their clients. Thanks also go to Caitlin Little for her assistance in editing the citations and other information in the manual.

Finally, special thanks go to Brian Stull, who early on encouraged and supported the idea of developing this manual.

Comments and suggestions are welcome. They may be sent to Sejal Zota at sejal@nipnlg.org or John Rubin at rubin@sog.unc.edu.

Sejal Zota
John Rubin
September 2017

About the North Carolina Indigent Defense Manual Series

The North Carolina Indigent Defense Manual Series is a collection of reference manuals addressing law and practice in areas in which indigent defendants and respondents are entitled to the representation of counsel at state expense. The series was created to address the need for comprehensive reference materials for public defenders and appointed counsel, who devote their time, skill, and effort to representing poor people. In addition to assisting indigent defenders with their responsibilities, the manuals also may be useful to others who work in the court system and who need a reference source on the law. In keeping with the School of Government's commitment to practical scholarship, the manuals are written by authors with subject-matter expertise in their respective fields, experience in developing effective educational materials, and knowledge of how things work in practice. The editor of the series is John Rubin, a member of the School of Government faculty who specializes in indigent defense education. Other manuals in the series can be found on our Indigent Defense Manual Series website. Production of the series is made possible by funding from the North Carolina Office of Indigent Defense Services, which is responsible for overseeing and enhancing the provision of indigent defense representation in North Carolina.

About the Authors of Immigration Consequences of a Criminal Conviction in North Carolina (2017 Edition)

Sejal Zota is the legal director of the National Immigration Project of the National Lawyers Guild. There, she engages in nationwide litigation, provides training and technical assistance on a broad range of immigration issues, and authors practice advisories and reference materials. She is based in Durham, North Carolina. Previously, she was a public defender with the Bronx Defenders, a teaching fellow at the Immigrant Rights Clinic of the New York University (NYU) School of Law, and an immigration law specialist at the School of Government. She was the lead author on the first edition of this manual. She earned a B.A. in economics and public policy studies from Duke University and a J.D. from NYU.

John Rubin joined the School of Government faculty in 1991. He specializes in criminal law and procedure and indigent defense education. Before joining the School, he practiced law for nine years in Washington, D.C., and Los Angeles, California. He has written extensively on criminal law and procedure and teaches and consults with indigent defenders, judges, magistrates, prosecutors, and others who work in the court system. He earned a B.A. from the University of California at Berkeley and a J.D. from UNC-Chapel Hill. In 2008, he received the Albert and Gladys Coates Term Award for Faculty Excellence. In 2012, he was named Albert Coates Professor of Public Law and Government.

Chapter 1
Obligations of Defense Counsel

1.1 Purpose of Manual   **1-2**

1.2 Obligations of Defense Counsel   **1-2**
   A. The U.S. Supreme Court Decides *Padilla v. Kentucky*
   B. North Carolina Follows *Padilla* in *State v. Nkiam*
   C. Impact on Duty to Advise Clients
   D. Impact on Duty to Negotiate
   E. Relevance of Practice Standards
   F. Severity of Immigration Consequences

1.3 How to Meet Your Obligations   **1-7**
   A. Identify Your Client's Citizenship and Immigration Status
   B. Investigate Your Client's Criminal History
   C. Analyze the Immigration Consequences of the Charged Offenses
      and Plea Offers and Advise Your Client
   D. Ascertain Your Client's Goals in the Case and Defend the Case
      According to the Client's Priorities
   E. Other Information

1.4 Important Terminology Used in this Manual   **1-8**
   A. Noncitizen
   B. Removal
   C. Conviction (for immigration purposes)
   D. Immigration and Nationality Act
   E. Department of Homeland Security
   F. Immigration Court

Neil is a 24-year old lawful permanent resident of the United States. Born in Pakistan, Neil came to the U.S. when he was 6 years old, but he has not yet become a U.S. citizen. His mother, father, two sisters, brother, and several cousins all live in the U.S. Neil is a graduate of community college and employed as an auto mechanic. After being taunted with racial slurs and threatened by some former customers, Neil purchases a gun for his safety. One night as he is driving home from work, Neil is stopped by a police officer for reckless driving—for passing a car in a no pass zone with the vehicle lights cut off. The officer searches Neil's car and finds the gun Neil recently purchased. Neil is charged with reckless driving and carrying a concealed gun. The prosecutor will dismiss the charge of reckless driving if Neil pleads guilty to the gun charge. Neil's attorney tells him that a reckless driving conviction could result in a suspension of his driver's license, which he needs to be able to drive to and from work, but not about the immigration consequences of the concealed weapon charge. Neil takes the deal. A few years later, Neil decides to become a citizen. After filing his citizenship application, Neil is notified by immigration officials that deportation proceedings are being initiated against him for a conviction of a firearm offense. His criminal lawyer was unaware that a misdemeanor firearm offense could lead to Neil's deportation and did not discuss these consequences with him. Had Neil negotiated a plea to the reckless driving offense rather than the carrying a concealed gun charge, or had he gone to trial and been acquitted, he would not be facing deportation today. He also might have succeeded in his application to become a U.S. citizen.

1.1   Purpose of Manual

For years, practice standards have recognized that defense counsel's role includes advising noncitizen defendants about the immigration consequences of a criminal conviction. The standards have recognized the serious impact a conviction can have on a person's immigration status. Now such advice is constitutionally required by the U.S. Supreme Court's landmark decision in *Padilla v. Kentucky*, 559 U.S. 356 (2010). A failure to competently advise noncitizen clients about the immigration consequences of a criminal conviction may constitute ineffective assistance of counsel. It is therefore essential for defense counsel either to learn enough about this area of law to advise their noncitizen clients about the impact of the criminal case or know when and how to consult with experts who can assist in them in providing that advice. The purpose of this manual is to help criminal defense counsel navigate this highly technical area of law and live up to their constitutional obligation.

This manual presents both the law on immigration consequences of a criminal conviction and options to assist clients in reducing or eliminating those consequences. The manual does not purport to provide specific legal advice in individual cases. Defense counsel and their clients should seek advice from an immigration expert as necessary.

1.2   Obligations of Defense Counsel

A. The U.S. Supreme Court Decides *Padilla v. Kentucky*

Seven years ago, in *Padilla v. Kentucky*, the U.S. Supreme Court established that criminal defense attorneys have an obligation, as part of the Sixth Amendment guarantee of effective assistance of counsel, to advise noncitizen clients about the immigration consequences of the criminal charges against them. The nature of the advice required varies according to the clarity of the immigration consequences. *Padilla*, 559 U.S. 356, 368–69. When the immigration consequences are clear, defense counsel must provide specific advice. In cases in which the immigration consequences are unclear or uncertain, defense counsel need only advise clients that the criminal charges may carry adverse immigration consequences. *A failure to provide any advice at all is constitutionally deficient representation under Padilla.*

B. North Carolina Follows *Padilla* in *State v. Nkiam*

The North Carolina Court of Appeals has confirmed the approach established in *Padilla*. In *State v. Nkiam*, ___ N.C. App. ___, 778 S.E.2d 863 (2015), the first North Carolina appellate decision to address the merits of a *Padilla* claim, the Court of Appeals found that the defendant's counsel failed to meet this obligation.

The defendant in *Nkiam*, an asylee turned lawful permanent resident, accepted a plea offer, after conferring with counsel, to aiding and abetting common law robbery and conspiracy to commit common law robbery. Although his attorney advised him that there was a risk of deportation—that is, that he *could* be deported as a result of the plea—his attorney did not advise him that deportation was presumptively mandatory—that is, that he *would* be deported. The plea, however, carried serious immigration consequences. Deportation was "presumptively mandatory" for the defendant's robbery conviction because it is an "aggravated felony" under federal immigration law. (Aggravated felonies include theft offenses when the person receives a one-year sentence of imprisonment, active or suspended.). Deportation was a paramount concern to the defendant, who feared political and ethnic persecution were he returned to the Democratic Republic of Congo.

Applying *Padilla*, the court in *Nkiam* agreed that the attorney's advice was insufficient. The court recognized that *Padilla* established a bifurcated duty for defense counsel—that is, "when the consequence of deportation is unclear or uncertain, counsel need only advise the client of the risk of deportation, but when the consequence of deportation is truly clear, counsel must advise the client in more certain terms." *Nkiam*, 778 S.E.2d at 868, *citing Padilla*, 559 U.S. at 369. The court found that deportation was a "truly clear" consequence in this case because it could be discerned from the plain language of the immigration statutes. *See Nkiam*, 778 S.E.2d at 870 (distinguishing cases in which the immigration consequences were not truly clear, as when the federal courts had divergent views or had not addressed the issue). The court rejected the State's argument that various forms of immigration relief were available to the defendant and therefore that the consequence of deportation was unclear. As the court recognized, such relief is rarely granted; its theoretical availability does not relieve counsel of the obligation to give "correct advice" about the likelihood of deportation. *Nkiam*, 778 S.E.2d at 871, *quoting Padilla*, 559 U.S. at 369.

C. Impact on Duty to Advise Clients

What do *Padilla* and *Nkiam* mean for defense counsel? The decisions have the following impact:

- When the immigration consequences are clear, counsel must give specific advice about those consequences; merely indicating that the consequences are possible or are a risk is not enough.

Practice Note: The following is an example of specific advice that would meet your Sixth Amendment obligations. Suppose your client is charged with cocaine distribution. You learn that she is a lawful permanent resident and that this is her first encounter with the criminal justice system. Cocaine distribution is a drug trafficking aggravated felony. *See infra* § 3.4A, Aggravated Felonies Generally. You should advise her that a conviction of the offense is a conviction for an aggravated felony and carries the most severe immigration consequences. Specifically, you should advise her that she faces almost certain removal (or words to that effect), that she is barred from most forms of relief from removal, that she is subject to mandatory detention, as well as the other consequences associated with an aggravated felony, discussed further in § 3.4A.

- Not giving any advice or referring the client to an immigration lawyer is insufficient. The Sixth Amendment, as interpreted in *Padilla* and *Nkiam*, places the obligation on defense counsel to provide effective advice about immigration consequences in connection with a guilty plea. Further, indigent clients are usually not in a position to hire separate immigration counsel to obtain the advice they need about the consequences of the criminal case. An indigent person does not have the right to appointed counsel in immigration proceedings.
- Attorneys cannot meet their Sixth Amendment obligations by telling all noncitizen clients that they *will* face immigration consequences as a result of the conviction. Where the consequences do not attach or are less certain, such advice is likewise inaccurate and could lead a client to reject a favorable plea in the mistaken belief that adverse immigration consequences would result. *See Lafler v. Cooper*, 566 U.S. 156 (2012) (holding that attorney may be found ineffective if advice led to improvident rejection of plea offer). Such blanket advice also could lead clients not to seek the assistance of an immigration attorney after the criminal proceedings in the mistaken belief that adverse immigration consequences are inevitable.
- A judge's general advisement during the plea colloquy about potential immigration consequences is not an adequate substitute for specific advice by counsel. *See Nkiam*, 778 S.E.2d 863, 872. Such judicial advisements do *not* satisfy counsel's Sixth Amendment obligations.
- As a practical matter, defense attorneys must do sufficient investigation and research to determine the specific immigration consequences of an offense. Or, they need to consult with an expert who can help them determine those consequences.

D. Impact on Duty to Negotiate

Padilla also has implications for defense counsel's role in negotiating a favorable plea for clients, one that best addresses the client's criminal and immigration concerns.

In *Padilla*, the Supreme Court explained that counsel's duty includes investigating the immigration consequences of the plea, not only to inform the defendant's choice regarding a guilty plea but also to inform defense negotiations: "Counsel who possess the most rudimentary understanding of the deportation consequences of a particular criminal offense may be able to plea bargain creatively with the prosecutor in order to craft a conviction and sentence that reduce the likelihood of deportation, as by avoiding a conviction for an offense that automatically triggers the removal consequence." *Padilla*, 559 U.S. at 373.

Two years later, the Supreme Court in *Missouri v. Frye* and *Lafler v. Cooper* reaffirmed that defense counsel's duty to provide effective assistance includes "the negotiation of a plea bargain." *Missouri v. Frye*, 566 U.S. 134, 141–44 (2012) ("In today's criminal justice system, therefore, the negotiation of a plea bargain, rather than the unfolding of a trial, is almost always the critical point for a defendant.") (citing *Padilla*); *Lafler v. Cooper*, 566 U.S. 156, 162 (2012).

More recently, in discussing the methodology for assessing whether a noncitizen is deportable, the Supreme Court in *Mellouli v. Lynch* again recognized defense counsel's role in negotiating and mitigating adverse immigration consequences. ___ U.S. ___, 135 S. Ct. 1980, 1987 (2015) (explaining that approach "enables aliens to anticipate the immigration consequences of guilty pleas in criminal court, and to enter 'safe harbor' guilty pleas [that] do not expose the [alien defendant] to the risk of immigration sanctions").

These cases support a Sixth Amendment duty to negotiate effectively to avoid or minimize immigration consequences. In addition, the professional standards relied on by *Padilla* in determining defense counsel's duties provide that immigration consequences should inform negotiation strategy. *See, e.g.*, National Legal Aid & Defender Assn., Performance Guidelines for Criminal Representation § 6.2 (1995) ("In order to develop an overall negotiation plan, counsel should be fully aware of, and make sure the client is fully aware of . . . other consequences of conviction such as deportation. . . . In developing a negotiation strategy, counsel should be completely familiar with . . . the advantages and disadvantages of each available plea according to the circumstances of the case."); ABA Standards for Criminal Justice, Prosecution Function and Defense Function, Standard 4-5.4 (4th ed. 2015). ("Defense counsel should include consideration of potential collateral consequences in negotiations with the prosecutor regarding possible dispositions, and in communications with the judge or court personnel regarding the appropriate sentence or conditions, if any, to be imposed).

Thus, if the preliminary investigation of the immigration consequences reveals that the proposed plea will result in adverse immigration consequences, counsel should assist the client in seeking to obtain an alternative disposition that would avoid or mitigate those consequences, particularly where the client has conveyed that the immigration consequences are a priority.

E. Relevance of Practice Standards

Both *Padilla* and *Nkiam* are consistent with a number of practice standards, which have long recognized that criminal defense counsel's role includes investigating and advising noncitizen clients about the potential immigration consequences of a criminal case. *See, e.g.*, ABA Standards for Criminal Justice, Pleas of Guilty, Standard 14-3.2(f) (3d ed. 1999) ("To the extent possible, defense counsel should determine and advise the defendant, sufficiently in advance of the entry of any plea, as to the possible collateral consequences that might ensue from entry of the contemplated plea."); Commentary to Standard 14-3.2(f) ("it may well be that many clients' greatest potential difficulty, and greatest priority, will be the immigration consequences of conviction").

Some of these standards reinforce *Padilla*. For example, in 2015 the American Bar Association (ABA) approved a new standard focused entirely on immigration consequences. It recognizes that defense counsel should determine a client's citizenship and immigration status; investigate and identify potential immigration consequences, including removal, exclusion, bars to relief from removal, immigration detention, and denial of citizenship; advise the client of all such potential consequences; and determine with the client the best course of action for the client's interests. *See* ABA Standards for Criminal Justice, Prosecution Function and Defense Function, Standard 4-5.5 (4th ed. 2015).

Other standards are weaker than what *Padilla* requires and no longer control. *See, e.g.,* IDS Performance Guidelines for Indigent Defense Representation in Non-Capital Criminal Cases at the Trial Level, Guideline 8.2(b) (2004) (counsel should be familiar with deportation and other possible immigration consequences that may result from the plea).

F. Severity of Immigration Consequences

It is essential for defense counsel to provide effective assistance to noncitizen clients because of the severity of the immigration consequences they face. Deportation is virtually automatic for certain convictions; in later immigration proceedings, the immigration judge does not have the ability to provide any relief or leniency, regardless of the client's equities. A noncitizen client may be subject to virtually automatic deportation even if he or she has been in this country since an early age, has been a lawful permanent resident (i.e., is a "green card" holder), and has no prior convictions. Thus, by the time the client gets to immigration court, the consequences may be set in stone. Even if the client has access to one, an immigration lawyer may be unable to mitigate the impact of the criminal disposition. For many, the adverse immigration effects of a criminal case may be far more important than the sentence imposed in the underlying criminal case.

A criminal conviction can also result in adverse immigration consequences other than deportation. A conviction can disqualify a person from legalizing his or her status, from obtaining admission back into the United States after traveling abroad, from becoming a U.S. citizen, from obtaining a grant of asylum, and from various forms of relief from removal. It can also result in extended civil detention.

Some attorneys assume that only felony offenses carry immigration consequences, but a person can be deported for relatively minor misdemeanor offenses, such as a minor theft or carrying a concealed gun. Sometimes it is possible for a client to avoid the adverse consequence by accepting a plea to a different violation, to a lesser included or related offense, or to the offense as charged but with a shorter sentence.

This manual is a guide to understanding the immigration consequences of convictions and advising noncitizen clients of all such consequences.

1.3   How to Meet Your Obligations

To satisfy your obligations under *Padilla v. Kentucky* and competently represent your noncitizen clients (and avoid potential ineffective assistance of counsel litigation in the future), criminal defense counsel should follow certain basic procedures in identifying, advising, and, where appropriate, negotiating alternative pleas that mitigate or do not carry the immigration consequences of concern to the client. At a minimum, defense counsel should take the following steps in each case involving a noncitizen client.

A. Identify Your Client's Citizenship and Immigration Status

In every case, you must identify whether your client is a noncitizen. Chapter 2 of this manual, *Determining Your Client's Citizenship and Immigration Status*, explains how to determine whether a particular client is a noncitizen and thus subject to the immigration laws. Once you have determined that a client is a noncitizen, Chapter 2 helps you identify the client's particular immigration status and gather information on his or her immigration history. Identifying your client's particular status and immigration history is necessary to understanding the possible adverse immigration consequences of the criminal case.

B. Investigate Your Client's Criminal History

You need to gather your client's entire criminal history as this information is essential to analyzing the potential immigration consequences.

C. Analyze the Immigration Consequences of the Charged Offenses and Plea Offers and Advise your Client

Using the client's prior immigration and criminal history, you need to analyze the specific immigration consequences of the charged offense and plea offers. Important considerations include whether the proposed disposition would qualify as a "conviction" for immigration purposes. Chapter 4 of this manual, *Conviction and Sentence for Immigration Purposes*, assesses whether various North Carolina dispositions are considered convictions for immigration law purposes.

Another important consideration is whether the charges or proposed plea come within a ground of removal or a bar to relief from removal. Chapter 3 of this manual, *Criminal Grounds of Removal and Other Immigration Consequences*, presents detailed information about the types and categories of crimes that can result in adverse immigration consequences. Appendix A of the manual, *Selected Immigration Consequences of North Carolina Offenses*, presents in chart form the immigration consequences of specific North Carolina offenses.

Chapter 5, *Determining Possible Immigration Consequences Based on Your Client's Immigration Status*, lays out the possible immigration consequences of the criminal case based on your client's particular immigration status. The chapter analyzes the consequences separately for lawful permanent residents, refugees, asylees, individuals with temporary status, and noncitizens without status.

After analyzing the immigration consequences, you must advise your client about them. As discussed *supra* in § 1.2, Obligations of Defense Counsel, the advice will vary based on the "clarity" of immigration consequences. In some cases, you may be able to advise that the plea is nearly certain to carry or not carry a specific immigration consequence. In other cases, you may only be able to advise that there is a risk that the plea will have a specific immigration consequence but that the law is not clear.

D. Ascertain Your Client's Goals in the Case and Defend the Case According to the Client's Priorities

You should discuss with your client the relative importance of any immigration consequences of conviction. Not every noncitizen client will have the same priorities or options with regard to immigration consequences. Some noncitizen defendants will care most about minimizing jail time. Others would be willing to plead to a more serious offense, take additional time, or even go to trial and risk a significantly higher sentence, if it meant that they might be able to remain in the U.S. with loved ones. Of course, a defendant can only make this crucial decision if he or she understands the potential criminal and immigration penalties. Thus, it is necessary to gauge the immigration goals of the case, as it will inform your ultimate strategy in the criminal proceeding.

For options for avoiding or mitigating adverse immigration consequences, consult Chapter 6 of this manual, *Options for Minimizing Adverse Immigration Consequences*.

E. Other Information

Also included in this manual are Chapter 7, *Procedures Related to Removal*, and Chapter 8, *State Post-Conviction Relief*. These chapters provide information about procedures, in immigration and criminal court, following conviction.

1.4   Important Terminology Used in this Manual

A. Noncitizen

The manual uses the term "noncitizen" to refer broadly to any individual who is not a citizen of the United States and who is therefore subject to potential immigration consequences as a result of criminal conviction. The term includes lawful permanent residents, refugees, asylees, temporary visa holders, and undocumented people. These categories are described in more detail in Chapter 2 of this manual.

B. Removal

Removal is the deportation or expulsion of a noncitizen from the United States. Before 1996, immigration law provided for two types of processes to eject noncitizens from the U.S.: "deportation" and "exclusion." Laws passed in 1996 ended the distinction and created a single process called removal (so that an individual is technically "removed" rather than "deported"). All immigration court proceedings that began on or after April 1, 1997, are called "removal" proceedings. Noncitizens can be removed from the U.S. because of certain criminal convictions. Removal and other adverse immigration consequences are described in more detail in Chapter 3 of this manual.

C. Conviction (for immigration purposes)

Immigration law defines "conviction" broadly. State law does *not* determine whether a state disposition will be considered a conviction for immigration law purposes. Chapter 4 discusses the immigration law definition of the term.

D. Immigration and Nationality Act

The Immigration and Nationality Act (INA) is the immigration statute. It is codified in Chapter 8 of the United States Code, and it establishes the basic structure of U.S. immigration law, including admission, exclusion, and naturalization. Section 212 of the INA, codified at 8 U.S.C. § 1182, enumerates the grounds of admissibility of noncitizens into the United States. Section 237 of the INA, codified at 8 U.S.C. § 1227, enumerates the grounds of deportability of noncitizens from the United States. When citing to the INA, this manual refers both to the pertinent INA section (e.g., INA § 212) and the codified section (e.g., 8 U.S.C. § 1182).

E. Department of Homeland Security

The Homeland Security Act of 2002 abolished the Immigration and Naturalization Service (INS) and created the Department of Homeland Security (DHS). The regulation and enforcement of immigration laws were placed under three new bureaus under DHS— U.S. Immigration and Customs Enforcement (ICE), U.S. Customs and Border Protection (CBP), and U.S. Citizenship and Immigration Services (USCIS), described below.

U.S. Immigration and Customs Enforcement (ICE). This branch of DHS is responsible for the detention and removal of noncitizens. ICE issues detainers (that is, holds) on noncitizens in jails and prisons and issues summonses for removal hearings. This is the branch of the Department of Homeland Security that defense attorneys and noncitizen defendants are most likely to deal with.

U.S. Customs and Border Protection (CBP). This branch of DHS conducts border inspections at ports of entry into the United States, including airports, seaports, and U.S. checkpoints. "Inspection" refers to inspection of travel documents from other countries, fingerprinting, and searches of people and belongings.

U.S. Citizenship and Immigration Services (USCIS). This branch of DHS has jurisdiction over the adjudication of applications for an immigration benefit, such as a visa, naturalization, asylum, and modification (called adjustment) of immigration status.

F. Immigration Court

Many removal proceedings are held in immigration court, which is an administrative court of the Department of Justice, Executive Office for Immigration Review. *See* INA § 240, 8 U.S.C. § 1229a. As part of the Department of Justice, immigration court is independent of the Department of Homeland Security. An individual placed into removal proceedings has a right to an attorney but at his or her own expense because such proceedings have been designated as civil, not criminal, in nature. One narrow exception exists for certain detained individuals who have a mental illness or disability rendering them incapable of representing themselves in detention or removal proceedings. *See Franco-Gonzalez v. Holder*, 2013 WL 3674492 (C.D. Cal. Apr. 23, 2013). An individual in removal proceedings also has a right to present any evidence on his or her own behalf, a right to cross-examine government witnesses and documents, and a right to appeal.

Either party can appeal the decision of the immigration judge to the Board of Immigration Appeals (BIA), an administrative court in Falls Church, Virginia. The noncitizen can appeal the decision of the BIA to the federal court of appeals in which the immigration court physically sits.

There is an immigration court in Charlotte, North Carolina. Removal proceedings for noncitizens who are not detained by DHS are generally held there. However, removal proceedings for noncitizens who are detained by DHS are generally held in Atlanta, in Stewart Detention Center in Lumpkin, Georgia, or other detention facility where a noncitizen may be detained. Removal hearings for a small number of individuals serving long sentences in North Carolina correctional facilities take place in Central Prison in Raleigh. A case arising out of a Georgia immigration court would be reviewed by the Eleventh Circuit Court of Appeals, and a case arising out of the Charlotte immigration court or Central Prison would be reviewed by the Fourth Circuit Court of Appeals. This difference can be important because the governing law varies by circuit.

Chapter 2
Determining Your Client's Citizenship and Immigration Status

2.1 Determining Whether Your Client Is a U.S. Citizen   **2-2**
  A. Generally
  B. Obstacles to Understanding Your Client's Status
  C. Who Are U.S. Citizens

2.2 Determining Your Noncitizen Client's Particular Immigration Status   **2-4**
  A. General Considerations
  B. Lawful Permanent Resident Status
  C. Refugee or Asylee Status
  D. Individuals with Temporary Lawful Status or Pending Application for Status
  E. Individuals without Immigration Status

2.3 Additional Interview Objectives for a Noncitizen Client   **2-8**
  A. Gather Additional Information from Your Client
  B. Gather Your Client's Criminal Record
  C. Assess Your Client's Goals in the Case
  D. Advise Your Clients of Their Rights

2.4 Sample Questions to Identify Client's Immigration Status and Eligibility for Relief   **2-10**

Appendix 2-1: Sample Images of Immigration Documents   **2-12**

Appendix 2-2: Sample Intake Form   **2-18**

When representing any new client in criminal court proceedings, a criminal defense attorney should as a preliminary matter determine whether or not the client is a U.S. citizen. If the client is *not* a U.S. citizen, the disposition of the criminal case may subject the client to adverse immigration consequences.

Do *not* make the mistake of assuming that your client is a U.S. citizen. Many noncitizens have lived in the United States their entire lives and do not exhibit an accent. Thus, it is paramount to ask every client about his or her citizenship, not just those clients with discernible accents or who appear "foreign." If the person was born in the U.S., the inquiry need go no further. Only if the person was not born in the U.S. will further questions be necessary.

2.1 Determining Whether Your Client Is a U.S. Citizen

A. Generally

If your client is a U.S. citizen or a U.S. national, he or she is not subject to removal or most other adverse immigration consequences (unless, in the case of a naturalized citizen, citizenship has been revoked because naturalization was obtained through some type of misrepresentation).[1]

A "national" is a broader term that not only refers to any person who is a U.S. citizen, but also covers a person born in "outlying possessions of the United States." *See* INA § 101(a)(22)(A), 8 U.S.C. § 1101(a)(22)(A); INA § 308, 8 U.S.C. § 1408. The outlying possessions of the United States are American Samoa and Swains Island. *See* INA § 101(a)(29), 8 U.S.C. § 1101(a)(29). Because "nationals" who are not U.S. citizens comprise such a small group, and because they are treated no differently than citizens for immigration purposes, this manual uses the term "citizen" to cover both U.S. citizens and noncitizen nationals.

B. Obstacles to Understanding Your Client's Status

Generally, identifying whether your client is not a U.S. citizen is a straightforward task. There are a few caveats, however. Criminal defendant clients do not always trust appointed attorneys, especially at the first meeting. They may fear that informing you of their noncitizen status could actually trigger immigration consequences.

Practice Note: Your client may have no familiarity with the adversarial process that is part of the U.S. criminal justice system—he or she may not understand that appointed counsel is independent of the government. When interviewing a client for the first time, it is helpful to reassure the client about confidentiality and that you have no association with U.S. Immigration and Customs Enforcement (ICE).

Other times, noncitizen clients may simply be unaware that they are not U.S. citizens, particularly those who came to the U.S. at a young age. They may mistakenly assume that they are citizens because they have lived in the United States for so long. Or, some

---

1. U.S. citizens can lose the ability, however, to submit a family visa petition for a noncitizen relative. The Adam Walsh Act, passed in 2006, imposes immigration penalties on U.S. citizens and permanent residents who are convicted of specified crimes relating to minors, including sex and kidnapping offenses. Certain convictions would prevent them from filing a visa petition on behalf of a close family member. *See* Section 402 of the Adam Walsh Act; INA § 204(a)(1)(A)(viii), (B)(i), 8 U.S.C. § 1154(a)(1)(A)(viii), (B)(i). For example, if your U.S. citizen client pleads guilty to indecent liberties, he may not be permitted to file a visa petition for a noncitizen relative.

noncitizens may interpret the question, "Are you a citizen," to be the same as "Are you here legally?" Thus, they may erroneously answer yes simply because they have a green card (for a discussion of people with green cards, see *infra* § 2.2B, Lawful Permanent Resident Status). It therefore may be necessary to clarify an affirmative response with follow-up questions.

Occasionally you will encounter a client who may be a citizen without realizing it, as in the case of someone who automatically derived citizenship from a family member without ever having taken any affirmative step. Therefore, some cases may require investigation beyond simply asking your client whether he or she is a citizen.

Practice Note: It is helpful to begin the citizenship inquiry by asking your client where he or she was born. If the person was not born in the U.S., then ask follow-up questions about citizenship and how, if at all, it was obtained. *See infra* § 2.4, Sample Questions to Identify Client's Immigration Status and Eligibility for Relief.

C. Who Are U.S. Citizens

Generally, your client is a U.S. citizen if he or she is within one of the following categories.

Place of Birth. Any person born in the United States is a U.S. citizen, except for certain children of foreign diplomats. *See* INA § 301(a), (b), 8 U.S.C. § 1401(a), (b). A person is also a U.S. citizen if he or she was born in Puerto Rico, the U.S. Virgin Islands, Guam, or American Samoa and Swains Island, as well as those born in the Northern Mariana Islands after November 4, 1988 and in many cases before. *See* INA §§ 301(a), (b), 302, 304–07, 8 U.S.C. §§ 1401(a), (b), 1402, 1404–07 (citizen by birth in the U.S., Puerto Rico, U.S. Virgin Islands, Guam, or Commonwealth of the Northern Mariana Islands); INA § 308, U.S.C. § 1408 (noncitizen national by birth in American Samoa and Swains Island).

Naturalization. A person who is born outside the United States may become a U.S. citizen by petitioning for and being granted citizenship through the "naturalization" process. This process generally involves passing a civics and English test, establishing "good moral character" for a specific period, and participating in a swearing-in ceremony. *See* INA §§ 310–319, 8 U.S.C. §§ 1410–1430.

"Acquired" Citizenship from U.S. Citizen Parent. A person is a U.S. citizen if he or she was born outside the United States but "acquired" U.S. citizenship at birth by having been born to a U.S. citizen parent or parents. The current law on "acquired" citizenship is contained in INA §§ 301(c), (d), (e), (g), (h), 303, 8 U.S.C. §§ 1401(c), (d), (e), (g), (h), 1403; and INA § 309, 8 U.S.C. § 1409 (child born out of wedlock). Thus, your client might be a U.S. citizen and not know it. Many people born in other countries unknowingly inherit U.S. citizenship from their parents under these provisions.

"Derivative" Citizenship from Naturalized U.S. Parent. A person is a U.S. citizen if he or she was born outside the United States but "derived" U.S. citizenship as a minor when one or both of his or her parents became a naturalized citizen. The current law on "derivative" citizenship is contained in INA § 320, 8 U.S.C. § 1431. Again, your client might be a U.S. citizen and not know it.

Practice Note: You should ask your client whether any of his or her parents or grandparents were born in the United States or at any point obtained U.S. citizenship, which could give your client "acquired" or "derivative" citizenship even if he or she was not born in the U.S. or U.S. territories. The rules surrounding "acquired" and "derivative" citizenship are complicated, however, and depend on several factors, including an ever-changing set of laws that are not retroactive. Because this is a particularly difficult area of law, if there is any question regarding your client's citizenship, you should contact an immigration expert for further assistance.

Documentation of U.S. Citizenship. U.S. citizens may have one of the following:

- U.S. Passport
- U.S. Birth Certificate
- U.S. Certificate of Citizenship
- U.S. Certificate of Naturalization

Sample images of some of these documents appear at the end of this chapter.

2.2   Determining Your Noncitizen Client's Particular Immigration Status

A. General Considerations

If you conclude that your client is not a citizen, you then must determine your client's particular immigration status. The immigration consequences will vary significantly depending on the client's particular immigration status. Many of your clients will have documentation indicating their immigration status. If possible, you should make arrangements to photocopy any such documents, especially in situations where your client is uncertain of his or her status. Also, have the client complete an immigration intake form. *See infra* Appendix 2-2, Sample Intake Form. Even if the client is not able or willing to answer all of the questions, any information that you gain will be helpful.

You are also likely to encounter clients without any immigration status who are unlawfully present in the U.S. Some of these clients may be able to gain lawful status in the future. Many avenues for status would be foreclosed, however, by certain types of criminal convictions. Additionally, criminal convictions can have other serious consequences, such as mandatory detention pending removal from the U.S. and enhanced criminal sentences for illegal reentry. Consequently, the immigration consequences of conviction may matter to some of these individuals as well.

The discussion below divides noncitizens into four broad categories of immigration status:

- Lawful permanent resident status
- Refugee and asylee status
- Individuals with temporary lawful status or pending applications for status
- Individuals with no status

This list focuses on the immigration statuses you are most likely to encounter, but it is not exhaustive. The immigration consequences of a criminal conviction for each of these categories are discussed *infra* in Chapter 5, Determining Possible Immigration Consequences Based on Your Client's Immigration Status.

B. Lawful Permanent Resident Status

Definition. A lawful permanent resident (LPR) is a noncitizen who has been lawfully admitted to the United States to live and work permanently (though an individual can lose this status). LPRs may travel in and out of the country. An LPR may apply to be naturalized as a U.S. citizen after meeting certain requirements, including a residency requirement. For most individuals, five years of lawful permanent residence is required. *See* INA § 316(a), 8 U.S.C. § 1427(a). *Regardless of numbers of years in the U.S. or U.S. citizen family relationships*, an LPR can be removed or face other immigration consequences because of a criminal conviction (for further discussion of impact of conviction on LPRs, see *infra* § 5.1, Lawful Permanent Resident).

Documentation of Status. An LPR will generally have one of the following:

- A "green card", which is the colloquial name for Form I-551. In May of 2017, USCIS began to issue a new version of the card. The new version states "PERMANENT RESIDENT" on the top left of the front of the card. The card is personalized with the bearer's photo on both sides, name, alien registration number ("A" number), date of birth, and laser-engraved fingerprint, as well as the card expiration date. Green cards now expire every ten years, and a replacement must be sought. An LPR does not lose legal status because the card expires or is misplaced. Conditional permanent residents (usually individuals who received their LPR status through a marriage less than two years old) are issued cards that are coded "CR" and that expire after two years.
- An I-551 stamp indicating "temporary evidence of lawful admission for permanent residence," and accompanying expiration date in a foreign passport.
- Foreign passport with a machine-readable immigrant visa. The machine-readable immigrant visa demonstrates permanent resident status for one year from the date of admission found in the foreign passport.

Sample images of some of these documents appear at the end of this chapter.

C. Refugee or Asylee Status

Definition. A refugee or a person granted asylum is a noncitizen who has been admitted conditionally to the U.S. due to a threat of persecution in his or her country of nationality. *See generally* INA §§ 207, 208, 8 U.S.C. §§ 1157, 1158. Refugee status is granted to an individual who applied from outside the United States. Upon application, he or she is granted a visa and then is allowed to come to the U.S. as a refugee. Asylum is granted to an individual *after* entry into the U.S. Thus, the person entered the U.S. in some other status or unlawfully, but then applied for and was granted asylum. Both refugees and asylees are allowed to work in the U.S. Refugees can apply to become lawful permanent residents after being present continuously for one year in the U.S., and asylees are eligible one year after being granted asylum. *See* INA §§ 209(a)(1), (b), 8 U.S.C. §§ 1159(a)(1), (b). Both refugees and asylees can be removed or face other immigration consequences because of a criminal conviction. *See infra* § 5.2, Refugee (who has not yet obtained LPR status), § 5.3, Person Granted Asylum (who has not yet obtained LPR status).

Documentation of Status. Refugees and asylees will generally have one of the following:

- Refugees should have an I-94 Arrival/Departure Record stating that they have been "admitted as a refugee pursuant to section 207 of the INA."[2] Some refugees may also have a Refugee Travel Document.
- Asylees will generally have a letter or other document from U.S. Citizenship and Immigration Services or the U.S. Department of Justice stating that the person has been granted asylum. They may also have a stamp in their I-94 document.
- Additionally, your client may have an employment authorization document indicating that he or she is in category A-3 (refugee) or A-5 (asylee). (Codes on the front of the card indicate the person's immigration status by referring to the applicable subsection of 8 C.F.R. § 274A.12, the regulation authorizing employment.)

Sample images of some of these documents appear at the end of this chapter.

Practice Note: If your client has merely *applied* for asylum, as opposed to having been *granted* asylum, refer to the discussion *infra* in § 2.2D, Individuals with Temporary Lawful Status or Pending Application for Status. Like a person granted asylum, an asylum applicant may also have an employment authorization document, but his or her card will be coded C-8 rather than A-3 or A-5.

---

2. The I-94 document used to be issued to almost all noncitizens on entry to the U.S. In April 2013, paper I-94 documents were no longer issued at airports and seaports; instead, they are maintained and can be accessed through the website of the U.S. Customs and Border Protection.

D. Individuals with Temporary Lawful Status or Pending Application for Status

The following discussion addresses people who have temporary lawful status in the U.S. or who have a pending application for status. Temporary status authorizes a person to remain in the U.S. for a discrete period, while having a pending application for status does not give a person any permission to remain in the U.S. either temporarily or permanently. All of these individuals can be removed or face other immigration consequences because of certain criminal convictions.

Nonimmigrant Visa Holders. Nonimmigrant visa holders are admitted to the United States on a time-limited temporary visa for a specific purpose (such as tourism, study, or temporary work). They are restricted to activity consistent with their visas. The visas are issued before entry by a U.S. consulate or embassy. It is possible for an individual to enter the U.S. as a temporary visa holder and eventually obtain another temporary or permanent status.

For example, an individual may come to the United States as a student, change to an employment-related temporary visa after graduation, and eventually obtain lawful permanent resident status based on an employment opportunity or a family relationship if he or she has the appropriate U.S. sponsor.

Documentation of Status

- Evidence of nonimmigrant status is documented on an I-94 document (paper or electronic). The expiration date on an I-94 document supersedes the visa expiration date. For example, an individual may have a tourist visa valid for ten years, but periods of stay in the U.S. are usually granted for no more than six months at a time (as indicated on the I-94 document).

Sample images of some of these documents appear at the end of this chapter

---

Temporary Protected Status. Temporary Protected Status (TPS) establishes a safe haven for and is conferred on an entire nationality based on dire situations such as civil wars, natural disasters, or other extraordinary conditions in their home country. *See* INA § 244, 8 U.S.C. § 1254a. Nationals of that country will not be forced to return there from the U.S. for a designated period of time, can travel outside the U.S. with special permission, and will receive employment authorization.

To acquire TPS status, the applicant must have been in the United States on or before the date of TPS country designation and must have properly registered within the period provided by the U.S. Attorney General. *See* INA § 244(c), 8 U.S.C. § 1254a(c). TPS is usually granted for only a year or 18 months at a time, but is often renewed several times. Since TPS is a temporary designation, the list of designated countries changes frequently. For information about which countries currently are designated for TPS, go to www.uscis.gov and click on Temporary Protected Status in the "Humanitarian" box. As of August 16, 2017, the countries designated for TPS were El Salvador, Haiti, Honduras,

Nepal, Nicaragua, Somalia, Sudan, South Sudan, Syria, and Yemen. However, designation for some of these countries has changed recently and may be discontinued in the near future so it is imperative to review USCIS's website for the most current information.

Individuals with Pending Applications for Status. This category includes individuals with pending applications for status, such as an asylum petition or an application for adjustment of status to a lawful permanent resident. It is important to note that a pending application does not constitute permission to remain in the U.S. Individuals with a pending application may, however, have a temporary employment authorization document and, as a result, erroneously assume that they have lawful status. While a pending application does not confer status, ICE may have more lenient policies with respect to removing such people.

E. Individuals without Immigration Status

These individuals do not have authorization to be present in the United States. This category includes undocumented people who entered the U.S. without inspection (crossed the border without permission), as well as individuals who entered the U.S. on a valid visa but remained past their authorized period of stay (a "visa overstay"). If your client is here unlawfully, he or she may be removed on that basis alone. The immigration consequences of conviction may still matter to some of these individuals because they may be eligible now or in the future to obtain lawful resident status, asylum, deferred action, or other protection from removal.

Certain convictions, such as an aggravated felony, can also result in enhanced criminal penalties should your client reenter the U.S. unlawfully after being removed. Many people who are removed re-enter the U.S. unlawfully after removal to join family members here. If the re-entrant is caught at the border, or picked up for any reason once inside, it is very likely that he or she will be prosecuted for a federal immigration offense. Illegal re-entry following removal is one of the most commonly prosecuted federal offenses today, comprising roughly 26% of all federal convictions in 2012 and resulting in an average sentence of two years. *See* Pew Hispanic Center, *The Rise of Federal Immigration Crimes* (Mar. 18, 2014).

2.3   Additional Interview Objectives for a Noncitizen Client

A. Gather Additional Information from Your Client

You should use the initial and later interviews to gather additional details about your client's immigration history, including length of residence in the U.S., any U.S. citizen family relationships, and potential fear of returning to his or her country of nationality. This information will be help you determine the immigration consequences of the potential conviction and whether your client will be eligible for any form of relief from deportation. *See infra* §3.2B, Relief from Removal.

B. Gather Your Client's Criminal Record

You will also need to gather your client's entire criminal record. A record of past convictions will be necessary to determine the immigration consequences of any potential conviction and whether your client will be eligible for any form of relief from removal.

C. Assess Your Client's Goals in the Case

After obtaining information to determine your client's immigration status, you should discuss with your client the relative importance of any immigration consequences of conviction. It may be that the traditional criminal defense goals of minimizing the severity of the conviction and sentence will conflict with the immigration-related goal of minimizing adverse immigration consequences. For example, in certain situations, your client may be able to plead guilty to a non-deportable offense in exchange for a longer sentence. Thus, it is necessary to gauge the immigration goals of the case, as it will inform your ultimate strategy in the criminal proceeding.

D. Advise Your Clients of Their Rights

U.S. Immigration and Customs Enforcement (ICE) prioritizes the removal of noncitizens who are in jails and prisons. ICE and cooperating law enforcement agents identify, question, and detain individuals who may be subject to removal based on criminal grounds or lack of immigration status. Admissions by noncitizen defendants may be used as evidence against them in deportation or criminal proceedings.

The client's Fifth Amendment privilege against self-incrimination covers immigration status if that information could lead to a criminal prosecution (certain immigration violations, including entering the U.S. without inspection, may carry criminal penalties). You should therefore advise all noncitizen clients not to discuss their immigration status, birthplace, or manner of entry into the U.S. with federal immigration agents or other law enforcement officers, except with the advice of counsel. You should also advise your noncitizen clients not to sign any documents while in custody, which could contain a stipulation that they are removable, except with the advice of counsel. If questioned by an immigration agent, your client may remain silent or ask for an attorney.

You should also advise your noncitizen clients not to lie or misrepresent their status, as they can be criminally prosecuted for making a false statement. *See* 18 U.S.C. § 1001 (false statements), § 911 (false claim to citizenship).

In addition, immigration agents may ask your clients to waive the opportunity for a removal hearing before an immigration judge. You should advise your clients not to waive their rights to a hearing ("stipulation of removal") until all of their options are fully evaluated.

2.4　Sample Questions to Identify Client's Immigration Status and Eligibility for Relief

Be sure to request copies of immigration documents to verify the information your client provides you. For a sample check-the-box intake form that gathers similar information, see *infra* Appendix 2-2, Sample Intake Form.

1. Where were you born? (if answer is U.S. or other U.S. territory such as Puerto Rico, end of inquiry; otherwise, continue)

2. Are you a United States citizen?
   a. If yes, how and when did you become a citizen? Do you have a U.S. passport? (to clarify whether the individual is in fact a citizen)
   b. If no, continue to #3

3. Were your parents or grandparents born in the United States? If not, did they ever become U.S. citizens?
   a. If your parents naturalized, were you under the age of 18 when they did? (If your client's parents or grandparents were born in the U.S. or your client's parents naturalized, you may have an acquired or derivative citizenship issue and should consult an immigration expert for further assistance in the case.)

4. When and how did you first enter the U.S. for the first time (unlawfully or through a visa)?

5. What is your current immigration status? When did you obtain it?
   a. Lawful permanent resident? Date obtained? On what basis (family visa, refugee, other)?
   b. Refugee?
   c. Asylee?
   d. Temporary protected status?
   e. Temporary visa, such as student visa?
   f. Deferred Action for Childhood Arrivals (DACA)?
   g. Valid work authorization card? Is there a pending application for status or relief? (Individuals with a pending application for status, such as an asylum petition, may have a temporary employment authorization card. A pending application, however, does not confer a lawful status.)
   h. Undocumented?
   i. Other?

6. Have you left the U.S. since your first arrived? If yes, list all dates left and returned.

7. Do you have any pending applications with immigration? If yes, what kind?

8. Have you been previously deported or ordered deported?[3] Have you ever had an encounter with immigration officials? What happened?

9. Do you have a prior criminal history? (Clients are not always aware of their entire criminal record; it is therefore important for counsel to separately obtain the client's criminal record.)

10. Do you have family here (including parents, children, spouse, and siblings)? What is their citizenship or immigration status?

11. Do you fear returning to your country? Why?

12. Have you been the victim of a violent crime? If yes, did you cooperate with the police?

---

3. If your client thinks that he or she may have been previously removed or is currently in removal proceedings but is not sure, you can call the U.S. Department of Justice Executive Office for Immigration Review (EOIR) automated information system (1.800.898.7180) to verify whether removal proceedings have commenced against your client or whether there is an outstanding removal order against your client. You will need your client's Alien Registration Number (also known as an "A Number," beginning with the letter A and followed by an 8 or 9 digit number). The Alien Registration Number may be found in your client's passport or other immigration documents. It will be printed on all Department of Homeland Security (DHS) and EOIR correspondence.

Appendix 2-1
Sample Images of Immigration Documents

Form N-560 or N-561—Certificate of United States Citizenship

Form N-550 or N-570—Certificate of Naturalization

Form I-551—Permanent Resident Card (Green Card)

Revised 1997

Revised 2011

Revised 2017

Foreign Passport with Temporary "Processed for I-551" Stamp (indicating "temporary evidence of lawful admission for permanent residence" and accompanying expiration date)

Foreign Passport with Machine-Readable Immigrant Visa

Form I-766—Employment Authorization Document

Revised 2017

Form I-94 – Arrival/Departure Record (this particular sample is for a nonimmigrant visa holder—note expiration date of April 23, 2009)

Electronic Copy of I-94

Appendix 2-2
Sample Intake Form

It is recommended that you use an intake form like this sample form for all noncitizen clients. The form will help you capture much of the information you (or an expert) will need to assess the immigration consequences of the criminal charges in a consistent and systematic way. This sample form was developed by the Immigrant Law Resource Center in California; it was modified slightly by the authors for the purpose of this manual.

Immigrant Defendant Questionnaire

This information is confidential and protected by attorney-client privilege.

Client's Name	A# (if possible)	Client's criminal case #
Client's Country of Birth	Client's Date of Birth	ICE Detainer/Hold
		__Yes __No __ Don't know

1. ENTRY:

Date first entered U.S.	Visa Type (or 'none')	Significant Departures (approximate OK; append list)
		Dates: Length of departures:

2. IMMIGRATION STATUS:

Lawful permanent resident?	Other Current Immigration status? (check one)
__Yes __No Date Obtained?_____ On what basis (e.g. family visa, refugee): Check one. To obtain green card, client: - Went to an interview in home country ____ - Processed ("adjusted status") in U.S. _____	__ Undocumented __Doesn't know __Has work permit but unsure of status (is there a pending application for status or relief?) __Refugee __Asylee __Temporary Protected Status __Deferred Action for Childhood Arrivals (DACA) Other: _____
Screen for possible US citizenship if: ____Grandparent or parents were US citizens at time of client's birth; OR ____Parent(s) were US citizens while client was under age 18 (Mark even if parents or grandparents are deceased).	

3. PRIOR REMOVAL/DEPORTATION/VOLUNTARY DEPARTURE:

Was Defendant ever deported?	Describe what happened to extent possible (e.g., saw an immigration judge? just signed form before leaving US? caught at the border?)	Where? When? (for each deportation)
__Yes __No		

4. FAMILY TIES & RELIEF

Family in U.S., including parents, spouses, children, siblings, or fiancé(e) (please list relationship to client, age, and immigration status):

Is your client afraid to return to his/her home country for any reason? Does he or she fear persecution or torture if removed from the U.S.? ___Yes ____No

Has the defendant been a victim of crime? ___Yes ___No   If yes, what type of crime?

5. DEFENSE GOALS & CRIMINAL HISTORY

Defendant's Goals Re: Immigration Consequences	Criminal History & Current Charges
___Avoid conviction that triggers deportation ___Preserve eligibility to apply for immigration status or relief from removal ___Get out of jail ASAP ___Immigration consequences/deportation not a priority ___Other goals re: imm consequences:	*Fill out below:* **List Prior Conviction/s from any jurisdiction** **List Current Charge/s and Plea Offer/s if any**

List Prior Convictions
(include statute section, date of conviction, and sentence)

List Current Charge(s), Plea Offer(s)

Chapter 3
Criminal Grounds of Removal and Other Immigration Consequences

3.1 Removal Defined   **3-2**

3.2 Deportability vs. Inadmissibility   **3-2**
  A. Consequences Distinguished
  B. Relief from Removal
  C. Long-Term Consequences of Removal Order

3.3 Determining Whether a State Offense Triggers Removal   **3-5**
  A. Categorical Approach and Variations
  B. Burden of Proof on ICE in Establishing Deportability
  C. Burden of Proof on Noncitizen in Applying for Relief and
      Demonstrating Admissibility

3.4 Crime-Related Grounds of Deportability   **3-8**
  A. Aggravated Felonies Generally
  B. Specific Types of Aggravated Felonies
  C. Conviction of a Crime Involving Moral Turpitude
  D. Conviction of Any Controlled Substance Offense
  E. Conviction of a Firearm or Destructive Device Offense
  F. Conviction of a Crime of Domestic Violence, Stalking, Child
      Abuse, Child Neglect, or Child Abandonment, or a Violation
      of a Protective Order
  G. Chart of Principal Deportable Offenses

3.5 Crime-Related Grounds of Inadmissibility   **3-23**
  A. Controlled Substance Offense
  B. Crime Involving Moral Turpitude
  C. Conviction of Two or More Offenses of Any Type with an
      Aggregate Sentence of Imprisonment of at Least Five Years
  D. Prostitution
  E. Significant Traffickers in Persons
  F. Money Laundering
  G. Chart of Principal Criminal Grounds of Inadmissibility

3.6   Criminal Bars to Naturalization   **3-26**

3.7   Criminal Bars to Deferred Action for Childhood Arrivals   **3-27**

3.1   Removal Defined

Before 1996, immigration law provided for two types of processes to eject noncitizens from the U.S.—"deportation" (if a noncitizen was found to be deportable) and "exclusion" (if a noncitizen was found to be inadmissible). *See infra* § 3.2, Deportability vs. Inadmissibility. Laws passed in 1996 ended the distinction and created a single process called removal.

There are several ways the government can remove a noncitizen. Before being removed, many noncitizens receive an administrative hearing before an immigration judge with the Department of Justice, Executive Office for Immigration Review. *See* INA § 240, 8 U.S.C. § 1229a. The immigration judge must make findings of fact and determine whether the noncitizen is removable under immigration law. If the immigration judge orders a noncitizen removed and that order becomes final, U.S. Immigration and Customs Enforcement (ICE) will physically remove that individual from the U.S. For a discussion of other procedures for removing a noncitizen, see *infra* § 7.4B, Removal Proceedings.

Removal from the U.S. is the immigration consequence that will probably be of most importance to your client. For a discussion of priorities based on the client's particular immigration status (e.g., lawful permanent resident, refugee, etc.), see *infra* Chapter 5, Determining Possible Immigration Consequences Based on Your Client's Immigration Status.

3.2   Deportability vs. Inadmissibility

A. Consequences Distinguished

A noncitizen can lose her status and be forced to leave the U.S. (removed) if she comes within a ground of *deportability*. In general, the grounds of deportability apply to noncitizens who have been lawfully "admitted"—that is, noncitizens who have entered the U.S. after inspection and authorization by an immigration officer. Lawful permanent residents and others who have a secure lawful immigration status fear becoming deportable.

A noncitizen can be denied admission to the U.S. (and thereby removed) or denied lawful permanent resident status (a green card) if he or she comes within a ground of *inadmissibility*. The grounds of inadmissibility generally apply to individuals who have not been "admitted" and are viewed as seeking admission to the U.S. Immigration law generally deems a person as seeking admission when:

- An individual present at the border or port of entry, including airports and seaports, seeks permission to enter the U.S.
- An individual is physically present in the U.S. but entered without inspection (e.g., crossed the border illegally).
- An individual applies to become a lawful permanent resident (LPR) (*see supra* § 2.2B, Lawful Permanent Resident Status).
- In some instances, a lawfully admitted individual travels abroad after being convicted of a crime and then returns to the U.S.

There are several criminal grounds of deportability and inadmissibility in the federal immigration statute. *See* INA § 212, 8 U.S.C. § 1182 (grounds of inadmissibility); INA § 237, 8 U.S.C. § 1227 (grounds of deportability). These grounds overlap somewhat, but they are not the same and do not have the same impact. It is critical to determine which consequences your client is concerned about, which will depend on your client's current status and on any future immigration status he or she may seek. For example, a noncitizen client with a non-immigrant work visa will be subject to the grounds of deportability because he or she has already been lawfully admitted to the U.S., but the client will also be concerned about the grounds of inadmissibility if he or she hopes to adjust status to an LPR in the future.

Key Terms: The following definitions may help counsel distinguish different immigration terms.

Admission means the lawful entry into the U.S. after inspection and authorization by an immigration officer. INA § 101(a)(13)(A), 8 U.S.C. § 1101(a)(13)(A).

Deportability applies to noncitizens who have been lawfully admitted to the U.S. (even if their lawful status has expired). LPRs who are in the U.S. and will not be traveling abroad will be most concerned about avoiding deportability.

Inadmissibility applies to people who are seeking admission into the U.S. Noncitizens who plan to adjust status/apply for a green card will be most concerned about avoiding inadmissibility. Also, LPRs convicted of crimes falling within the grounds of inadmissibility who travel abroad may be viewed as seeking admission on their return and thus subject to the grounds of inadmissibility.

B. Relief from Removal

If an immigration judge finds that an individual is deportable or inadmissible, the individual will be removed from the U.S. unless he or she is granted some form of relief from removal.

There are several forms of relief from removal codified in the immigration statute, each with its own specific eligibility requirements. Most forms of relief are discretionary and will depend on an individual's ties to the U.S and other factors. In most cases, an immigration judge will determine whether relief from removal will be granted and the individual allowed to remain in the U.S. Certain convictions will make noncitizens ineligible for relief from removal, regardless of ties to the U.S., demonstrated rehabilitation, contributions to the community (including military service), and hardship to family members. For a discussion of different forms of relief, see Immigrant Legal Resource Center, Immigration Relief Toolkit for Criminal Defenders: How to Quickly Spot Possible Immigration Relief for Noncitizen Defendants (Jan. 2016). The main types of convictions that bar relief from removal are discussed in Chapter 5, Determining Possible Immigration Consequences Based on Your Client's Immigration Status.

Practice Note: Except as noted, a person convicted of one of the offenses discussed below may be eligible for limited forms of relief from removal. However, because it can be difficult to get relief, your client should *not* count on it. When possible, it is best for a noncitizen to avoid convictions that provide grounds for removal.

C. Long-Term Consequences of Removal Order

Noncitizens who have been ordered removed face a number of obstacles in returning to the U.S. Once deported, most individuals will not be able to return lawfully to the U.S.

Generally speaking, clients who are removed from the U.S. will be barred from future admission into the U.S. for a statutory period. An individual ordered removed after a removal hearing will generally be barred from the U.S. for ten years. *See* INA § 212(a)(9)(A)(ii), 8 U.S.C. § 1182(a)(9)(A)(ii). In the case of a second or subsequent removal, an individual will be barred from the U.S. for twenty years. *See id.* Although an individual may request permission from the government to return to the U.S. before the end of the statutory time period, such permission is difficult to obtain. *See* 8 C.F.R. § 212.2. Even after the statutory period has passed, it will not be easy for your client to return to the U.S.—your client will still have to establish eligibility for an immigrant visa.

The most drastic consequences are for clients who are removed on the basis of an aggravated felony conviction, discussed further below. These clients will generally not be able to return to the U.S. for life unless special permission to return is authorized by the Attorney General. *See* INA § 212(a)(9)(A)(ii)&(iii), 8 U.S.C. § 1182(a)(9)(A)(ii)&(iii).

Noncitizens who return or attempt to return unlawfully are subject to federal prosecution for illegal reentry and face lengthy prison sentences. *See* INA § 276, 8 U.S.C. § 1326. Prison sentences run up to twenty years if the noncitizen was removed after a conviction of an aggravated felony. *See* INA § 276(b)(2), 8 U.S.C. § 1326(b)(2). In recent years, the U.S. Attorneys' offices have significantly increased enforcement of these federal immigration crimes.

3.3   Determining Whether a State Offense Triggers Removal

A. Categorical Approach and Variations

Minimum culpable conduct. To determine whether a state conviction qualifies as an offense that triggers removal, the immigration court employs the "categorical approach." Under this approach, the factfinder compares the elements of the statute of conviction to the federal removal ground. *See Moncrieffe v. Holder*, 569 U.S. 184, 133 S. Ct. 1678 (2013). The actual conduct that led to the defendant's prosecution is irrelevant. What matters is whether the "least of the acts" criminalized by the statute necessarily comes within the ground of removal. *Id.*, 133 S. Ct. at 1684. For example, in *Castillo v. Holder*, 776 F.3d 262 (4th Cir. 2015), the Fourth Circuit considered whether the defendant's conviction for unauthorized use of a vehicle under Virginia law was an aggravated felony theft offense. The aggravated felony theft ground of removal requires that an element of the offense be a non-consensual taking. In *Castillo*, the Court found that the minimum culpable conduct criminalized under the Virginia statute is where the car is entrusted to the defendant but is used in a manner not specifically authorized by the owner. The Court found that the statute was not a categorical match because the minimum culpable conduct under the statute did not involve a taking without the owner's consent and thus did not come within the aggravated felony theft ground. Thus, no convictions under the Virginia unauthorized-use statute qualify as an aggravated felony theft offense. It does not matter that the noncitizen may in fact have taken the car without the owner's consent because the immigration court is required to presume that the conviction rested on the least of the acts under the statute.

As part of this analysis, the immigration court must consider whether a "realistic probability" exists that the convicting jurisdiction actually prosecutes the minimum culpable conduct. *Moncrieffe*, 133 S. Ct. at 1684–85. If there is a "realistic probability" that the state would apply the statute of conviction to conduct falling outside the federal removal ground, the immigration consequence is not triggered.

How have courts determined whether a realistic probability of prosecution exists? The Supreme Court has explained that a noncitizen can satisfy this standard by pointing to a case in which the state courts applied the statute to conduct falling outside the removal ground. *See Gonzalez v. Duenas-Alvarez*, 549 U.S. 183, 193 (2007). The Eleventh Circuit has held that where the statute on its face expressly reaches conduct that falls outside the generic ground of removability, the statute satisfies the standard. *Ramos v. Attorney General*, 709 F.3d 1066, 1071–72 (11th Cir. 2013) (concluding that where a Georgia theft statute expressly covered alternative intents, one of which did not satisfy the elements of an aggravated felony theft crime, the statute's language created the realistic probability that it would punish crimes beyond generic theft). The BIA, however, does not apply this express language rule. *Matter of Ferreira*, 26 I&N Dec. 415, 419 (BIA 2014). The Fourth Circuit has held that even where the language of the statute does not expressly include the minimum conduct, but the case law interpreting the statutory language does, the realistic probability standard is satisfied. *United States v. Aparicio-Soria*, 740 F.3d 152, 158 (4th Cir. 2014) (en banc).

Modified categorical approach. The above approach includes an additional step, called the "modified categorical approach," if the statute of conviction is *divisible*—that is, it defines more than one offense, at least one of which comes within the removal ground and one of which does not. *Descamps v. U.S.*, ___ U.S. ___, 133 S. Ct. 2276 (2013). In these cases, the immigration judge cannot perform the required categorical analysis until it has been determined which offense the individual was convicted of. For this limited purpose, the immigration judge can look beyond the language of the statute to a limited set of official court documents from the defendant's criminal case, called the "record of conviction." The defendant's particular conduct remains irrelevant under this analysis; the only issue is which of the multiple offenses defined by the statute was the basis of the conviction. *Id.* The specific documents that comprise the record of conviction are listed below.

Until recently, it was unclear when the immigration court could look to the record of conviction in applying the modified categorical approach. Some statutes contain a disjunctive list of acts, which are considered alternative ways of committing a single crime. In other statutes, the acts are considered elements, which are part of separate crimes. In identifying the offense committed by the defendant, can the immigration court look at the record of conviction in both instances or only when the statute creates separate crimes?

For example, suppose a statute defines burglary as unlawfully breaking and entering into a *building, car, or boat* with the intent to commit a felony. For immigration purposes, burglary of a car or boat is not an aggravated felony burglary offense. Can the immigration court look to the record of conviction to determine whether the defendant was guilty of burglary of a building (which is an aggravated felony burglary) or burglary of a car (which is not an aggravated felony burglary). The U.S. Supreme Court recently held that this question turns on whether the items in the list (building, car, or boat) are "elements" of the offense, which must be found unanimously and beyond a reasonable doubt, or are alternative means of committing a single offense. *See United States v. Mathis*, ___ U.S. ___, 136 S. Ct. 2243 (2016). If the former, then the immigration court may look to the record of conviction, If the latter, the immigration court cannot because the statute creates only one offense. This is an important distinction because if "building, car, or boat" are alternative means of committing one offense, then the minimum conduct punished under the statute does not come within the burglary aggravated felony ground and does not trigger removal on that basis.

Assume instead that "building, car, or boat" are three different elements, defining three different crimes. In that case, because the statute defines more than one offense, the immigration judge would be permitted to consult the record of conviction to determine for which offense the defendant was convicted. If the record indicates that he was convicted of entering a building, the client would be deportable. If the record of conviction is silent, then the immigration court should conclude that the noncitizen is not deportable because the burden of proof lies with the government. *See infra* § 3.3B, Burden of Proof on ICE in Establishing Deportability. Similarly, if the defendant takes an *Alford* plea, there is an argument that the government cannot meet its burden of establishing under which prong of a divisible statute the defendant was convicted. *See infra* § 6.1C, Categorical Approach and Record of Conviction.

A practitioner would generally look to state law to make this determination. Researching state case law and examining the state criminal statute's text is therefore an essential and critical first step to ascertaining whether a criminal statute is divisible and permits review of the record of conviction. For a discussion of this issue in the context of pleading requirements, see 1 North Carolina Defender Manual § 8.5G, Disjunctive Pleadings (2d ed. 2013); Robert L. Farb, The "Or" Issue in Criminal Pleadings, Jury Instructions, and Verdicts; Unanimity of Jury Verdict (Feb. 1, 2010).

Record of Conviction. The Board of Immigration Appeals and U.S. Supreme Court have determined that the following documents make up the record of conviction:

- statute of conviction,
- charging document (such as the indictment or information),
- written plea agreement,
- transcript of plea colloquy,
- any factual findings by the judge to which the defendant agreed
- stipulations to the factual basis for the offense, and
- jury instructions if the defendant is convicted after a jury trial.

The following documents are beyond the record of conviction and ordinarily may not be considered by the immigration court:

- police reports,
- probation or pre-sentence reports, and
- statements by the noncitizen outside the judgment and sentence transcript.

The record of conviction can be affected by counsel's handing of the case, discussed *infra* in § 6.1C, Categorical Approach and Record of Conviction.

Non-categorical exceptions. In a few limited contexts, the immigration court may take a non-categorical, "circumstance-specific" approach, which permits an inquiry into the facts of a conviction without regard to the elements of the statute of conviction. In *Nijhawan v. Holder*, 557 U.S. 29 (2009), the U.S. Supreme Court held that some aggravated felony definitions are made up of two parts: one or more "generic" offenses that are subject to the categorical approach, and one or more "circumstance-specific" factors that are not. *Nijhawan* concerned the aggravated felony of a crime of fraud or deceit in which the loss to the victim exceeds $10,000. INA § 101(a)(43)(M), 8 U.S.C. § 1101(a)(43)(M). The Court found that the amount of loss is circumstance-specific and need not be proved under the categorical approach, while fraud and deceit are generic offenses that are subject to the categorical approach. Thus, in determining whether the loss was greater than $10,000, the immigration court is permitted to look at documents beyond the record of conviction, such as presentence reports. Other areas in which this approach applies include the exception to deportability for an offense involving possession of thirty grams or less of marijuana (*see Matter of Davey*, 26 I&N 37 Dec. (BIA 2012); *see also infra* § 3.4D, Conviction of any Controlled Substance Offense) and proof of a domestic relationship for purposes of the domestic violence ground of deportability. *See Hernandez-Zavala v. Lynch*, 806 F.3d 259 (4th Cir. 2015); *see infra* § 3.4F, Conviction of a Crime of Domestic Violence, Stalking, Child Abuse, Child Neglect, or Child Abandonment, or a Violation of a Protective Order

B. Burden of Proof on ICE in Establishing Deportability

In removal proceedings, ICE has the burden of establishing that the noncitizen is deportable. *See* INA § 240(c)(3), 8 U.S.C. § 1229a(c)(3); 8 C.F.R. § 1240.8(a). Thus, ICE must demonstrate that the offense of conviction falls into a ground of removal. If the statute of conviction defines multiple offenses (some of which come within the immigration ground and some of which do not), and there is insufficient information in the record of conviction to determine the offense of conviction, the government would be unable to demonstrate that the noncitizen is deportable. *See Matter of Almanza-Arenas*, 24 I&N Dec. 771 (BIA 2009); *see also infra* § 6.1C, Categorical Approach and Record of Conviction (discussing *Alford* pleas).

C. Burden of Proof on Noncitizen in Applying for Relief and Demonstrating Admissibility

If ICE establishes that a noncitizen is deportable, the noncitizen may be able to apply for some form of relief from removal. In general, the noncitizen has the burden of proving that he or she is eligible for a form of relief from removal. *See* 8 C.F.R. § 1240.8(d); *Matter of Almanza-Arenas*, 24 I&N Dec. 771 (BIA 2009). Also, noncitizens subject to grounds of inadmissibility generally bear the burden of demonstrating that they are admissible. *See* INA § 240(c)(2), 8 U.S.C. § 1229a(c)(2). Thus, in some instances, the noncitizen has the burden of documenting necessary information in the record of conviction. For example, an individual convicted of Class 1 misdemeanor marijuana possession in North Carolina is inadmissible on controlled substance grounds. But, the individual may qualify for relief from removal for such an offense by demonstrating that the conviction involved 30 grams or less of marijuana. Because Class 1 misdemeanor possession of marijuana covers quantities of more and less than 30 grams, the noncitizen must ensure that the record of conviction indicates that the amount of possession was 30 grams or less. Counsel may be able to take steps to safeguard the record. *See infra* § 6.1C, Categorical Approach and Record of Conviction.

3.4   Crime-Related Grounds of Deportability

This section reviews the main features of the different categories of criminal offenses that trigger deportability. The criminal grounds of deportability generally require that a "conviction" exist. There is a statutory definition of conviction for immigration purposes. State law does *not* determine whether a state disposition will be considered a conviction for immigration law purposes. For example, dispositions involving drug treatment court, deferral of prosecution, expunction, and prayers for judgment continued may be treated as convictions for immigration purposes. For the definition of conviction, see *infra* § 4.1, Conviction for Immigration Purposes.

A. Aggravated Felonies Generally

Definition. A noncitizen is deportable if convicted of an aggravated felony any time after admission. INA § 237(a)(2)(A)(iii), 8 U.S.C. § 1227(a)(2)(A)(iii). "Aggravated felony" is an immigration law term that includes an expanding list of offenses defined in INA § 101(a)(43), 8 U.S.C. § 1101(a)(43). The label is somewhat misleading, as an offense classified as an "aggravated felony" does not have to be either "aggravated" (as that term may be commonly understood) or a "felony" under state law. As a result of broad interpretations of the statutory language, the term may include some state misdemeanors, such as maintaining a place of prostitution.

The long list of aggravated felony offenses can generally be classified into the following groupings:

- specific offenses, regardless of sentence, such as murder, rape, sexual abuse of a minor, drug trafficking, and firearm trafficking;
- specific offenses for which an active or suspended sentence of imprisonment of one year or more is imposed (for definition of sentence length, see *infra* § 4.3, Sentence to a Term of Imprisonment), such as theft, burglary, forgery, crimes of violence, perjury, and obstruction of justice;
- specific offenses where a specific circumstance (other than the elements of the crime) is met, such as fraud or deceit offenses in which the loss to the victim exceeds $10,000; and
- any attempt or conspiracy to commit any of the enumerated aggravated felony offenses.

The following table lists the broad categories of offenses classified as aggravated felonies. Offenses that do not meet these criteria may still constitute deportable or inadmissible offenses, discussed further below, but they do not trigger the severe consequences associated with aggravated felony convictions.

Aggravated Felonies Regardless of Sentence
- Murder
- Rape
- Sexual abuse of a minor (including indecent liberties with a minor under N.C. law)
- Drug trafficking
- Firearm trafficking and certain other firearm offenses
- Certain ransom offenses
- Certain child pornography offenses
- Offenses related to prostitution business
- Offenses related to slavery or involuntary servitude

- National security offenses
- Alien smuggling offenses, with an exception for spouse, parents, and children
- Illegal reentry after being previously deported for an aggravated felony
- Miscellaneous federal offenses, including racketeering and certain gambling offenses
- Offenses related to failure to appear for service of sentence if the underlying offense is punishable by five years or more imprisonment
- Offenses related to bail jumping if underlying offense is a felony punishable by two or more years imprisonment

Aggravated Felonies Triggered by a One-Year Term of Imprisonment (Active or Suspended) or More
- Crimes of violence
- Theft or burglary offenses (including possession or receipt of stolen property)
- Passport or document fraud offenses
- Offenses related to counterfeiting
- Offenses related to forgery
- Offenses related to commercial bribery
- Offenses related to trafficking in vehicles with altered identification numbers
- Offenses related to obstruction of justice
- Offenses related to perjury or subornation of perjury
- Offenses related to bribery of a witness

Aggravated Felonies Triggered by More than a $10,000 Loss
- Offenses involving fraud or deceit with a loss to the victim of more than $10,000
- Money laundering offenses involving more than $10,000
- Tax evasion with a loss to the government of more than $10,000

Consequences. Convictions for aggravated felonies carry the most severe immigration consequences. A conviction for an aggravated felony not only triggers deportability, it also bars eligibility for almost all forms of relief from removal, effectively subjecting the individual to mandatory removal without any consideration of his or her equities. When removed on the basis of an aggravated felony conviction, an individual is permanently inadmissible and thus permanently barred from returning to the U.S. (unless special permission from the government is obtained, which is quite difficult). *See* INA § 212(a)(9)(A)(ii), 8 U.S.C. § 1182(a)(9)(A)(ii). In addition, an individual removed on the basis of an aggravated felony conviction who returns to the U.S. unlawfully may be imprisoned for up to twenty years if federally prosecuted for illegal reentry. *See* INA § 276(b)(2), 8 U.S.C. § 1326(b)(2).

B. Specific Types of Aggravated Felonies

Crime of Violence Aggravated Felonies. Offenses that constitute "crimes of violence" within the meaning of immigration law are aggravated felonies if a sentence of imprisonment (active or suspended) of one year or more is imposed (for definition of sentence length, see *infra* § 4.3, Sentence to a Term of Imprisonment). *See* INA § 101(a)(43)(F), 8 U.S.C. § 1101(a)(43)(F).

The definition of crime of violence is broad in scope. It is defined in 18 U.S.C. § 16 as:

> (a) an offense that has as an element the use, attempted use, or threatened use of physical force against the person or property of another, or
> (b) any other offense that is a felony and that, by its nature, involves a substantial risk that physical force against the person or property of another may be used in the course of committing the offense.

The definition has been the subject of much federal litigation. Note the distinction between § 16(a), which requires that force be an element of the offense, and § 16(b), which refers to force but does not require that it be an element. For example, the U.S. Supreme Court has said that felony burglary would come within § 16(b) because there is an inherent risk that the burglar may encounter the homeowner and use force against her in that confrontation. Offenses that have been found to constitute crimes of violence include intentional violent assaults, kidnappings, robberies, and burglaries.

Five federal courts of appeals have found that 18 U.S.C. § 16(b) is void for vagueness. *See Dimaya v. Lynch*, 803 F.3d 1110 (9th Cir. 2015) (holding that 18 U.S.C. § 16(b) is void for vagueness under reasoning of *Johnson v. United States*, ___ U.S. ___, 135 S. Ct. 2551 (2015)); *United States v. Vivas-Ceja*, 808 F.3d 719, 722–23 (7th Cir. 2015); *Shuti v. Lynch*, 828 F.3d 440 (6th Cir. 2016); *Golicov v. Lynch*, 837 F.3d 1065 (10th Cir. 2016); *Baptiste v. Atty. Gen.*, 841 F.3d 601 (3d Cir. 2016). The U.S. Supreme Court has granted cert. on this issue in *Dimaya v. Lynch* and will decide by the end of the 2018 term whether § 16(b) is unconstitutionally vague. If it is found to be unconstitutionally vague, federal court and BIA cases finding that certain offenses are crimes of violence under § 16(b) will be overruled.

A misdemeanor assault does not constitute a crime of violence aggravated felony because under North Carolina law the sentence cannot exceed 150 days for even the most serious misdemeanor assault.

The Supreme Court has held that an offense requiring only proof of accidental or negligent conduct, even when involving serious physical injury or death, is not purposeful enough to qualify as an aggravated felony "crime of violence," as defined in 18 U.S.C. § 16. *Leocal v. Ashcroft*, 543 U.S. 1 (2004) (holding that a state offense of driving under the influence of alcohol and causing serious bodily injury, which does not have a mens rea component or requires only a showing of negligence in the operation of a vehicle, is not crime of violence under 18 U.S.C. § 16). For example, a conviction of felony serious injury by vehicle, G.S. 20-141.4(a3), which penalizes unintentionally causing serious injury when driving while impaired (G.S. 20-138.1 or G.S. 20-138.2), should not qualify as a crime of violence aggravated felony even if the person receives a sentence of imprisonment of one year or more.

The U.S. Supreme Court has not resolved whether a state offense that requires proof of reckless use of force qualifies as a crime of violence. *See Leocal v. Ashcroft*, 543 U.S. 1, 13 (2004); *Voisine v. United States*, ___ U.S. ___, 136 S. Ct. 2272, 2280 n.4 (2016). Most federal courts of appeals, including the Fourth and Eleventh Circuits, however, have held that such an offense is not sufficiently purposeful to qualify as a crime of violence. *See, e.g., Garcia v. Gonzalez*, 455 F.3d 465 (4th Cir. 2006) (holding that conviction for reckless assault in the second degree is not a crime of violence aggravated felony); *United States v. Palomino Garcia*, 606 F.3d 1317, 1336 (11th Cir. 2010).

Also, the Board of Immigration Appeals has held that the crime of battery by offensive touching does not require "violent" force and thus is not a crime of violence. *Matter of Velasquez*, 25 I&N Dec. 278, 282–83 (BIA 2010) (treating the rule in *Johnson v. United States*, 559 U.S. 133 (2010), as controlling authority in interpreting whether an offense is a "crime of violence" under § 16(a)).

Drug Trafficking Aggravated Felonies. Drug trafficking offenses within the meaning of immigration law are aggravated felonies regardless of the length of the sentence imposed.

Federal law, not state law, determines whether a state offense constitutes an aggravated felony "drug trafficking" offense. *See* INA § 101(a)(43)(B), 8 U.S.C. § 1101(a)(43)(B) (drug trafficking crime is defined at 18 U.S.C. § 924(c)). "Controlled substance" is defined by federal law and refers to substances covered by the federal drug schedules in 21 U.S.C. § 802. At the time of this revised edition, it appears that all of the drugs listed in the North Carolina state drug schedules are covered by the federal drug schedules, with one exception. Schedule III of the N.C. controlled substance schedules regulates chorionic gonadotropin, which steroid users employ to avoid testicular atrophy, a side effect from steroids. G.S. 90-91(k). This is not a federally controlled substance, so a conviction for such an offense would not come within this ground of removal. The U.S. Supreme Court has held that where the state drug statute is broader than the federal drug statute (by encompassing drugs that are not on the federal list), and the record of conviction does not reveal the identity of the drug involved, the government would not be able to meet its burden of proof to show that the immigrant is deportable for a controlled substance offense. *See Mellouli v. Lynch*, ___ U.S. ___, 135 S. Ct. 1980 (2015); *see infra* § 3.4D, Conviction of Any Controlled Substance Offense.

Below are examples from the cases of what are and are not drug trafficking aggravated felonies.

- A misdemeanor or felony conviction for simple possession of a controlled substance—except for possession of any amount of flunitrazepam (colloquially known as the "date rape drug")— is not a "drug trafficking" aggravated felony offense. *Lopez v. Gonzalez*, 549 U.S. 47 (2006).
- Under *Lopez*, there is a strong argument, as evidenced by an unpublished administrative BIA decision, that North Carolina possession by trafficking should not qualify as an aggravated felony. *See infra* Appendix B, Relevant Immigration Decisions.

- Federal law punishes straight possession as a misdemeanor, regardless of quantity (although a federal prosecutor might charge the offense as possession with intent to distribute if the amount is large). Thus, where the state offense, like North Carolina possession by trafficking, proscribes straight possession (even where the quantity is large), it should not constitute a felony under federal criminal law and thus should not qualify as drug trafficking aggravated felony. *See Lopez v. Gonzales*, 549 U.S. 47, 60 (2006).
- A second North Carolina drug possession conviction, if prosecuted as a recidivist offense under G.S. 90-95(e)(3), may be deemed a drug trafficking aggravated felony. *See Carachuri-Rosendo v. Holder*, 560 U.S. 563 (2010).
- A conviction of any drug sale or possession with intent to sell continues to qualify as a drug trafficking aggravated felony. *See Lopez v. Gonzales*, 549 U.S. 47.
- The U.S. Supreme Court has also held that a statute that punishes conduct that includes the transfer of small amounts of marijuana for no remuneration is not a "drug trafficking" aggravated felony. *See Moncrieffe v. Holder*, 569 U.S. 184 (2013). Under *Moncrieffe*, there is a good argument that a conviction for delivery of marijuana or possession of marijuana with intent to manufacture, sell, or deliver under G.S. 90-95(b)(1) is not a drug trafficking aggravated felony. The reason is that a defendant can be convicted of possession with intent to manufacture, sell, or deliver without any evidence of remuneration and without the State establishing the amount of the marijuana. *See State v. Pevia*, 56 N.C. App. 384 (1982) (holding that it is not necessary for the State to prove remuneration or quantity of marijuana transferred for offense of delivery.)[1] The Board of Immigration Appeals adopted this argument in an unpublished decision. *See infra* Appendix B, Relevant Immigration Decisions.

"Drug Trafficking" Aggravated Felony Offenses in North Carolina

- Any manufacture, sale, or delivery of controlled substance offense (except delivery of marijuana or involving chorionic gonadotropin)
- Any possession of controlled substance with intent to manufacture, sell, or deliver offense (except possession of marijuana with intent to manufacture, sell, or deliver or involving chorionic gonadotropin)
- Any N.C. drug trafficking offense (except possibly trafficking by possession or involving chorionic gonadotropin)
- Possibly a second N.C. drug possession offense prosecuted as a recidivist drug offense (except involving chorionic gonadotropin)

---

1. The North Carolina General Statutes contain a specific provision for the social sharing of marijuana, but only for up to 5 grams of marijuana. *See* G.S. 90-95(b)(2) ("the transfer of less than 5 grams of marijuana . . . for no remuneration shall not constitute a delivery in violation of G.S. 90-95(a)(1)"). In *Moncrieffe*, the Court suggested that a "small amount" covers up to 30 grams of marijuana, so someone who delivered 25 grams of marijuana would still come within the *Moncrieffe* exception (but not within G.S. 90-95(b)(2)). The actual amount of marijuana involved does not matter under *Moncrieffe* because the immigration court cannot go beyond the elements of the statute. *See supra* § 3.3A, Categorical Approach and Variations.

Not "Drug Trafficking" Aggravated Felony Offenses

- Possession of controlled substance, whether felony or misdemeanor, with the exception of any amount of flunitrazepam (date rape drug)
- Possession of drug paraphernalia
- Delivery of marijuana or possession with intent to manufacture, sell, or deliver
- Possibly trafficking by possession

Practice Note: The above does not necessarily mean that a conviction for simple drug possession, delivery of marijuana, or other drug offenses is an "immigration-safe" plea. Any controlled substance conviction is a separate ground of deportability except for a one-time exception for possession of 30 grams or less of marijuana. *See infra* § 3.4D, Conviction of Any Controlled Substance Offense. However, these pleas may be beneficial because clients can avoid the harsh consequences of an aggravated felony and preserve the possibility of relief from removal.

Firearm Aggravated Felonies. There are two categories of firearm aggravated felonies. The first category covers certain offenses involving trafficking in firearms or destructive devices. *See* INA § 101(a)(43)(C), 8 U.S.C. § 1101(a)(43)(C). The Board of Immigration Appeals has found in an unpublished case that a single sale may constitute "trafficking." The second aggravated felony category covers miscellaneous firearm and explosives offenses, such as possession of a machine gun and possession of a firearm by felon. *See* INA § 101(a)(43)(E), 8 U.S.C. § 1101(a)(43)(E).

C. Conviction of a Crime Involving Moral Turpitude

A noncitizen may be deportable for a conviction of a crime involving moral turpitude (CMT) depending on the potential length of sentence, the number of CMT convictions, and the date the offense was committed in relation to when the noncitizen was admitted to the U.S. (discussed under Consequences, below).

Definition. There is no statutory definition for the immigration term "crime involving moral turpitude" (CMT). There is, however, a considerable amount of case law governing what constitutes a CMT. As a general rule, a crime involves "moral turpitude" if it is inherently base, vile, or depraved, and contrary to the accepted rules of morality and the duties owed between persons or to society in general. *See, e.g., Matter of Olquin-Rufino*, 23 I&N Dec. 896 (BIA 2006). Also, the Board of Immigration Appeals requires some form of scienter (at least recklessness) coupled with reprehensible conduct. *See, e.g., Matter of Leal*, 26 I&N Dec. 20 (BIA 2012); *Matter of Tavdidishvili*, 27 I&N Dec. 142 (BIA 2017) (holding that criminally negligent homicide under New York law is categorically not a crime involving moral turpitude because it does not require that a perpetrator have a sufficiently culpable mental state). The CMT label covers a broad category of criminal offenses and generally includes:

- offenses in which either an intent to steal or defraud is an element (such as theft and forgery offenses),

- many aggravated assaults (depending on whether infliction of bodily injury is an element), and
- many sex offenses

Examples of crimes *not involving moral turpitude* include simple assault, misdemeanor breaking and entering, carrying a concealed weapon, trespass, unauthorized use of a vehicle, drunk and disruptive, disorderly conduct, and regulatory offenses.

There has been much litigation about whether the categorical approach applies to determining whether an offense qualifies as a CMT. Both the Fourth and Eleventh Circuits have held that the categorical approach applies. *See Prudencio v. Holder*, 669 F.3d 472 (4th 2012); *Fajardo v. U.S. Att'y Gen.*, 659 F.3d 1303 (11th Cir. 2011).

To determine whether a specific crime constitutes a CMT, consult Appendix A, Selected Immigration Consequences of North Carolina Offenses, at the end of this manual.

Assault Offenses. The cases are mixed on assault offenses—they are not all consistent and rely on different factors. Below is the recommended analysis.

- North Carolina simple assault does not qualify as a CMT for multiple reasons. First, simple assault or battery is generally not deemed to involve moral turpitude for purposes of immigration law because it requires general intent only. *See Matter of Short,* 20 I&N Dec. 136 (BIA 1989). Second, the Fourth Circuit has found that the minimum conduct for a simple assault under North Carolina law requires only culpable negligence. *United States v. Vinson*, 805 F.3d 120, 126 (4th Cir. 2015). This mental state is sufficient for either an assault (essentially, an attempted battery) or a battery (essentially, unlawful physical contact), which are both covered by North Carolina's assault statute. Because culpable negligence does not rise to recklessness, the minimum scienter required for a CMT, North Carolina simple assault does not qualify as a CMT. *See id.* (holding that culpable negligence as defined in North Carolina is a lesser standard of culpability than recklessness, which requires at least "a *conscious* disregard of risk").
- An intentional or knowing assault involving some aggravating dimension that increases the culpability of the offense, such as the offender's use of a deadly weapon or infliction of serious injury on a person whom society views as deserving of special protection, such as children, domestic partners, or peace officers, is a CMT. *See Matter of Sanudo*, 23 I&N Dec. 968 (2006). North Carolina assault with a deadly weapon is possibly a CMT offense for that reason. This rule arguably should not apply to the simple forms of assault on a female, assault on an officer, and assault on a child because under *Vinson*, the minimum conduct under those statutes involves culpable negligence, which does not rise to a CMT. Accordingly, the BIA in an unpublished decision has found that assault on a female does not qualify as a CMT. *See infra* Appendix B, Relevant Immigration Decisions. Moreover, these offenses do not require infliction of bodily injury. Beware, however, that the Eleventh Circuit has held that no requirement of bodily injury is necessary. *See Gelin v. U.S. Atty. Gen.*, 837 F.3d 1236 (11th Cir. 2016) (holding that Florida abuse of an elderly or disabled

person is a CMT because of the statutory elements of a vulnerable victim and a knowing or willful mental state). Additionally, an assault on an officer should not qualify as a CMT because the minimum conduct punished can be mere offensive touching, such as spitting at an officer. *See State v. Mylett*, ___ N.C. App. ___, 799 S.E.2d 419 (2017) (upholding conviction for assault on an officer where defendant spat at officer); *Matter of Sanudo*, 23 I&N Dec. 968 (2006) (where minimum conduct punished under statute is battery by offensive touching against a protected class, the offense does not rise to a CMT).

Impaired Driving Offenses. A conviction for impaired driving may be a CMT depending on the presence of aggravating or grossly aggravating factors. The Board of Immigration Appeals has held that a simple driving while impaired offense is not a CMT. *See Matter of Torres-Varela*, 23 I&N Dec. 78 (BIA 2001). Further, an offense of driving while impaired with two or more prior convictions for simple driving while impaired under an Arizona statute has been held not to be a CMT. *See id.* In contrast, the BIA has held that a conviction for an aggravated DWI offense containing an element of driving with a revoked license is a CMT. *Matter of Lopez-Meza*, 22 I&N Dec. 1188 (BIA 1999).

Under this case law, an impaired driving conviction under North Carolina law will not constitute a CMT offense if there are no aggravating sentencing factors. An impaired driving conviction with an aggravating sentencing factor of driving with a revoked license is possibly a CMT offense. It is unclear because the case law requires that the driving with a revoked license component be an element of the offense as opposed to a sentencing factor. Under *Apprendi v. New Jersey*, 530 U.S. 466 (2000), aggravating factors that increase the penalty for a crime must be proven beyond a reasonable doubt and are considered to be elements of the offense. If viewed as offense elements, some of North Carolina's aggravating sentencing factors may make a DWI conviction a CMT. This manual does not address the impact of other sentencing factors.

Consequences. A noncitizen is deportable if convicted of one CMT committed within five years of admission to the U.S. and *punishable* by at least one year in prison. *See* INA § 237(a)(2)(A)(i), 8 U.S.C. § 1227(a)(2)(A)(i). The Fourth Circuit Court of Appeals has held that to determine whether a North Carolina offense is punishable by at least one year in prison for purposes of the federal sentencing guidelines, courts consider the maximum sentence that a defendant could receive in state court based on the defendant's prior record level under North Carolina law. *See United States v. Simmons*, 649 F.3d 237, 240, 249–50 (4th Cir. 2011) (en banc). The North Carolina Justice Reinvestment Act, effective for offenses committed on or after December 1, 2011, introduced a new nine-month period of mandatory post-release supervision (PRS) for Class F through I felonies, the lowest felony classes in North Carolina. *See* G.S. 15A-1368.2(c). As a result, the sentence that "may be imposed" for any North Carolina felony conviction will be greater than a one year sentence. *See United States v. Barlow*, 811 F.3d 133 (4th Cir. 2015).

A noncitizen is also deportable if convicted of two or more CMTs, not arising out of a single scheme of criminal misconduct, committed at any time after admission and regardless of the actual or potential sentence. *See* INA § 237(a)(2)(A)(ii), 8 U.S.C. §

1227(a)(2)(A)(ii). Two CMTs that arose out of a separate scheme and that are consolidated for judgment or are run concurrently, will likely still be considered separate convictions for immigration purposes and will trigger deportability. Conversely, if a person is convicted of two or more CMTs arising out of a single scheme, the convictions should not trigger deportability.

Practice Note: In North Carolina, because misdemeanors are generally not punishable by a year or more of imprisonment, the commission of one misdemeanor CMT will not trigger deportability.

D. Conviction of Any Controlled Substance Offense

Conviction of Any Controlled Substance Offense. A noncitizen is deportable for any violation of law "relating to" a controlled substance, whether felony or misdemeanor, except for a single offense of simple possession of 30 grams or less of marijuana (discussed further below). *See* INA § 237(a)(2)(B)(i), 8 U.S.C. § 1227(a)(2)(B)(i).

"Controlled substance" is defined by federal law and refers to substances covered by the federal drug schedules in 21 U.S.C. § 802. At the time of this revised edition, it appears that all of the drugs listed in the North Carolina state drug schedules are covered by the federal drug schedules, with one exception. Schedule III of the N.C. controlled substance schedules regulates chorionic gonadotropin, which steroid users employ to avoid testicular atrophy, a side-effect from steroids. G.S. 90-91(k). This is not a federally controlled substance, so a conviction for such an offense would not come within this ground of removal. The U.S. Supreme Court has held that where the state drug statute is broader than the federal drug statute (by encompassing drugs that are not on the federal list), and the record of conviction does not reveal the identity of the drug involved, the government would not be able to meet its burden of proof to show that the immigrant is deportable for a controlled substance offense. *See Mellouli v. Lynch*, ___ U.S. ___, 135 S. Ct. 1980 (2015). Thus, if your client pleads guilty to possession of a Schedule III drug and the record of conviction does not reveal the specific drug, there is a strong argument that your client is not deportable for a controlled substance offense under *Mellouli*. However, if the charging document names a controlled substance other than chorionic gonadotropin, the client will be deportable.

Conviction of Drug Paraphernalia. The government will likely argue that a conviction for drug paraphernalia is a controlled substance offense, but that may not be so.

In *Mellouli*, the Supreme Court held that a drug paraphernalia conviction is only a deportable controlled substance offense where a federally controlled drug is an element of the offense. Thus, a conviction for paraphernalia related to an unnamed Schedule III drug should not be a deportable offense, and for that reason defenders may want to negotiate such language where appropriate.

Additionally, there is an argument that no North Carolina conviction for drug paraphernalia is a deportable offense. Under *United States v. Mathis*, ___ U.S. ___, 136

S. Ct. 2243 (2016), the identity of the controlled substance is arguably not an *element* of the North Carolina paraphernalia statute (except when the paraphernalia involves marijuana under G.S. 90-113.22A). Because the state schedules are broader than the federal ones (because North Carolina's covers chorionic gonadotropin), a state paraphernalia conviction is arguably never a controlled substance offense. *See supra* § 3.3A, Categorical Approach and Variations.

Exception for Possession of Small Amount of Marijuana. A noncitizen is not deportable if she or he has been convicted of only "a single offense involving possession for one's own use of thirty grams or less of marijuana." 8 U.S.C. § 1227(a)(2)(B)(i), INA § 237(a)(2)(B)(i). A North Carolina possession conviction for less than 30 grams of marijuana will fall within this exception if the noncitizen has no prior drug convictions. In *Matter of Davey*, 26 I&N Dec. 37, 39 (BIA 2012), the Board of Immigration Appeals held that the immigration court is *not* limited to the elements of the offense and to the record of conviction; instead, the 30 grams exception calls for a circumstance-specific inquiry into the noncitizen's actual conduct. Thus, to meet its burden of proof, the government can look to court documents outside of the record of conviction to establish that more than 30 grams of marijuana was in fact involved. *See supra* § 3.3A, Categorical Approach and Variations.

Exception for Possession of Drug Paraphernalia Related to a Small Amount of Marijuana. The Board in *Davey* also found that the 30 grams exception would cover the possession of drug paraphernalia where the paraphernalia was merely an adjunct to the noncitizen's simple possession or use of 30 grams or less of marijuana. *Id.* at 40–41. Thus, a client who pleads guilty to marijuana paraphernalia related to less than 30 grams of marijuana should not be deportable (assuming she has no other drug convictions). In 2014, North Carolina enacted a separate statute on marijuana drug paraphernalia, G.S. 90-113.22A. If a defendant violates that statute in a case involving 30 grams or less of marijuana, defenders should ensure that the record reflects that fact.

Practice Note: A conviction for a Class 3 misdemeanor possession of marijuana should not make a noncitizen with no prior drug convictions deportable under the 30 grams or less exception discussed above. A conviction for a Class 1 misdemeanor possession of marijuana also should not make a noncitizen deportable, unless the record of conviction or other documents, like the lab report, establish possession of more than 30 grams of marijuana. Consequently, if your client is charged with a Class 1 misdemeanor involving possession of marijuana, you should document in the record that the amount involved was 30 grams or less.

Drug Abuse or Addiction. A noncitizen is also deportable if he or she is or has been a drug abuser or addict at any time after being admitted to the U.S. *See* INA § 237(a)(2)(B)(ii), 8 U.S.C. § 1227(a)(2)(B)(ii). This ground of deportability does not require a conviction. Drug abuse or addiction is determined in accordance with U.S. Department of Health and Human Services regulations. *See* INA § 212(a)(1)(A)(iv), 8 U.S.C. § 1182(a)(1)(A)(iv). Drug abuse is broadly defined as "current substance use disorder or substance-induced disorder, mild, as defined in the most recent edition of the

Diagnostic and Statistical Manual for Mental Disorders (DSM) as published by the American Psychiatric Association, or by another authoritative source as determined by the Director of Centers for Disease Control and Prevention, of a substance listed in Section 202 of the Controlled Substances Act." 42 C.F.R. § 34.2(h). This ground generally requires a medical determination and should not be triggered by a mere admission by the defendant.

E. Conviction of a Firearm or Destructive Device Offense

A noncitizen is deportable for a single conviction of purchasing, selling, offering for sale, exchanging, using, owning, possessing, or carrying in violation of any law, whether felony or misdemeanor, a firearm or destructive device (including part or accessory) as defined in 18 U.S.C. § 921(a). *See* INA § 237(a)(2)(C), 8 U.S.C. § 1227(a)(2)(C). The federal definition of firearm includes explosive-powered firearms and destructive devices (as defined in 18 U.S.C. § 921(a)(4)). The federal definition does not cover air-powered weapons like BB or pellet guns. There is also a federal exception for antique firearms. *See* 18 U.S.C. § 921(a)(3).

There is not a single definition of firearm under the North Carolina criminal law statutes. Some of the firearm definitions may be broader than the federal law, while others seem to match. For example, with regard to carrying a concealed pistol or gun under G.S. 14-269(a1), neither the statute nor the pattern jury instructions define "pistol" or "gun." Case law suggests that a gun or pistol must be a "firearm," *see, e.g., State v. Best*, 214 N.C. App. 39 (2011), which other North Carolina statutes have defined as a weapon that "expels a projectile by action of an explosion." Because there is no exception for an antique firearm as under federal law, there is an argument that this state offense is broader than the federal firearm ground of removal. *See Moncrieffe v. Holder*, 569 U.S. 184, 133 S. Ct. 1678, 1693 (2013); *see also supra* § 3.3A, Categorical Approach and Variations.

Where the use of a firearm (as defined in the federal statute) is an element of a crime, the conviction will be considered a firearm offense. *See, e.g., Matter of P-F-*, 20 I&N Dec. 661 (BIA 1993) (holding that convictions for first-degree armed burglary and robbery with a firearm under Florida statute constituted a firearm conviction where the use of firearm was an essential element of the crime). A conviction under a divisible statute (where the elements define both firearms offenses and non-firearms offenses) is not a deportable offense unless the record of conviction establishes that the conviction was under the firearms subsection. *See Matter of Pichardo-Sufren*, 21 I&N Dec. 330 (BIA 1996); *Matter of Teixeira*, 21 I&N Dec. 316 (BIA 1996); *Matter of Madrigal-Calvo*, 21 I&N Dec. 323 (BIA 1996); *see also supra* § 3.3A, Categorical Approach and Variations.

Practice Note: If your client is convicted of an offense where a weapon is an element of the offense, and the record of conviction does not establish that the weapon involved was a firearm, he or she should not be deportable for a firearm offense.

Federal law also criminalizes the possession of a firearm by noncitizens unlawfully present in the U.S. and by certain nonimmigrant visa holders. *See* 18 U.S.C. § 922(g)(5). Noncitizens in North Carolina have been federally prosecuted for this offense.

F. Conviction of a Crime of Domestic Violence, Stalking, Child Abuse, Child Neglect, or Child Abandonment, or a Violation of a Protective Order

A noncitizen is deportable if convicted of a crime of domestic violence, stalking, child abuse, child neglect, or child abandonment, whether felony or misdemeanor. *See* INA § 237(a)(2)(E) (i), 8 U.S.C. § 1227(a)(2)(E)(i).

These grounds of deportability only apply to convictions or violations occurring after September 30, 1996. *See* Section 350(b) of the Illegal Immigration Reform and Immigrant Responsibility Act of 1996, Pub. L. 104-208, Division C, 110 Stat. 3009-546.

Crime of Domestic Violence. A crime of domestic violence has two main requirements. First, the offense must be a crime of violence as defined in 18 U.S.C. § 16. The definition of crime of violence for a crime of domestic violence is the same as for aggravated felonies, discussed *supra* in § 3.4B, Specific Types of Aggravated Felonies. However, there is *not* a requirement of a one-year sentence here. Second, the offense must be against a current or former spouse, co-parent of a child, a person with whom the defendant is or has cohabited as a spouse, any other individual similarly situated to a spouse, or other individual protected under federal, state, tribal, or local domestic or family violence laws. *See* INA § 237(a)(2)(E)(i), 8 U.S.C. § 1227(a)(2)(E)(i).

The Fourth Circuit has found that the North Carolina offense of assault on a female is *not* a crime of domestic violence for purposes of 18 U.S.C. § 922(g)(9). *See United States v. Vinson*, 805 F.3d 120 (4th Cir. 2015). Section 922(g)(9) is a federal criminal statute that prohibits anyone who has previously been "convicted . . . of a misdemeanor crime of domestic violence" from possessing firearms or ammunition. It has a broader definition of force than 18 U.S.C. § 16. If an offense is not a crime of domestic violence for purposes of 18 U.S.C. § 922(g)(9), then it cannot be a crime of violence under the narrower definition of 18 U.S.C. § 16. *Cf. United States. v. Castleman*, ___ U.S. ___, 134 S. Ct. 1405, 1411 n.4 (2014) (finding "misdemeanor crime of domestic violence" under 18 U.S.C. § 922(g)(9) to have a more expansive definition than crimes of violence under 18 U.S.C. § 16, which denotes "active and violent force"). The Board of Immigration Appeals in an unpublished case has found that assault on a female is not a crime of domestic violence for immigration purposes. *See infra* Appendix B, Relevant Immigration Decisions.

While the categorical approach applies to "crime of violence," the fact-based circumstance-specific approach applies to the requirement of a domestic relationship. *See Hernandez-Zavala v. Lynch*, 806 F.3d 259 (4th Cir. 2015); *see also Matter of Estrada*, 26 I&N Dec. 749 (BIA 2016). Thus, the relationship between the offender and the victim need not be an element of the crime of conviction. Moreover, the immigration court will be permitted to look to documents beyond the record of conviction, such as sentencing and pre-sentence documents, to determine whether the victim was a protected party. *See supra* § 3.3A, Categorical Approach and Variations.

Crime of Child Abuse. The Board of Immigration Appeals treats "child abuse, child neglect, or child abandonment" as a "unitary concept," not as three different categories of offenses. *See Matter of Soram*, 25 I&N Dec. 378, 381 (BIA 2010). The immigration statute does not define this child abuse concept, but the BIA has interpreted it broadly to include "any offense involving an intentional, knowing, reckless, or criminally negligent act or omission that constitutes maltreatment of a child or that impairs a child's physical or mental well-being, including sexual abuse or exploitation." *Matter of Velazquez-Herrera*, 24 I&N Dec. 503, 512 (BIA 2008). The BIA defines "child" as anyone under age 18 and does not require that the offender be a parent or guardian caring for the child. *Id.*

In *Matter of Soram*, 25 I&N Dec. 378 (BIA 2010), the Board held that no proof of actual harm or injury to the child is required. *Id.*; *see also Matter of Mendoza Osorio*, 26 I&N Dec. 703 (BIA 2016). As a result, whether a child abuse offense involves an omission or negligent conduct, this definition would appear to apply without proof of actual harm. *But see Ibarra v. Holder*, 736 F.3d 903, 915-16 (10th Cir. 2013) (rejecting the BIA's broad interpretation and finding that child abuse ground of removal does not encompass criminally negligent conduct with no resulting injury to a child).

The categorical approach still applies here. *See Matter of Velazquez-Herrera*, 24 I&N Dec. 503, 513. Therefore, convictions for offenses that do *not* contain as an element "minor" or "child" should not come within this ground of removal.

Violation of a Protective Order. A noncitizen is also deportable if enjoined by a protective order to prevent acts of domestic violence and found by a civil *or* criminal court to have violated the portion of a protective order that protects against credible threats of violence, repeated harassment, or bodily injury. *See* INA § 237(a)(2)(E)(ii), 8 U.S.C. § 1227(a)(2)(E)(ii). The Board of Immigration Appeals has found that violation of a no-contact order falls within this ground of removal because the purpose of a no-contact order is to protect "against credible threats of violence, repeated harassment, or bodily injury" within the meaning of INA § 237(a)(2)(E)(ii). *See Matter of Strydom*, 25 I&N Dec. 507 (BIA 2011). However, a violation of an order requiring attendance at and payment for a counseling program or requiring the payment of costs for supervision during parenting time is *not* covered by the removal provision. *Id.* at 511.

In North Carolina, for protective order purposes, domestic violence is broadly defined to include persons of the opposite sex who have lived together, parents and children, grandparents and grandchildren, current or former household members, and persons involved in non-cohabiting romantic relationships. *See* G.S. 50B-1(b). A violation of such a no-contact protective order is a deportable offense.

Practice Note: Under certain circumstances, the grounds of deportability for a crime of domestic violence, stalking, and violation of a protective order may be waived by immigration authorities when the defendant has been battered or subjected to extreme cruelty and is not and was not the primary perpetrator of violence in the relationship. *See* INA § 237(a)(7), 8 U.S.C. § 1227(a)(7). If these circumstances seem to apply to your client, any documentation in court that the particular incident was part of a larger pattern of abuse against your client may be helpful to your client in future immigration proceedings.

G. Chart of Principal Deportable Offenses

The following chart lists the principal categories of deportable offenses. It does not include some miscellaneous grounds involving infrequently charged federal crimes, which are generally not of concern to state law practitioners. An interested reader can find the complete list of the criminal grounds of deportability at INA § 237(a)(2), 8 U.S.C. § 1227(a)(2). There is also a growing list of security-related grounds of deportability and inadmissibility linked to criminal activity. This is a complicated and developing area of immigration law and covers alleged acts of terrorism, which a state law practitioner is unlikely to encounter. *See* INA § 237(a)(4), 8 U.S.C. § 1227(a)(4); INA § 212(a)(3), 8 U.S.C. § 1182(a)(3).

Keep in mind that one offense can be classified under multiple categories of deportability. For example, a conviction of assault with a deadly weapon with intent to kill against a spouse may be an aggravated felony, crime involving moral turpitude, and crime of domestic violence.

Ground of Deportability	Significant Features	Exceptions
Conviction of aggravated felony	• Includes felonies and some misdemeanors • Carries most severe immigration consequences • Includes 21 broad categories of offenses as set forth in immigration statute (*see supra* § 3.4A, Aggravated Felonies Generally)	
Conviction of crime involving moral turpitude (CMT)	• Committed within 5 years of admission to U.S. • Punishable by at least 1 year in jail	All misdemeanors, other than certain impaired driving offenses
Conviction of 2 or more CMTs	• Committed at any time after admission • Length of sentence immaterial	CMTs arising out of a single scheme
Conviction relating to a controlled substance	• Includes felonies and misdemeanors • May include drug paraphernalia offenses	An offense of simple possession of 30 grams or less of marijuana if no prior drug convictions
Firearm conviction	• Includes purchasing, selling, offering for sale, exchanging, using, owning, possessing, or carrying a "firearm or destructive device" as defined under federal law • Includes felonies and misdemeanors • Includes carrying a concealed gun	

Conviction of domestic violence, stalking, child abuse, child neglect, or child abandonment	• Includes felonies and misdemeanors • Domestic violence crime must be a crime of violence (*see supra* § 3.4B, Specific Types of Aggravated Felonies) • Domestic violence crime must be directed against a protected party under state or federal domestic violence laws	Convictions or violations occurring before September 30, 1996
Violation of a protective order	• Violation of the portion of order that protects against credible threats of violence, repeated harassment, or bodily injury • Violation may be found in civil or criminal court	Convictions or violations occurring before September 30, 1996

3.5   Crime-Related Grounds of Inadmissibility

This section reviews the main crime-related grounds of inadmissibility. The criminal grounds of inadmissibility are generally broader than the grounds of deportability and include offenses that are not covered under the comparable deportability grounds. For example, a conviction of simple possession of 30 grams or less of marijuana triggers inadmissibility, but not deportability. There is some overlap with the deportability grounds, but the grounds are different and require close scrutiny. For example, the crime involving moral turpitude ground of inadmissibility covers the same offenses as the crime involving moral turpitude deportability ground, but different rules apply depending on the length of sentence and number of convictions.

Certain criminal grounds of inadmissibility do not require a conviction—mere "bad acts" or status can trigger the penalty. Examples include engaging in prostitution or if the government has "reason to believe" the person has been a drug trafficker, as discussed below.

The controlled substance and moral turpitude grounds of inadmissibility also allow for a finding of inadmissibility without a conviction where a noncitizen *admits* the essential elements of a controlled substance offense or of a crime involving moral turpitude. *See* INA §§ 212(a)(2)(A)(i)(I)&(II), 8 U.S.C. §§ 1182(a)(2)(A)(i)(I)&(II). Generally, this ground has come into play when a noncitizen has made certain admissions to an immigration judge or an ICE officer; it does not apply to an admission in a criminal case that does not result in a conviction. *See Matter of Seda,* 17 I&N Dec. 550 (BIA 1980), *overruled in part on other grounds Matter of Ozkok,* 19 I&N Dec. 546 (BIA 1988).

A. Controlled Substance Offense

A noncitizen is inadmissible for any conviction of an offense related to any controlled substance, whether felony or misdemeanor. *See* INA § 212(a)(2)(A)(i)(II), 8 U.S.C. § 1182(a) (2)(A)(i)(II). (A noncitizen can also be inadmissible for an admission of committing such an offense, usually to an immigration judge or immigration officer.) With one exception, the language of this ground is almost identical to the controlled substance ground of deportability discussed *supra* in § 3.4D, Conviction of Any Controlled Substance Offense. The inadmissibility ground does not contain the exception for a single offense of simple possession of 30 grams of marijuana. In other words, a conviction for possession of any amount of marijuana will make your client inadmissible.

Drug offenses carry serious consequences for non-LPR clients. Drug offenses trigger inadmissibility and permanently preclude noncitizens from obtaining LPR status. The one offense that can be waived by an immigration judge in certain circumstances is simple possession of 30 grams or less of marijuana if the defendant has no prior drug convictions.

Practice Note: If your client is pleading guilty to a Class 1 misdemeanor possession of marijuana, which includes quantities of more and less than 30 grams of marijuana, it is important to document in the record of conviction that your client possessed 30 grams or less of marijuana, if applicable. *See supra* § 3.3C, Burden of Proof on Noncitizen in Applying for Relief and Demonstrating Admissibility.

A person is also inadmissible if the U.S. government knows or has reason to believe that the person is an illicit trafficker, or knowing aider, abettor, assister, conspirator, or colluder with others in illicit trafficking, in a controlled substance (as defined in 21 U.S.C. § 802). *See* INA § 212(a)(2)(C), 8 U.S.C. § 1182(a)(2)(C). No conviction (or admission) is necessary. Cases have held "drug trafficking" to mean that a person must have been a knowing and conscious participant or conduit in the transfer, passage, or delivery of narcotic drugs.

B. Crime Involving Moral Turpitude

A noncitizen is inadmissible for a conviction of a crime involving moral turpitude (CMT). *See* INA § 212(a)(2)(A)(i)(I), 8 U.S.C. § 1182(a)(2)(A)(i)(I). (A noncitizen can also be inadmissible for an admission of such an offense, usually to an immigration judge or immigration officer.) The types of offenses constituting CMTs are described *supra* in § 3.4C, Conviction of a Crime Involving Moral Turpitude.

For purposes of inadmissibility, there is an exception for a petty offense. A conviction is considered a petty offense if the noncitizen has no prior CMT convictions and the maximum *possible* sentence for that offense is one year or less and the *actual* sentence of imprisonment, active or suspended, is six months or less. *See* INA § 212(a)(2)(A)(ii)(II), 8 U.S.C. § 1182(a)(2) (A)(ii)(II). For discussion of what constitutes the maximum possible sentence, see *supra* § 3.4C, Conviction of a Crime Involving Moral Turpitude.

Practice Note: Because misdemeanors in North Carolina other than impaired driving are not punishable by one year or more of imprisonment under structured sentencing, the commission of one misdemeanor CMT offense will fall within the petty offense exception and not make your client inadmissible. Two CMTs will not fall within the petty offense inadmissibility exception, however, even if they arise out of the same transaction

---

or are consolidated for judgment or run concurrently. The reason is that the petty offense exception is limited to one CMT.

C. Conviction of Two or More Offenses of Any Type with an Aggregate Sentence of Imprisonment of at Least Five Years

A noncitizen who has been convicted of two or more offenses of any type with an aggregate sentence of imprisonment, active or suspended, of five years or more is inadmissible. *See* INA § 212(a)(2)(B), 8 U.S.C. § 1182(a)(2)(B).

D. Prostitution

Prostitutes or persons who have engaged in or sought to engage in prostitution or to procure prostitution within 10 years of application for admission are inadmissible. *See* INA § 212(a)(2)(D), 8 U.S.C. § 1182(a)(2)(D); 22 C.F.R. § 40.24. The Board of Immigration Appeals has held that to "engage in" prostitution, one must have engaged in a regular pattern of behavior and conduct. *See Matter of T-*, 6 I&N Dec. 474 (BIA 1955); *Matter of Gonzalez-Zoquiapan*, 24 I&N Dec. 549 (BIA 2008) (noncitizen convicted of a single act of solicitation of prostitution did not come within inadmissibility ground for prostitution). A conviction of a prostitution offense is also a crime involving moral turpitude and may trigger inadmissibility on that ground, possibly even if only a one-time occurrence. *See, e.g., Rohit v. Holder*, 670 F.3d 1085 (9th Cir. 2012).

E. Significant Traffickers in Persons

Any noncitizen is inadmissible if he or she commits or conspires to commit human trafficking offenses in the U.S. or outside of the U.S. *See* INA § 12(a)(2)(H), 8 U.S.C. § 1182(a)(2)(H). A person is also inadmissible if the government knows or has reason to believe that the individual has been a knowing aider, abettor, assister, conspirator, or colluder with such a trafficker in severe forms of trafficking in persons. *See id.*

F. Money Laundering

A noncitizen is inadmissible if the government knows or has reason to believe that the individual has engaged, is engaging, or seeks to enter the U.S. to engage in money laundering, or who is or has been a knowing aider, abettor, assister, conspirator, or colluder with others in money laundering. *See* INA § 212(a)(2)(I), 8 U.S.C. § 1182(a)(2)(I).

G. Chart of Principal Criminal Grounds of Inadmissibility

The following chart lists the principal criminal grounds of inadmissibility. It does not include two other grounds involving foreign government officials and diplomats, which are not of concern to state law practitioners. An interested reader can find the complete list of the criminal grounds of inadmissibility at INA § 212(a)(2), 8 U.S.C. § 1182(a)(2).

Ground of Inadmissibility	Significant Features	Exceptions
Crime involving moral turpitude (CMT)	• Conviction (or admission) • Committed at any time	Petty offense, including almost all misdemeanors, if • client has no prior CMTs, • maximum *potential* prison sentence is one year or less, and • *actual* sentence is six months or less
Controlled substance offense	• Conviction (or admission) • Includes felonies or misdemeanors • Includes drug paraphernalia offenses • Includes single offense of simple possession of 30 grams or less of marijuana (even though it is not an offense triggering deportation)	Controlled substance offenses render an individual permanently inadmissible, except for a single possession of 30 grams or less of marijuana if the defendant has no prior drug convictions; such an offense can be waived by an immigration judge under certain circumstances
Trafficking in controlled substance	• No conviction (or admission) necessary • May be based on government knowledge or reason to believe	
Conviction of multiple offenses	• Includes offenses of any type • Must be at least 2 convictions • Aggregate sentence of imprisonment (active or suspended) of 5 years or more	
Prostitution	• No conviction (or admission) necessary (however, immigration officers generally rely on a conviction or an admission)	
Trafficking in persons	• No conviction necessary • May be based on government knowledge or reason to believe	
Money laundering	• No conviction necessary • May be based on government knowledge or reason to believe	

3.6   Criminal Bars to Naturalization

In addition to removal, there are other potential adverse immigration consequences of a conviction. For many noncitizens, the potential for naturalization is a big concern.

Naturalization requires a showing of good moral character for a qualifying period of time, in many cases five years. *See* INA § 316(a)(3), 8 U.S.C. § 1427(a)(3). If an LPR client is convicted of or admits certain crimes, he or she is statutorily precluded for up to five years (or permanently in the case of an aggravated felony conviction) from demonstrating good moral character for naturalization purposes. The convictions listed below have this effect.

Immigration authorities still have discretion to find that your client lacks the requisite moral character for U.S. citizenship based on other dispositions, but they do not automatically preclude your client from demonstrating good moral character.

- Conviction of an aggravated felony, entered on or after November 29, 1990. This makes your client permanently ineligible for citizenship, *see* INA § 101(f)(8), 8 U.S.C. § 1101(f)(8), and will almost certainly result in your client's removal from the U.S. as well. *See supra* § 3.4A, Aggravated Felonies Generally.
- Conviction or admitted commission of any controlled substance offense except one offense of simple possession of 30 grams or less of marijuana if no prior drug convictions. *See* INA § 101(f)(3), 8 U.S.C. § 1101(f)(3).
- Conviction or admitted commission of a crime involving moral turpitude, except if the client does not have a prior conviction for a crime involving moral turpitude and the offense is not subject to a potential prison sentence of more than one year and does not carry an actual sentence of imprisonment, active or suspended, of more than six months. *See* INA § 101(f)(3), 8 U.S.C. § 1101(f)(3).
- Conviction of two or more offenses of any type, plus an aggregate sentence of imprisonment, active or suspended, of five years or more. *See* INA § 101(f)(3), 8 U.S.C. § 1101(f)(3).
- Conviction of two or more gambling offenses. *See* INA § 101(f)(5), 8 U.S.C. § 1101(f)(5).
- Confinement, as a result of conviction, to a penal institution for an aggregate period of 180 days or more. *See* INA § 101(f)(7), 8 U.S.C. § 1101(f)(7).

For additional grounds barring a finding of good moral character, see INA § 101(f), 8 U.S.C. § 1101(f).

3.7   Criminal Bars to Deferred Action for Childhood Arrivals

Some individuals without status might be eligible for Deferred Action for Childhood Arrivals (DACA). On June 15, 2012, the Obama Administration announced that it would not deport certain undocumented people who entered the U.S. as children. Deferred action means that even though the noncitizen is here without status and subject to deportation, the government agrees to "defer" any actions to remove them. Individuals granted DACA receive a two year deferral of deportation and are able to apply for work authorization and a social security number. While deferred action does not provide a pathway to getting LPR status or citizenship, it does allow noncitizens without status to stay and work legally in the U.S.

Practice Note: The Trump administration is considering repealing DACA but hasn't taken action as of release of this edition of the manual.

To qualify, the individual must:

- be younger than 31 years old as of June 15, 2012;
- have entered the U.S. when he or she was under age 16;
- have been physically present in the U.S. on June 15, 2012, and have continuously resided in the U.S. during the preceding five years (except for brief, casual, and innocent absences); and
- currently be in school or have graduated from high school or obtained a GED, or been honorably discharged from the coast guard or armed forces.

Convictions of a broad array of criminal offenses will bar eligibility unless a person can show "exceptional circumstances" (but such approvals are very rare). Such convictions will also bar someone who already has DACA from renewing his or her status, which must be done every two years. The convictions below have this effect:

- conviction of any felony (federal, state, or local offense that is punishable by imprisonment of more than one year);
- conviction of a "significant misdemeanor," which means an offense that is punishable by imprisonment of one year or less but more than five days and is an offense of
  - domestic violence,
  - sexual abuse or exploitation,
  - burglary,
  - unlawful possession or use of a firearm,
  - drug distribution or trafficking,
  - driving under the influence of alcohol or drugs, or
  - any conviction for which the individual was sentenced to a jail sentence of more than 90 days (suspended sentences do not count toward the 90 days);
- conviction of three or more non-significant misdemeanors that do not occur on the same day or arise from the same act or scheme of conduct. (Minor traffic offenses, such as driving without a license, will not count against the limit of three nonsignificant misdemeanors.)

The following dispositions will *not* automatically disqualify someone, but the Department of Homeland Security (DHS) will consider them on a case by case basis:

- any state immigration-related felony or misdemeanor (to the extent any exist),
- juvenile delinquency adjudications, and
- expunged convictions.

For more information on the DACA criminal bars, see Immigrant Legal Resource Center, Understanding the Criminal Bars to the Deferred Action Policy for Childhood Arrivals (Oct. 2012).

Chapter 4
Conviction and Sentence for Immigration Purposes

4.1 Conviction for Immigration Purposes   4-2
A. Conviction Defined
B. Conviction without Formal Judgment
C. Finality of Conviction

4.2 Effect of North Carolina Dispositions   4-3
A. Deferred Prosecution
B. Drug Treatment Court Disposition
C. 90-96 and 15A-1341 Deferrals
D. Prayer for Judgment Continued
E. Expungement
F. Juvenile Delinquency Adjudication
G. Conviction Vacated via Post-Conviction Relief

4.3 Sentence to a Term of Imprisonment   4-8
A. Imprisonment Defined
B. Sentence Modification
C. Implications for an Aggravated Felony
D. Comparison to Potential Sentence

Most of the crime-related grounds of deportability and some of the crime-related grounds of inadmissibility require a conviction to make a noncitizen deportable or inadmissible. Even where criminal conduct may be sufficient for removal without a conviction, the U.S. Immigration and Customs Enforcement (ICE) may not be able to establish the conduct without a conviction. Therefore, in practice, ICE usually relies on convictions to establish deportability and inadmissibility.

Criminal defense attorneys should be aware that there is a statutory definition of conviction for immigration purposes. State law does *not* determine whether a state disposition will be considered a conviction for immigration law purposes. For example, a state disposition that results in the dismissal of all criminal charges may still be a conviction for immigration purposes in some instances.

Chapter 3 describes the offenses that trigger the principal immigration consequences for a defendant. *See also* Appendix A, Selected Immigration Consequences of North Carolina Offenses. Once you have determined that a particular offense is one that may trigger immigration consequences for your client, you must then determine whether the potential disposition in the case would be considered a conviction for immigration purposes. You must also consider whether the potential sentence is of the type or length that would trigger adverse consequences.

4.1   Conviction for Immigration Purposes

A. Conviction Defined

In 1996, Congress adopted a statutory definition of conviction for immigration purposes. The definition of conviction was made deliberately broad in scope. It is set out in INA § 101(a)(48)(A), 8 U.S.C. § 1101(a)(48)(A), as follows:

> The term "conviction' means, with respect to an alien, a formal judgment of guilt of the alien entered by a court or, if adjudication of guilt has been withheld, where—
> (i)   a judge or jury has found the alien guilty or the alien has entered a plea of guilty or nolo contendere or has admitted sufficient facts to warrant a finding of guilt, and
> (ii) the judge has ordered some form of punishment, penalty, or restraint on the alien's liberty to be imposed.

Under this definition, a disposition may constitute a conviction with or without the entry of a formal judgment.

B. Conviction without Formal Judgment

Generally. A state court disposition without a formal judgment will constitute a conviction if there has been both a finding, plea, or admission of guilt *and* the court has ordered some form of "punishment, penalty, or restraint on liberty."

Under this prong of the definition, certain court proceedings in which a defendant enters a guilty plea or makes an admission of sufficient facts to warrant a finding of guilt and is ordered by the court to complete probation or some other condition will likely be treated as a conviction for immigration law purposes even if the plea is later vacated or charges dismissed. In contrast, a pre-plea diversion arrangement, in which no plea is entered or admission made but some form of pretrial probation or community service is ordered, should not be considered a conviction for immigration purposes. The application of this definition to different North Carolina dispositions is discussed *infra* in § 4.2, Effect of North Carolina Dispositions.

Plea of Guilty. The term "plea" includes a no contest plea as well as a guilty plea. The definition has also been interpreted as including an *Alford* plea even though the defendant does not admit guilt with that type of plea. (In an *Alford* plea, the defendant asserts his or her innocence but admits that sufficient evidence exists with which the prosecution could likely convince a judge or jury to find the defendant guilty.) *See Abimbola v. Ashcroft*, 378 F.3d 173, 180–81 (2d Cir. 2004).

Punishment or Restraint on Liberty. In addition to incarceration, the term "punishment" or "restraint on liberty" includes a variety of community corrections alternatives, such as probation, treatment alternatives to street crime (TASC), drug education school (DES), house arrest with electronic monitoring, community service, and anger management and substance abuse programs. It also includes other restraints, such as restitution and a fine. *See Matter of Cabrera*, 24 I&N Dec. 459 (BIA 2008).

The punishment or restraint must be imposed by the court for the disposition to qualify as a conviction for immigration purposes. An agreement with a prosecutor to attend a drug treatment program or anger management program, for example, should not qualify as a restraint on liberty if not ordered by the court.

C. Finality of Conviction

Traditionally, a conviction was deemed effective for immigration purposes only when the judgment of conviction was final. *See Pino v. Landon*, 349 U.S. 901 (1955). A conviction is final for immigration purposes when the direct appeal has been exhausted or waived. A pending state or federal post-conviction challenge, however, does not affect the finality of the conviction.

The Ninth Circuit has found that Congress, in adopting a statutory definition of conviction, eliminated the requirement of finality. *Planes v. Holder*, 652 F.3d 991, 996 (2011), *reh'g denied*, 686 F.3d 1033 (9th Cir. 2012). In contrast, the Third Circuit has held that the finality rule survives, at least with regard to a "formal judgment of guilt"— that is, the conviction is not considered final until direct appeal has been exhausted or waived. *Orabi v. Att'y Gen. of U.S.*, 738 F.3d 535 (3d Cir. 2014). Although the law is in flux, the traditional requirement of finality appears to continue to apply in the Fourth and Eleventh Circuits, which review cases arising from the North Carolina and Georgia immigration courts involving North Carolina defendants.

4.2   Effect of North Carolina Dispositions

A. Deferred Prosecution

In North Carolina, a "deferred prosecution" occurs when the State agrees to cease prosecution on the defendant's successful completion of certain conditions. The court does not enter judgment against the defendant, and the deferred prosecution is generally not considered a conviction under state law. If the person fails to live up to the conditions, the State then reinstitutes the prosecution and seeks a conviction.

Types of Deferred Prosecution. There are two basic forms of deferred prosecution, formal and informal. Formal deferred prosecution is governed by G.S. 15A-1341(a1) and generally requires a written agreement and approval of the court. Formal deferrals may vary county by county. When a person is placed on formal deferred prosecution, the conditions of the deferral may be made a part of probation. Prosecutors also informally "defer" prosecution by dismissing the case on the defendant's promise to abide by certain conditions.

In both instances, the defendant ordinarily does not enter a plea but may be asked to sign a statement admitting the charged conduct.

Immigration Consequences. Whether a deferral constitutes a conviction for immigration purposes depends on the structure of the deferred prosecution. The key factors are whether the defendant made an *admission of* having committed the essential elements of an offense and the *court imposed conditions* as part of the deferred prosecution.

In a formal deferral, if the defendant is required to admit the essential elements of the offense and the court imposes conditions that the defendant must fulfill, the disposition will almost certainly be treated as a conviction for immigration purposes, even if the charges are later dismissed on successful completion of the conditions. In this instance, though the defendant does not enter a guilty plea and only admits the essential elements of the offense, that is sufficient to trigger a conviction under immigration law.

If, however, the court imposes conditions *without* an admission to the factual allegations, the deferral *should* not be considered a conviction for immigration purposes. Counsel should be wary of box # 9 of AOC-CR-626 (Dec. 2016) (deferred prosecution), which states that "the admission of responsibility given by me and any stipulation of facts shall be used against me and admitted into evidence without objection in the State's prosecution against me for this offense. . . ." If checked, the document would suggest that the defendant had made an admission when, in fact, he or she may not have. In appropriate cases, therefore, strike the language or leave the box unchecked.

The Fourth Circuit recently stated that a "deferred prosecution agreement is not by itself a sufficient 'admission of facts,' given that it seems to merely describe the anticipated admission of responsibility and stipulation to take place. . . ." *Boggala v. Sessions*, 866 F.3d 563, 568 n.3 (4th Cir. 2017). In *Boggala*, the Court found that the deferred prosecution agreement at issue was a conviction under immigration law because the defendant stipulated to sufficient facts as part of the deferral, in that instance during the hearing at which the court accepted the deferral. *Id.* (finding that petitioner was informed in writing of the facts to be used against him and then later stipulated to those facts underlying each element of the crime). Thus, a deferral agreement, unaccompanied by a written or oral admission or stipulation of sufficient facts, should not rise to a conviction under immigration law.

There is still some risk to a defendant with a formal deferral even if he or she makes no admission. If ICE learns of the deferral, it might institute removal proceedings on the assumption that an admission of guilt is often made in formal deferrals, but a defendant armed with this law should ultimately prevail before an immigration judge.

An informal deferral by the prosecutor should not constitute a conviction for immigration purposes because ordinarily the defendant does not make an admission as a condition of such an arrangement. Further, there are no court-ordered restraints in an informal deferral—the second requirement—as the court is generally not involved in such an arrangement.

B. Drug Treatment Court Disposition

In North Carolina, there are both post-plea and pre-plea drug treatment courts. The practices vary from county to county. In a post-plea drug court, a defendant is required to plead guilty before the court will order the defendant to participate in a drug treatment program. Even if the court does not enter a judgment of conviction, such a disposition will almost certainly constitute a conviction for immigration purposes. This is true even if the State eventually dismisses the criminal charges because the combination of admission of guilt and restraint on the defendant's liberty would be considered a conviction for immigration purposes. *See Matter of Salazar-Regino*, 23 I&N Dec. 223 (BIA 2002).

Drug treatment courts that require a guilty plea up front raise difficult issues for a noncitizen client. On the one hand, diversion to a drug treatment program may provide a way of getting all drug charges dismissed in the end. Moreover, if the individual suffers from drug addiction, the treatment program may assist the person to overcome the addiction. On the other hand, the drug treatment court proceeding is almost certain to constitute a conviction for immigration purposes.

In a pre-plea drug court, a client typically must make an admission of guilt as part of a deferred prosecution agreement; thus, the first requirement is met. If the court then imposes treatment or other restraints, the disposition will probably qualify as a conviction for immigration purposes. *See supra* § 4.2A, Deferred Prosecution. In some counties, the court does not order the treatment or other restraints but simply approves the deferred prosecution agreement. If the court does not order drug treatment or other restraints on the defendant, it is possible that such a disposition would not constitute a conviction for immigration purposes. It is not clear how an immigration court would treat such a procedure.

C. 90-96 and 15A-1341 Deferrals

A deferral under G.S. 90-96, called a conditional discharge or discharge and dismissal in North Carolina, is available for a narrow class of drug offenses. If the defendant pleads guilty or is found guilty, a court may defer further proceedings and place the defendant on probation without entering judgment. *See* G.S. 90-96(a). If the defendant fulfills the conditions of probation, the proceedings are dismissed and the defendant does not have a conviction under state law. However, the deferral will almost certainly constitute a conviction for immigration purposes because the statute requires that the defendant plead or be found guilty and that the court impose conditions.

North Carolina recently created a similar conditional discharge procedure for Class H and I felonies and misdemeanors other than impaired driving offenses. *See* G.S. 15A-1341(a4); *see also* G.S. 15A-1341(a3) (conditional discharge for prostitution offenses).

For the above reasons, these dispositions would probably constitute convictions for immigration purposes.

D. Prayer for Judgment Continued

A prayer for judgment continued (PJC) granted by a North Carolina court will almost always be treated as a conviction for immigration purposes.

A PJC occurs when the court accepts the defendant's guilty plea or finds the defendant guilty after trial but withholds judgment in the case. A PJC is considered a conviction under state law for many purposes, whether or not the court imposes any conditions or costs.

For immigration purposes, if a PJC is granted and the court imposes conditions amounting to punishment, such as performance of community service or payment of a fine, then the definition of conviction has been met. A PJC in which court costs alone have been imposed is a conviction as well. Even though North Carolina law does not treat court costs as punishment (*State v. Popp*, 197 N.C. App. 226 (2009)), the immigration courts do. *See Matter of Cabrera*, 24 I&N Dec. 459 (BIA 2008) (imposition of court costs in the criminal sentencing context constitutes a form of punishment for immigration purposes). It is unclear whether a PJC without the imposition of costs or other conditions would be treated as a conviction for immigration purposes.

E. Expungement

A North Carolina conviction that has been expunged will continue to constitute a conviction for immigration purposes. The Board of Immigration Appeals considered the issue of an Idaho expungement in *Matter of Roldan-Santoya* and held that no effect would be given in immigration proceedings to any state action that purports to expunge, dismiss, cancel, vacate, discharge, or otherwise remove a guilty plea or other record of guilt or conviction by operation of a state rehabilitative procedure. 22 I&N Dec. 512 (1999).

F. Juvenile Delinquency Adjudication

Adjudication of Delinquency Not a Conviction. A juvenile delinquency adjudication is not a conviction for immigration purposes. *See Matter of Devison-Charles*, 22 I&N Dec. 1362 (BIA 2001); *Matter of Ramirez-Rivero*, 18 I&N Dec. 135 (BIA 1981). Thus, regardless of the nature of the offense, a juvenile delinquency adjudication should not trigger any adverse immigration consequences based on conviction of a crime.

Under the North Carolina Juvenile Code, jurisdiction of a juvenile may be transferred to superior court for prosecution as an adult for some felonies. A conviction of a juvenile resulting from a transfer to superior court likely constitutes a conviction for immigration purposes. *See, e.g., Singh v. U.S. Att'y Gen.*, 561 F.3d 1275, 1278–79 (11th Cir. 2009) (finding that a 15-year old tried as an adult under state law was convicted for immigration purposes).

Practice Note: Because it is settled law that a juvenile delinquency adjudication is not a conviction for immigration purposes, and a conviction in superior court has other adverse consequences for a juvenile (such as a criminal record for state law purposes), defense counsel should ordinarily resist transfer of a juvenile case to superior court.

Other Potential Consequences of Adjudication. Counsel representing juveniles should be aware that a finding of juvenile delinquency could still have adverse consequences for a noncitizen. First, it could be considered an adverse factor if the juvenile applies for any discretionary benefit under the immigration laws, such as adjustment of status to a lawful permanent resident. *See Wallace v. Gonzales*, 463 F.3d 135 (2d Cir. 2006) (upholding BIA and immigration judge's consideration of noncitizen's New York youthful offender adjudication when evaluating his application for adjustment of status).

Second, certain grounds of inadmissibility and deportability do not require a conviction; mere "bad acts" or status can trigger the penalty. Examples include engaging in prostitution, being a drug addict or abuser, using false documents, smuggling aliens, or the government having "reason to believe" the person has ever been a drug trafficker. Thus, a juvenile delinquency adjudication involving one of these offenses could support a finding of inadmissibility, in particular an adjudication involving drug trafficking. *See Matter of Favela*, 16 I&N 753 Dec. (BIA 1979) (holding that individuals who pled guilty to drug trafficking in juvenile proceedings are inadmissible as drug traffickers even though there is no conviction). Adjudications involving these offenses can also be used to deny an application for Special Immigrant Juvenile Status (SIJS), which helps certain undocumented children in the state juvenile/foster care system obtain lawful immigration status. An adjudication involving drug trafficking will bar SIJS relief.

Additionally, defense counsel should be aware that immigration officers sometimes question clients in North Carolina juvenile detention centers. Admissions to immigration officers by juvenile clients could lead to removal proceedings. *See supra* § 2.3D, Advise Your Clients of Their Rights.

G. Conviction Vacated via Post-Conviction Relief

The BIA has ruled that when a state court vacates a judgment of conviction based on a procedural or legal defect, the state court order must be given full faith and credit, and the conviction is eliminated for immigration purposes. *See Matter of Rodriguez-Ruiz*, 22 I&N Dec. 1378 (BIA 2001). For example, if a conviction is vacated for ineffective assistance of counsel through a motion for appropriate relief, there is no longer a conviction for immigration purposes.

The conviction is not eliminated for immigration purposes, however, if it was vacated for reasons "solely related to rehabilitation or immigration hardships, rather than on the basis of a procedural or substantive defect in the underlying criminal proceedings." *Matter of*

Pickering, 23 I&N Dec. 621 (BIA 2003), *rev'd on other grounds*, 465 F.3d 263 (6th Cir. 2006); *cf. Yanez-Popp v. I.N.S.*, 998 F.2d 231, 235 (4th Cir. 1993) ("[U]nless a conviction is vacated on its merits, a revoked state conviction is still a 'conviction' for federal immigration purposes.").

For a further discussion of the impact of post-conviction relief, see *infra* Chapter 8, State Post-Conviction Relief.

4.3   Sentence to a Term of Imprisonment

In some cases, adverse immigration consequences are triggered by the length of imprisonment ordered. For example, a burglary offense that carries a term of imprisonment of one year or more results in an aggravated felony conviction and most likely mandatory removal.

A. Imprisonment Defined

For immigration purposes, a "term of imprisonment" includes "the period of incarceration or confinement ordered by a court of law regardless of any suspension of the imposition or execution of all or part of the sentence." INA § 101(a)(48)(B), 8 U.S.C. § 1101(a)(48)(B).

The actual length of confinement ordered by the court is what counts as the sentence for immigration law purposes, even if the execution of sentence is suspended and the defendant does not serve any actual time in jail. *See Matter of Esposito*, 21 I&N Dec. 1 (BIA 1995). For example, in a misdemeanor case, a defendant who receives a sentence of 150 days suspended and supervised probation will be treated as having been sentenced to 150 days in jail for immigration purposes. The duration of probation does not count as a term of imprisonment.

Further, a sentence is considered to be a sentence for the maximum term actually imposed, even if the defendant is released before serving the maximum term. *See Matter of D*, 20 I&N Dec. 827 (BIA 1994); *Matter of Chen*, 10 I&N Dec. 671 (BIA 1964). In North Carolina, a period of post-release supervision is added to every felony sentence of imprisonment for felony offenses committed on or after December 1, 2011. *See* Justice Reinvestment Act of 2011, 2011 N.C. Sess. Laws 192; G.S. 15A-1340.17(d). The Fourth Circuit has found that the post-release supervision term counts toward the maximum term. *See United States v. Barlow*, 811 F.3d 133, 139–40 (4th Cir. 2015) (finding that "state law renders post-release supervision part of the term of imprisonment"). Thus, a defendant who is sentenced to 3 months minimum and 13 months maximum in a felony case will be treated as having been sentenced to 13 months in jail for immigration purposes, even if he or she ultimately serves only 3 months in jail and nine months on post-release supervision.

B. Sentence Modification

A trial court's order modifying or reducing a noncitizen's criminal sentence is recognized as valid for purposes of immigration law without regard to the trial court's reasons for the modification or reduction. *See Matter of Cota-Vargas*, 23 I&N Dec. 849 (BIA 2005) (trial court's reduction of defendant's prison sentence from 365 days to 240 days, *nunc pro tunc*, to the date of his original sentencing was recognized by the BIA, and defendant was no longer deportable for an aggravated felony because his receipt of stolen property offense was no longer one "for which the term of imprisonment [was] at least one year").

C. Implications for an Aggravated Felony

One Year Rule. The definition of term of imprisonment has important consequences for the aggravated felony ground of deportability because the immigration statute defines certain offenses as aggravated felonies only if the defendant receives a sentence of imprisonment of one year or more. *See supra* § 3.4A, Aggravated Felonies Generally.

The North Carolina Justice Reinvestment Act introduced a new nine-month period of mandatory post-release supervision (PRS) for class F through I felonies, effective for offenses committed on or after December 1, 2011. As a result, the lowest possible maximum term of imprisonment (including the PRS period) for a felony conviction in North Carolina, regardless of offense class or prior record level, is thirteen months. *See* 2011 N.C. Sess. Laws 192; G.S. 15A-1340.17(d). The Fourth Circuit has found that the PRS term counts towards the sentence. *See United States v. Barlow*, 811 F.3d 133, 139-40 (4th Cir. 2015). Thus, defense counsel should treat an active or suspended sentence of 3 months minimum and 13 months maximum (or longer) for specified offenses as an aggravated felony, subjecting a noncitizen client to mandatory removal.[1]

A judge may impose a fine, without a sentence of imprisonment, for felonies that authorize a community or "C" punishment under structured sentencing. A judge also may enter a prayer for judgment continued or PJC, without a sentence of imprisonment. Even though a sentence of imprisonment of one year or more is authorized, a fine or PJC would be the sentence imposed in those circumstances and therefore would not make the offense an aggravated felony under the one-year rule.

Consecutive Sentences. Consecutive sentences cannot be combined to satisfy the statutory one year requirement for aggravated felony offenses that depend on a minimum one-year sentence of imprisonment. *Compare* INA § 101(a)(43)(F), 8 U.S.C. § 1101(a)(43)(F) (requiring sentence of one year or more to trigger aggravated felony definition) *with* INA § 241(b)(3) (B), 8 U.S.C. § 1231(b)(3)(B) (providing that noncitizen

---

1. For offenses committed before December 1, 2011, a low level felony may have an imposed sentence of less than one year. For example, a defendant may have been sentenced to 8 months minimum and 10 months maximum under structured sentencing for a Class H felony larceny. Because the imposed sentence is less than one year, the defendant would not have an aggravated felony conviction related to theft.

sentenced to aggregate term of imprisonment of five years or more is ineligible for relief of withholding of removal) and INA § 212(a)(2)(B), 8 U.S.C. § 1182(a)(2)(B) (providing that noncitizen convicted of two or more offenses for which the aggregate sentence of imprisonment is five years or longer is inadmissible). As long as no individual count results in a maximum sentence of one year or longer, a total term of imprisonment (active or suspended) of more than one year will not satisfy the statutory definition for this type of aggravated felony offense.

This concept does not come into play often in North Carolina because under structured sentencing all felony sentences of imprisonment now exceed one year.[2] For a discussion of practical considerations in cases in which sentence length is critical, see *infra* § 6.2A, Aggravated Felonies Triggered by a One Year Term of Imprisonment.

D. Comparison to Potential Sentence

In some instances, the immigration statute focuses on the potential sentence that *may* be imposed—that is, whether the offense is punishable by a certain term of imprisonment. This approach is used in limited instances—specifically, with the grounds of removal involving crimes involving moral turpitude (CMT). *See* INA § 237(a)(2)(A)(i), 8 U.S.C. § 1227(a)(2) (A)(i) (an individual is deportable if convicted of one CMT committed within five years of admission to the U.S., for which a sentence of one year or longer *may* be imposed); INA § 212(a)(2)(A)(ii)(II), 8 U.S.C. § 1182(a)(2)(A)(ii)(II) (a noncitizen is inadmissible for a conviction or admitted commission of a CMT, unless the maximum *possible* sentence for the offense is one year or less, the actual sentence of imprisonment is six months or less, and the person has no prior CMT convictions). For those immigration grounds, the actual sentence imposed, even if less than the maximum, is not determinative.

In those instances, the sentence that "may be imposed" under structured sentencing for a felony means the maximum sentence a defendant could receive in state court based on the defendant's prior record level under North Carolina's structured sentencing statutes. *See* *United States v. Simmons*, 649 F.3d 237, 240, 249-50 (4th Cir. 2011) (en banc). The Justice Reinvestment Act, effective for offenses committed on or after December 1, 2011, introduced a nine-month period of mandatory post-release supervision (PRS) for Class F through I felonies, the lowest felony classes in North Carolina. *See* Justice Reinvestment

---

2. There may be an argument that a person convicted of multiple felony offenses and sentenced to consecutive terms has not received a sentence of one year or more *for the second and subsequent offense*. For the second and subsequent offense, North Carolina law reduces the maximum sentence to be served by the period of post-release supervision for that offense. *See* G.S. 15A-1354(b). This argument may be helpful only where a non-aggravated felony is the first in the string of consecutive judgments (because the maximum sentence for the first-sentenced offense *will* include post-release supervision), followed by the potential aggravated felony offense (so that the reduction rule of G.S. 15A-1354(b) is applied to the potential aggravated felony). This argument may not succeed, as the maximum sentence "imposed" by the judge on the second and subsequent offense still includes the extra time for post-release supervision even though the defendant will never serve it.

Act of 2011, 2011 N.C. Sess. Laws 192. As a result, the sentence that "may be imposed" for any North Carolina felony conviction will be greater than a one year sentence. *See United States v. Barlow*, 811 F.3d 133, 139–40 (4th Cir. 2015).

Chapter 5
Determining Possible Immigration Consequences Based on Your Client's Immigration Status

5.1 Lawful Permanent Resident   **5-2**
A. LPR Client's Immigration Priorities
B. Impact on LPR of an Aggravated Felony Conviction
C. Impact on LPR of Other Dispositions Triggering Deportability
D. Impact on LPR of a Criminal Disposition Triggering Inadmissibility
E. Forms of Relief Depending on Offense
F. Impact on LPR of a Criminal Disposition Barring Naturalization

5.2 Refugee (who has not yet obtained LPR status)   **5-6**
A. Refugee Client's Immigration Priorities
B. Impact on Refugee of a Criminal Disposition Triggering Deportability
C. Impact on Refugee of a Criminal Disposition Triggering Inadmissibility
D. Forms of Relief Depending on Offense

5.3 Person Granted Asylum (who has not yet obtained LPR status)   **5-9**
A. Asylee Client's Immigration Priorities
B. Impact on Asylee of an Aggravated Felony Conviction
C. Impact on Asylee of a Criminal Disposition Triggering Inadmissibility
D. Forms of Relief Depending on Offense

5.4 Nonimmigrant Visa Holder   **5-11**
A. Immigration Priorities for Nonimmigrant Visa Holder
B. Impact on Nonimmigrant Visa Holder of a Criminal Disposition Triggering Deportability
C. Impact on Nonimmigrant Visa Holder of a Criminal Disposition Triggering Inadmissibility
D. Forms of Relief Depending on Offense

5.5 Noncitizens with Temporary Protected Status   **5-14**

5.6   Noncitizens without Immigration Status   **5-14**

    A. Immigration Priorities for Noncitizen Client without Immigration Status

    B. Impact on Noncitizen without Immigration Status of a Criminal Disposition Triggering Inadmissibility

    C. Impact on Noncitizen without Immigration Status of Controlled Substance and Certain Other Dispositions

    D. Impact on Noncitizen without Immigration Status of an Offense that Bars Persecution-Based Claims

    E. Impact on Noncitizen without Immigration Status of a Conviction that Bars Deferred Action of Childhood Arrivals (DACA)

    F. Impact on Noncitizen without Immigration Status of a Conviction that Bars Voluntary Departure

    G. Enhanced Liability for Illegal Reentry after Removal

5.7   Summary of Priorities in Representing Noncitizen   **5-20**
Clients by Status

The immigration consequences of a criminal conviction or other disposition vary largely with the noncitizen's particular immigration status. This chapter discusses and prioritizes adverse immigration consequences of a criminal disposition based on the client's particular immigration status. For the purposes of presenting the various immigration consequences, noncitizens are divided into five broad categories:

- Lawful permanent residents (LPRs) (*see* § 5.1)
- Refugees (who have not yet obtained LPR status) (*see* § 5.2)
- Persons granted asylum (who have not yet obtained LPR status (*see* § 5.3)
- Nonimmigrant visa holders (*see* § 5.4)
- Noncitizens with Temporary Protected Status (*see* § 5.5)
- Noncitizens without immigration status (*see* § 5.6)

These are the immigration statuses you are most likely to encounter, but they are not exhaustive.

5.1   Lawful Permanent Resident

A lawful permanent resident, or LPR, is a person allowed to live and work in the U.S. permanently. *See supra* § 2.2B, Lawful Permanent Resident Status. Such a client may have immigrated to this country as a child, may have lived and worked in this country for many years, and may have most, if not all, of his or her family in the U.S.

An LPR can be removed or face other adverse immigration consequences because of a criminal conviction, regardless of number of years in the U.S. or U.S. citizen family relationships.

A. LPR Client's Immigration Priorities

An LPR can be removed from the U.S. for an offense triggering deportability. *See supra* § 3.2A, Consequences Distinguished. Generally, since LPRs want to remain in the U.S., such a conviction will be their greatest immigration concern. In particular, an LPR will be concerned about an aggravated felony conviction, which carries the most severe consequences, including being barred from most forms of relief from removal.

A second concern is a conviction that triggers inadmissibility. Generally, an LPR cannot be removed for an offense that triggers inadmissibility. However, if an LPR travels outside of the U.S. after being convicted of such an offense, he or she may be placed in removal proceedings on attempting to return to the U.S. While an LPR can avoid this consequence by not traveling outside of the U.S., this is easier said than done, as many noncitizens travel to visit family members outside of the U.S.

Third, if your client cannot avoid an offense triggering deportability, he or she may still be able to remain in the U.S. permanently by seeking relief from removal. Dispositions to avoid include aggravated felonies and particularly serious crimes, explained further below.

In addition, an LPR may be concerned about eligibility to become a naturalized citizen, which has numerous benefits. Once an LPR has lawfully obtained citizenship, it generally cannot be revoked; he or she can remain in the U.S. without fear of removal. Therefore, if your client is able to avoid a deportable offense, he or she may also want to avoid a disposition that bars a showing of good moral character necessary for naturalization.

Last, certain convictions where the victim is a minor will bar a permanent resident (or U.S. citizen) from being able to sponsor a family member for immigration in the future.[1]

B. Impact on LPR of an Aggravated Felony Conviction

Generally, an LPR's greatest immigration priority will be to avoid a conviction for an aggravated felony. It not only makes your client deportable, but it also bars eligibility for most forms of relief from removal, resulting in virtually mandatory removal for most clients. If an individual is deportable, a grant of relief from removal allows an individual to remain in the U.S. and keep his or her green card. Most forms of relief are

---

1. The Adam Walsh Act passed in 2006 imposes immigration penalties on U.S. citizens and permanent residents who are convicted of specified crimes relating to minors, including sex and kidnapping offenses. Certain convictions would prevent them from filing a visa petition on behalf of a close family member. *See* Section 402 of the Adam Walsh Act; INA §§ 204(a)(1)(A)(viii), (B)(i), 8 USC §§ 1154(a)(1)(A)(viii), (B)(i). For example, if your LPR client is convicted of indecent liberties, he may not be permitted to file a visa petition for a noncitizen relative.

discretionary and will depend on an individual's ties to the U.S and other factors. Certain convictions will make noncitizens ineligible for relief from removal. An aggravated felony conviction bars almost all forms of immigration relief.

An aggravated felony carries other serious immigration consequences, including:

- It subjects a person to mandatory detention during the removal process.
- It subjects a person to up to twenty years in prison if he or she is prosecuted and convicted of reentering the U.S. without permission after removal.
- It permanently bars immigration to the U.S. in the future.

For a table of the categories of offenses classified as aggravated felonies, see *supra* § 3.4A, Aggravated Felonies Generally.

C. Impact on LPR of Other Dispositions Triggering Deportability

In addition to an aggravated felony, an LPR will be concerned about offenses that trigger deportability on other grounds. *See supra* § 3.4G, Chart of Principal Deportable Offenses. If not convicted of an aggravated felony, a deportable client may remain eligible for relief from removal.

D. Impact on LPR of a Criminal Disposition Triggering Inadmissibility

If your client plans to travel abroad in the future, an additional concern is a criminal disposition that triggers inadmissibility.

The criminal grounds of inadmissibility are generally broader than the grounds of deportability and include offenses that are not covered under the comparable deportability grounds. For example, a conviction of simple possession of 30 grams or less of marijuana triggers inadmissibility but not deportability. As a result, an LPR client convicted of such an offense would not be subject to removal and could remain in the U.S. unless he or she traveled outside of the U.S. and on return was considered inadmissible. Inadmissible LPR clients should be warned of the consequences of leaving the United States.

For the principal criminal grounds of inadmissibility, see *supra* § 3.5G, Chart of Principal Criminal Grounds of Inadmissibility.

E. Forms of Relief Depending on Offense

If your client cannot avoid deportability, he or she may still be able to remain in the U.S. and keep his or her green card by seeking relief from removal. Below are three principal forms of relief for an LPR client. It may be helpful to consult with an immigration lawyer to determine whether your client is otherwise eligible for these forms of relief.

Cancellation of Removal (if not convicted of an aggravated felony). This is one of the most common forms of relief for a deportable LPR. To be eligible, the person must have lived in the U.S. for at least seven years (since being admitted in any status, e.g., as a tourist or LPR)[2] and must have been an LPR for at least five of those years. *See* INA § 240A(a), 8 U.S.C. § 1229b(a). A conviction for an aggravated felony will bar such relief. *Id.* Cancellation of removal does not require a showing of any particular level of hardship, either to the applicant or his or her family; however, more serious crimes require more substantial equities to warrant cancellation.

Adjustment of Status (if not convicted of an inadmissible offense). If your client cannot avoid an offense triggering deportability, he or she may still be able to remain in the U.S. if he or she is able to "re-immigrate" through a U.S. citizen or LPR family member. Adjusting status is a defense to deportation and requires that the noncitizen be admissible. *See Matter of Rainford*, 20 I&N Dec. 598 (BIA 1992). Note that the criminal grounds of inadmissibility do not include some crimes that would render a person deportable— namely, firearm and domestic violence offenses. (If, however, the firearm or domestic violence offense constitutes a crime of moral turpitude, which is one of the crimes of inadmissibility, the offense could still render the person inadmissible.) Therefore, a conviction for carrying a concealed firearm would not render your client inadmissible and would not bar adjustment of status.

Withholding of Removal (if not convicted of a particularly serious offense). If your client cannot avoid an offense triggering deportability, and fears persecution in the country of removal, he or she may still be able to remain in the U.S. by seeking "withholding of removal." *See* § INA 241(b)(3); 8 U.S.C. § 1231(b)(3). It is a less beneficial form of persecution-based relief and requires a higher threshold showing of persecution than asylum.

Withholding of removal is barred by a conviction of a "particularly serious crime." In this context, a particularly serious crime includes one or more aggravated felony convictions with an aggregate sentence of imprisonment (active or suspended) of five years or more. *See* INA § 241(b)(3)(B), 8 U.S.C. § 1231(b)(3)(B). The five-year sentence may be for one conviction or different convictions, whether or not resolved at the same time. A particularly serious crime presumptively includes an aggravated felony conviction involving trafficking in a controlled substance. *See Matter of Y-L-, A-G-, R-S-R-*, 23 I&N Dec. 270 (A.G. 2002) (recognizing that presumption of particularly serious crime is rebuttable). Other offenses may be considered particularly serious crimes in the discretion of the immigration judge. *See Matter of M-H-*, 26 I&N Dec. 46 (BIA 2012); *Matter of N-A-M-*, 24 I&N Dec. 336 (BIA 2007). The relevant factors include the nature and underlying facts of the conviction and the type of sentence imposed.

---

2. The clock for the seven year residence requirement stops—that is, the person does not get any credit for any of the time—following the *commission* of an offense triggering inadmissibility. *See* INA § 240A(d)(1), 8 U.S.C. § 1229b(d)(1). For example, if your client commits an inadmissible offense six years after moving to the United States (and even if she continues to live here for five more years before being placed in removal proceedings), she will be unable to apply for cancellation of removal.

F. Impact on LPR of a Criminal Disposition Barring Naturalization

LPRs seek to naturalize and become U.S. citizens for several reasons. Once lawfully obtained, citizenship generally cannot be revoked and LPRs can remain in the U.S. without fear of removal. There are also a number of other benefits of citizenship, such as the right to vote, the right to travel freely, the right to sponsor relatives for immigration to the U.S., and eligibility for certain state and federal jobs. If an LPR client is able to avoid a deportable offense, which will generally be the client's highest immigration priority, a secondary concern may be avoiding a disposition that bars eligibility for naturalization.

In many cases, naturalization requires a showing of good moral character for five years. *See supra* § 3.6, Criminal Bars to Naturalization. If an LPR client is convicted of *or* admits certain crimes, he or she is precluded from demonstrating good moral character for up to five years. The convictions listed below bar a showing of good moral character:

- Convictions triggering inadmissibility that involve crimes involving moral turpitude (subject to the petty offense exception), drugs, prostitution, and multiple criminal convictions.
- Conviction, on or after November 29, 1990, of an aggravated felony. Such a conviction makes your client *permanently* ineligible for citizenship.
- Conviction of two or more gambling offenses.
- Actual confinement, as a result of one or more convictions during the five-year period, to a penal institution for an aggregate period of 180 days or more.

Bear in mind that if your client is convicted of one of these offenses (if it is not an aggravated felony), he or she may still be eligible for naturalization five years *after* the date of conviction or the completion of any jail sentence (whichever is later).

5.2   Refugee (who has not yet obtained LPR status)

Refugees have been conditionally admitted to the U.S. based on a fear of persecution in their country of nationality on account of race, religion, nationality, membership in a particular social group, or political opinion. *See supra* § 2.2C, Refugee or Asylee Status.

Refugees can be removed because of a criminal conviction and thus can be returned to a country where they may be harassed, imprisoned, tortured, or even killed. There is much at stake in a criminal case for a client with refugee status.

Both refugees and asylees (discussed *infra* in § 5.3, Person Granted Asylum (who has not yet obtained LPR status)) have been admitted to the U.S. due to a threat of persecution. Both groups can work in the U.S. and adjust to LPR status. Refugee status, however, is granted to an individual *before* entering the U.S., based on U.S. refugee policy and priorities. Upon application, he or she is granted a visa, and then is admitted to the U.S. as a refugee. In contrast, asylum is granted to an individual *after* entry into the U.S. Thus, the individual entered the U.S. in some other status or unlawfully, but then applied for and was granted asylum.

A. Refugee Client's Immigration Priorities

Refugees may be removed from the U.S. based on an offense that triggers deportability. *See Matter of D-K-*, 25 I&N Dec. 761 (BIA 2012). Such offenses are their primary immigration concern.

A secondary concern is an offense that triggers inadmissibility. Refugees who have been in the U.S. for at least one year are eligible to adjust to LPR status. *See* INA § 209(a), 8 U.S.C. § 1159(a). These individuals will be concerned about offenses that trigger inadmissibility, which would preclude them from becoming an LPR and remaining in the U.S. permanently.

Third, if your refugee client cannot avoid an offense triggering deportability, he or she may still be able to remain in the U.S. permanently by seeking relief from removal. Dispositions to avoid include drug trafficking, violent offenses, and particularly serious crimes, explained further below.

B. Impact on Refugee of a Criminal Disposition Triggering Deportability

The principal concern for a refugee client is a disposition triggering deportability, as he or she can be removed from the U.S. for such offenses. For the principal criminal grounds of deportability, see *supra* § 3.4G, Chart of Principal Deportable Offenses.

C. Impact on Refugee of a Criminal Disposition Triggering Inadmissibility

Another significant concern for a refugee client is an offense that renders him or her inadmissible. Because refugee status does not confer a permanent right to reside in the U.S., a refugee may want to adjust to LPR status. To adjust his or her status, a refugee must avoid the crime-related grounds of inadmissibility. For the principal criminal grounds of inadmissibility, see *supra* § 3.5G, Chart of Principal Criminal Grounds of Inadmissibility. Other offenses can result in a denial of adjustment of status in the discretion of the immigration judge or officer, but they are not automatic bars.

D. Forms of Relief Depending on Offense

If your client cannot avoid deportability, he or she may still be able to remain in the U.S. by seeking relief from removal. Below are three principal forms of relief for a refugee client. It may be helpful to consult with an immigration lawyer to determine whether your client is otherwise eligible for these forms of relief.

209(c) Waiver (if not convicted of drug trafficking or violent offense). If your refugee client cannot avoid an offense triggering deportability, he or she may still be able to remain in the U.S. permanently by seeking a 209(c) waiver, a special form of relief for refugees and asylees for humanitarian purposes, to assure family unity, or when it is otherwise in the public interest. *See* INA § 209(c), 8 U.S.C. § 1159(c). Such relief is barred by any conviction that provides the government "reason to believe" that the refugee has been involved in drug trafficking. *See id; see also supra* § 3.5A, Controlled Substance Offenses.

In addition, since 2002, a conviction of a "violent or dangerous" crime will presumptively bar such discretionary relief. *See Matter of Jean,* 23 I&N Dec. 373, 381–84 (A.G. 2002). Neither the statute nor regulations define "violent and dangerous" crime, but both court and agency decisions indicate that it may include crimes of assault, manslaughter, robbery, and sex offenses.

Adjustment of status (if not convicted of inadmissible offense). If your refugee client cannot avoid an offense triggering deportability, he or she may still be able to remain in the U.S. permanently by seeking adjustment of status and becoming an LPR. Adjusting status is a defense to deportation, and refugees are otherwise eligible to adjust status after one year of residence in the U.S. Note that the criminal grounds of inadmissibility do not include some crimes that would render a person deportable—namely, firearm and domestic violence offenses. (If, however, the firearm or domestic violence offense constitutes a crime of moral turpitude, which is one of the crimes of inadmissibility, the offense could still render the person inadmissible.) Therefore, a conviction for carrying a concealed firearm would not render your client inadmissible and would not bar adjustment of status.

Withholding of Removal (if not convicted of a particularly serious offense). If your refugee client cannot avoid an offense triggering deportability, he or she may still be able to remain in the U.S. by seeking "withholding of removal" based, again, on the client's previously determined fear of persecution in the country of removal. *See* § INA 241(b)(3); 8 U.S.C. § 1231(b)(3). It is a less beneficial form of persecution-based relief and requires a higher threshold showing of persecution than asylum.

Withholding of removal is barred by a conviction of a "particularly serious crime." In this context, a particularly serious crime includes one or more aggravated felony convictions with an aggregate sentence of imprisonment (active or suspended) of five years or more. The five-year sentence may be for one conviction or different convictions, whether or not resolved at the same time. *See* INA § 241(b)(3)(B), 8 U.S.C. § 1231(b)(3)(B). A particularly serious crime presumptively includes an aggravated felony conviction involving trafficking in a controlled substance. *See Matter of Y-L-, A-G-, R-S-R-,* 23 I&N Dec. 270 (A.G. 2002) (recognizing that presumption of particularly serious crime is rebuttable). Other offenses may be considered particularly serious crimes in the discretion of the immigration judge. *See Matter of M-H-,* 26 I&N Dec. 46 (BIA 2012); *Matter of N-A-M-,* 24 I&N Dec. 336 (BIA 2007). The relevant factors include the nature and underlying facts of the conviction and the type of sentence imposed.

5.3   Person Granted Asylum (who has not yet obtained LPR status)

A person granted asylum has been admitted indefinitely to the U.S. due to a threat of persecution in his or her country of nationality. *See supra* § 2.2C, Refugee or Asylee Status. Asylees can be removed because of a criminal conviction and thus returned to a country where they may be harassed, imprisoned, tortured, or even killed. There is much at stake in a criminal case for a client who has been granted asylum.

Both refugees (discussed *supra* in § 5.2, Refugee (who has not yet obtained LPR status)) and asylees have been admitted to the U.S. due to a threat of persecution. Both groups can work in the U.S. and adjust to LPR status. Refugee status, however, is granted to an individual *before* entering the U.S., based on U.S. refugee policy and priorities. Upon application, he or she is granted a visa, and then is admitted to the U.S. as a refugee. In contrast, asylum is granted to an individual *after* entry into the U.S. Thus, the individual entered the U.S. in some other status or unlawfully, but then applied for and was granted asylum.

For technical immigration law reasons pertaining to their status, a refugee can be removed for an offense triggering deportability (*see supra* § 5.2A, Refugee Client's Immigration Priorities), while an asylee's status can be terminated only if convicted of a "particularly serious crime." However, both groups are also concerned about adjusting to LPR status and therefore with avoiding offenses that trigger inadmissibility.

A. Asylee Client's Immigration Priorities

An asylee's greatest concern is conviction of a "particularly serious crime," including any aggravated felony. Such a conviction may result in the termination of his or her asylum status, after which he or she can be removed for grounds of inadmissibility. *See* INA § 208(c)(2)(B)&(3), 8 U.S.C. § 1158(c)(2)(B)&(3); 8 C.F.R. § 1208.22(2013). An asylee will not be removed based on the crime-related grounds of deportability. *See Matter of V-X-*, 26 I&N Dec. 147 (BIA 2013).

Another significant concern for asylees is an offense triggering inadmissibility. An asylee has been given conditional, not permanent, permission to reside in the U.S. An asylee can lose his or her status if conditions in the country of nationality change. To remain permanently in the U.S., an asylee must adjust status to an LPR. If the asylee has been convicted of a crime making him or her inadmissible, he or she is ineligible to become an LPR.

Third, if your asylee client cannot avoid an aggravated felony, he or she may still be able to remain in the U.S. permanently by seeking relief from removal. Dispositions to avoid include drug trafficking, violent offenses, and particularly serious crimes (as defined for the purposes of withholding), explained further below.

B. Impact on Asylee of an Aggravated Felony Conviction

An asylee's primary immigration concern is a conviction of a "particularly serious crime," for which his or her status can be terminated. *See* INA § 208(c)(2)&(3), 8 U.S.C. § 1158(c)(2)&(3). There is no statutory definition of a particularly serious crime. However, in the context of determining whether an asylee can be deported, an aggravated felony conviction is *per se* a conviction for a "particularly serious crime." *See* INA § 208(b)(2)(B)(i), 8 U.S.C. § 1158(b)(2)(B)(i). For a table of the categories of offenses classified as aggravated felonies, see *supra* § 3.4A, Aggravated Felonies Generally.

Other offenses may be considered particularly serious crimes in the discretion of the immigration judge. *See Matter of M-H-*, 26 I&N Dec. 46 (BIA 2012); *Matter of N-A-M,* 24 I&N Dec. 336 (BIA 2007). The relevant factors include the nature and underlying circumstances of the conviction and the type of sentence imposed.

C. Impact on Asylee of a Criminal Disposition Triggering Inadmissibility

Another significant concern for an asylee client is an offense that renders him or her inadmissible. Because asylum does not confer a permanent right to reside in the U.S., an asylee may want to adjust to LPR status. To adjust his or her status, a person granted asylum must avoid the crime-related grounds of inadmissibility. *See supra* § 3.5G, Chart of Principal Criminal Grounds of Inadmissibility. Other offenses can result in a denial of adjustment of status in the discretion of the immigration judge or officer, but they are not automatic bars.

D. Forms of Relief Depending on Offense

If your client cannot avoid an aggravated felony, he or she may still be able to remain in the U.S. by seeking relief from removal. Below are two principal forms of relief for an asylee client. It may be helpful to consult with an immigration lawyer to determine whether your client is otherwise eligible for these forms of relief.

209(c) Waiver (if not convicted of drug trafficking or violent offense). If your asylee client cannot avoid an aggravated felony, he or she may still be able to remain in the U.S. permanently by seeking a § 209(c) waiver, a special form of relief for refugees and asylees for humanitarian purposes, to assure family unity, or when it is otherwise in the public interest. *See* INA § 209(c), 8 U.S.C. § 1159(c). Such relief is barred by any conviction that provides the government "reason to believe" that the refugee has been involved in drug trafficking. *See id; see also supra* § 3.5A, Controlled Substance Offense (discussing meaning of drug trafficking in this context).

In addition, a conviction of a "violent or dangerous" crime will presumptively bar such discretionary relief. *See supra* "209(c) Waiver (if not convicted of drug trafficking or violent offense)" in § 5.2D, Forms of Relief Depending on Offense.

Withholding of Removal. If your asylee client cannot avoid an aggravated felony, he or she may be able to seek "withholding of removal" based, again, on the client's previously determined fear of persecution in the country of removal. *See* § INA 241(b)(3); 8 U.S.C. § 1231(b)(3). It is a less beneficial form of persecution-based relief and requires a higher threshold showing of persecution than asylum.

Withholding of removal is barred by a conviction of a "particularly serious crime." In this context, a particularly serious crime includes one or more aggravated felony convictions with an aggregate sentence of imprisonment (active or suspended) of five years or more. *See* INA § 241(b)(3)(B), 8 U.S.C. § 1231(b)(3)(B). The five-year sentence may be for one conviction or different convictions, whether or not resolved at the same time A particularly serious crime presumptively includes an aggravated felony conviction involving trafficking in a controlled substance. *See Matter of Y-L-, A-G-, R-S-R-,* 23 I&N Dec. 270 (A.G. 2002) (recognizing that presumption of particularly serious crime is rebuttable). Other offenses may be considered particularly serious crimes in the discretion of the immigration judge. *See Matter of M-H-,* 26 I&N Dec. 46 (BIA 2012); *Matter of N-A-M-,* 24 I&N Dec. 336 (BIA 2007). The relevant factors include the nature and underlying circumstances of the conviction and the type of sentence imposed.

5.4 Nonimmigrant Visa Holder

Nonimmigrant visa holders are admitted to the U.S. on a temporary visa for a specific purpose, such as tourism, study, or temporary work. *See supra* § 2.2D, Individuals with Temporary Lawful Status or Pending Application for Staus. These noncitizens may have only temporary status, but like LPRs they may have come to this country many years ago and may have lived and worked in this country for many years. They can be removed because of a criminal conviction.

A. Immigration Priorities for Nonimmigrant Visa Holder

A nonimmigrant visa holder may be removed from the U.S. based on an offense that triggers deportability. Such offenses are, therefore, their primary immigration concern.

A secondary concern is an offense that triggers inadmissibility. Certain nonimmigrant visa holders may be able to become LPRs based on a family relationship or employer sponsor. These individuals will be concerned about offenses that trigger inadmissibility, which would preclude them from becoming an LPR and remaining in the U.S permanently.

Third, if your client cannot avoid an offense triggering deportability, he or she may still be able to remain in the U.S. by seeking relief from removal. Dispositions to avoid include controlled substance offenses, violent offenses, and particularly serious crimes, explained further below.

B. Impact on Nonimmigrant Visa Holder of a Criminal Disposition Triggering Deportability

Concern about Deportable Offenses. The greatest immigration concern for lawfully admitted noncitizens are dispositions triggering deportability, as they can be removed from the U.S for such offenses. *See supra* § 3.4G, Chart of Principal Deportable Offenses.

Additional Concern for Nonimmigrant Visa Holder Client. As a practical matter, a criminal disposition of any kind can potentially trigger a separate ground of deportability for nonimmigrant visa holders. A nonimmigrant who has failed to meet the conditions for continued nonimmigrant status is deportable. *See* INA § 237(a)(1)(C)(i), 8 U.S.C. § 1227(a)(1)(C)(i). For example, a student who has failed to maintain a full course of study because he or she was sentenced to six months in jail may be deportable on this ground, even if the conviction itself is not a deportable offense. Similarly, a nonimmigrant with "visitor" status who is sentenced to active time in jail or prison will be deemed to have failed to maintain that status. *See Matter of A-*, 6 I&N Dec. 762 (BIA 1955) (visitor status cannot be pursued in jail).

Practice Note: If your client has a nonimmigrant visa other than a visitor visa, your client should consult with an immigration attorney before addressing the pending criminal charges. The consequences for each nonimmigrant status vary substantially and are beyond the scope of this manual.

C. Impact on Nonimmigrant Visa Holder of a Criminal Disposition Triggering Inadmissibility

A second concern for a nonimmigrant is an offense that triggers inadmissibility, which would prevent them from becoming an LPR. Some noncitizens may have a pending application for LPR status or some basis for acquiring LPR status in the future. *See supra* § 3.5G, Chart of Principal Criminal Grounds of Inadmissibility.

Practice Note: The routes to LPR status are a complicated and constantly changing area of law. If your client is in the process of seeking LPR status, you should consult with his or her immigration attorney regarding the status of the application.

D. Forms of Relief Depending on Offense

If your client cannot avoid deportability, he or she may still be able to remain in the U.S. by seeking relief from removal. Here are three principal forms of relief. It may be helpful to consult with an immigration lawyer to determine whether your client is otherwise eligible for these forms of relief.

Adjustment of Status (if not convicted of inadmissible offense). If your client cannot avoid an offense triggering deportability, he or she may still be able to remain in the U.S.

permanently by seeking adjustment of status and becoming an LPR. Adjusting status is a defense to deportation, but your client would need a route to seek such status. Note that the criminal grounds of inadmissibility do not include some crimes that would render a person deportable—namely, firearm and domestic violence offenses. (If, however, the firearm or domestic violence offense constitutes a crime of moral turpitude, which is one of the crimes of inadmissibility, the offense could still render the person inadmissible.) Therefore, a conviction for carrying a concealed firearm would not render your client inadmissible and would not bar adjustment of status.

212(h) Waiver (if not convicted of controlled substance offense). If your client cannot avoid a crime of inadmissibility and is otherwise able to adjust status, he or she may still be able to obtain LPR status by seeking a form of relief known as a 212(h) waiver. *See* INA § 212(h), 8 U.S.C. § 1182(h). In many cases, to obtain this waiver, the noncitizen would need to demonstrate that she is the spouse, parent, son, or daughter of a U.S. citizen or lawful permanent resident and that denial of the waiver would result in "extreme hardship" to that relative. A conviction of a controlled substance offense (other than a single offense of simple possession of 30 grams or less of marijuana if the client has no prior controlled substance convictions) is a bar to a 212(h) waiver and consequently a permanent bar to obtaining LPR status.

In addition, Department of Homeland Security (DHS) regulations provide that a conviction of a "violent or dangerous" crime will presumptively bar a 212(h) waiver. *See* 8 C.F.R. 212.7(d); *see also supra* "209(c) Waiver (if not convicted of drug trafficking or violent offense)" in § 5.2D, Forms of Relief Depending on Offense.

Practice Note: A conviction for a Class 1 misdemeanor possession of marijuana may involve more or less than 30 grams of marijuana. If your client is pleading guilty to a Class 1 misdemeanor possession of marijuana, it is important to document in the record of conviction that your client possessed 30 grams or less of marijuana, if applicable, for purposes of 212(h) relief. *See supra* § 3.3C, Burden of Proof on Noncitizen in Applying for Relief and Demonstrating Admissibility.

Withholding of Removal (if not convicted of a particularly serious offense). If your client cannot avoid an offense triggering deportability, and fears persecution in the country of removal, he or she may still be able to remain in the U.S. by seeking "withholding of removal." *See* § INA 241(b)(3); 8 U.S.C. § 1231(b)(3). It is a less beneficial form of persecution-based relief and requires a higher threshold showing of persecution than asylum.

Withholding of removal is barred by a conviction of a "particularly serious crime." In this context, a particularly serious crime includes one or more aggravated felony convictions with an aggregate sentence of imprisonment (active or suspended) of five years or more. *See* INA § 241(b)(3)(B), 8 U.S.C. § 1231(b)(3)(B). The five-year sentence may be for one conviction or different convictions, whether or not resolved at the same time. A particularly serious crime presumptively includes an aggravated felony conviction involving trafficking in a controlled substance. *See Matter of Y-L-, A-G-, R-S-R-,* 23 I&N

Dec. 270 (A.G. 2002) (recognizing that presumption of particularly serious crime is rebuttable). Other offenses may be considered particularly serious crimes in the discretion of the immigration judge. *See Matter of M-H-*, 26 I&N Dec. 46 (BIA 2012); *Matter of N-A-M-,* 24 I&N Dec. 336 (BIA 2007). The relevant factors include the nature and underlying facts of the conviction and the type of sentence imposed.

5.5   Noncitizens with Temporary Protected Status

Temporary Protected Status (TPS) provides temporary protection to nationals of countries experiencing dire and extraordinary conditions that make it too dangerous to return. *See supra* § 2.2D, Individuals with Temporary Lawful Status or Pending Application for Status. The countries designated for TPS as of August 16, 2017 are El Salvador, Haiti, Honduras, Nepal, Nicaragua, Somalia, Sudan, South Sudan, Syria, and Yemen. These noncitizens may have only temporary status, but like LPRs they may have come to this country many years ago and may have lived and worked in this country for many years. They can be removed because of a criminal conviction.

For technical immigration law reasons pertaining to their status, individuals with TPS will lose their status and face removal if convicted of:

- Any felony conviction or two or more misdemeanor convictions (whether the convictions are entered separately or consolidated for judgment). *See* INA § 244(c)(2)(B)(i), 8 U.S.C. § 1254a(c)(2)(B)(i).
- A "particularly serious crime." *See* INA § 244(c)(2)(B)(ii), 8 U.S.C. § 1254a(c)(2)(B)(ii). There is no statutory definition of a particularly serious crime. However, in this context, an aggravated felony conviction is *per se* a conviction for a "particularly serious crime." *See* INA § 208(b)(2)(B)(i), 8 U.S.C. § 1158(b)(2)(B)(i). For a table of the categories of offenses classified as aggravated felonies, see *supra* § 3.4A, Aggravated Felonies Generally. Other offenses may be considered particularly serious crimes in the discretion of the immigration judge. *See Matter of M-H-*, 26 I&N Dec. 46 (BIA 2012); *Matter of N-A-M-,* 24 I&N Dec. 336 (BIA 2007). The relevant factors include the nature and underlying circumstances of the conviction and the type of sentence imposed.
- Specific offenses that come within the crime-related grounds of inadmissibility: a crime involving moral turpitude (except for an offense that falls within the petty offense exception), a drug offense (except for a single offense of possession of 30 grams or less of marijuana), or evidence that supports a charge of drug trafficking. *See* INA § 244(c)(2)(A) (iii), 8 U.S.C. § 1254a (c)(2)(A)(iii).

5.6   Noncitizens without Immigration Status

Noncitizens without lawful status have no government authorization to be present in the United States. *See supra* § 2.2E, Individuals without Immigration Status. This category includes undocumented people who entered the U.S. without inspection (crossed the border illegally), as well as individuals who entered the U.S. on a valid visa but remained past their authorized period of stay. Some of these individuals may have pending applications for status or may be able, now or in the future, to obtain LPR status or persecution-based relief.

These noncitizens may have no current immigration status, but like LPRs they may have come to this country many years ago and may have lived and worked in this country for many years. An individual without status can be removed because of a criminal conviction. If an individual does not have lawful immigration status, he or she also may be removed immediately on that basis alone.

Because a client without status can be removed for being here unlawfully, sometimes criminal defense attorneys assume that the outcome of the criminal case does not matter. However, a removal based on criminal grounds (especially aggravated felony grounds) carries many more adverse consequences than a removal based on unlawful presence in the U.S. Thus, the outcome of the criminal case may still be important.

A. Immigration Priorities for Noncitizen Client without Immigration Status

Some individuals without immigration status may have a pending application for status or may be able, now or in the future, to obtain LPR status through a U.S. citizen spouse, relief from removal, or persecution-based relief. Even if an individual is currently ineligible to obtain lawful status, that circumstance could change in the future, so the client may still be concerned about offenses that bar eligibility for lawful status in the future.

A client who wants to acquire LPR status, now or in the future, will be most concerned about offenses that trigger inadmissibility. To qualify for LPR status, the noncitizen must not be convicted of an offense that triggers inadmissibility.

If your client cannot avoid an offense that triggers inadmissibility, he or she may still be able to become an LPR by seeking 212(h) relief, which allows noncitizens to adjust to LPR status despite such a conviction (if the noncitizen is otherwise eligible to obtain LPR status). A controlled substance offense bars 212(h) relief.

If your client has a fear of persecution in the country of nationality, he or she will also be concerned about any disposition that bars persecution-based relief, in particular a conviction of an aggravated felony or drug trafficking offense.

If your client is potentially eligible for Deferred Action for Childhood Arrivals (DACA) (see further description below in Section E.), he or she will be concerned about any felony conviction and certain misdemeanors, which bar eligibility for the DACA program.

In addition, your client may be concerned about "voluntary departure." Voluntary departure allows an individual to leave the U.S. voluntarily at his or her own expense in lieu of being removed by the government. If eligibility for voluntary departure is a concern, your client should avoid an aggravated felony conviction, which is a bar to voluntary departure.

Clients who cannot avoid serious convictions should be warned of enhanced prison penalties should they return to the U.S. illegally after removal.

B. Impact on Noncitizen without Immigration Status of a Criminal Disposition Triggering Inadmissibility

Your client may have a pending application for LPR status or may be otherwise concerned about his or her ability to obtain LPR status in the future. If this is a priority for your client, he or she should avoid offenses that trigger inadmissibility. *See supra* § 3.5G, Chart of Principal Criminal Grounds of Inadmissibility.

In most cases, the grounds of deportability are irrelevant to an undocumented person because he or she has not been admitted to the U.S.[3] Note that the criminal grounds of inadmissibility do not include some crimes that would render a person deportable— namely, firearm and domestic violence offenses. (If, however, the firearm or domestic violence offense constitutes a crime of moral turpitude, which is one of the crimes of inadmissibility, the offense could still render the person inadmissible.) Therefore, a conviction for carrying a concealed firearm would not render your client inadmissible and bar adjustment to LPR status.

C. Impact on Noncitizen without Immigration Status of Controlled Substance and Certain Other Dispositions

If your client cannot avoid a crime of inadmissibility and is otherwise eligible to adjust status, he or she may still be able to obtain LPR status by seeking 212(h) relief. *See supra* "212(h) Waiver (if not convicted of controlled substance offense)" in § 5.4D, Forms of Relief Depending on Offense.

A conviction of a controlled substance offense (other than a single offense of simple possession of 30 grams or less of marijuana if the client has no prior controlled substance convictions) is a bar to 212(h) relief and consequently a permanent bar to obtaining LPR status.

In addition, a conviction of a "violent or dangerous" crime may make it more difficult to obtain 212(h) relief. *See supra* "209(c) Waiver (if not convicted of drug trafficking or violent offense)" in § 5.2D, Forms of Relief Depending on Offense.

---

3. The main exception is if the person will apply for non-permanent resident cancellation of removal, based upon 10-years residence in the U.S. and exceptional hardship to citizen or permanent resident relatives. *See* INA § 240A(b)(1), 8 USC § 1229b(1). A conviction for an offense described in the grounds of deportability would bar this relief.

Practice Note: A conviction for a Class 1 misdemeanor possession of marijuana may involve more or less than 30 grams of marijuana. If your client is pleading guilty to a Class 1 misdemeanor possession of marijuana, it is important to document in the record of conviction that your client possessed 30 grams or less of marijuana, if applicable, for purposes of 212(h) relief. *See supra* § 3.3C, Burden of Proof on Noncitizen in Applying for Relief and Demonstrating Admissibility.

D. Impact on Noncitizen without Immigration Status of an Offense that Bars Persecution-Based Claims

Generally. Your client may have a pending application for asylum. Or, your client may be someone who fears persecution in his or her country of nationality but never applied for asylum. Or, your client may be a national of a country designated as experiencing civil strife, environmental disaster, or other extraordinary and temporary conditions, and thus be eligible for Temporary Protected Status (TPS).

If your client has a pending application for asylum, fears persecution in the country of removal, or is a national of a TPS-designated country, it may be an important goal to avoid offenses that bar persecution-based claims.

Practice Note: The law of asylum and other persecution-based relief from removal is a complicated and constantly changing area of law. In addition, the countries that are designated for temporary grants of TPS constantly change. If your client has already begun the process of seeking asylum or TPS, and has an immigration attorney or other representative, you should consult with that representative regarding the current status of the application. If not, and your client wants to remain in the U.S., you or your client may consider contacting an immigration lawyer to determine what options are available to your client under the current immigration laws. Once you have been able to determine more precisely your client's immigration prospects, you and your client will be in a better position to determine appropriate strategies for the criminal case.

Asylum. A conviction of a "particularly serious crime" bars asylum. *See* INA § 208(b)(2)(A) (ii), 8 U.S.C. § 1158(b)(2)(A)(ii). There is no statutory definition of a "particularly serious crime." For *asylum* purposes, an aggravated felony conviction is considered a "particularly serious crime." *See* INA § 208(b)(2)(B)(i), 8 U.S.C. § 1158(b)(2)(B)(i). Other offenses may be considered a conviction of a particularly serious crime in the discretion of the immigration judge. *See Matter of M-H-*, 26 I&N Dec. 46 (BIA 2012); *Matter of N-A-M-,* 24 I&N Dec. 336 (BIA 2007). The relevant factors include the nature and underlying facts of the conviction and the type of sentence imposed.

In addition, a conviction of a "violent or dangerous" crime will make it more difficult to obtain asylum. *See supra* "209(c) Waiver (if not convicted of drug trafficking or violent offense)" in § 5.2D, Forms of Relief Depending on Offense.

Withholding of Removal. Even if your client is not eligible for asylum, he or she may be eligible for withholding of removal. *See* § INA 241(b)(3); 8 U.S.C. § 1231(b)(3). It is a less beneficial form of persecution-based relief and requires a higher threshold showing of persecution than asylum.

Withholding of removal is barred by a conviction of a "particularly serious crime." In this context, a particularly serious crime includes one or more aggravated felony convictions with an aggregate sentence of imprisonment (active or suspended) of five years or more. *See* INA § 241(b)(3)(B), 8 U.S.C. § 1231(b)(3)(B). The five-year sentence may be for one conviction or different convictions, whether or not resolved at the same time. A particularly serious crime presumptively includes an aggravated felony conviction involving trafficking in a controlled substance. *See Matter of Y-L-, A-G-, R-S-R-,* 23 I&N Dec. 270 (A.G. 2002) (recognizing that presumption of particularly serious crime is rebuttable). Other offenses may be considered particularly serious crimes in the discretion of the immigration judge. *See Matter of M-H-,* 26 I&N Dec. 46 (BIA 2012); *Matter of N-A-M-,* 24 I&N Dec. 336 (BIA 2007). The relevant factors include the nature and underlying facts of the conviction and the type of sentence imposed.

Temporary Protected Status (TPS). Your client may be eligible for the temporary relief of TPS if he or she is a national of a designated country. The countries designated for TPS as of August 16, 2017 are El Salvador, Haiti, Honduras, Nepal, Nicaragua, Somalia, Sudan, South Sudan, Syria, and Yemen.

Obtaining TPS is barred by any felony conviction, two or more misdemeanor convictions, or a conviction for a particularly serious crime. *See* INA § 244(c)(2)(B), 8 U.S.C. § 1254a(c)(2)(B); *see also supra* § 5.5, Noncitizens with Temporary Protected Status. Obtaining TPS is also barred by a crime involving moral turpitude (except for an offense that falls within the petty offense exception), a drug offense (except for a single offense of possession of 30 grams or less of marijuana), or evidence that supports a charge of drug trafficking. *See* INA § 244(c)(2)(A) (iii), 8 U.S.C. § 1254a (c)(2)(A)(iii).

Practice Note: TPS country designations constantly change; the designations of the countries listed above may expire or new countries may be added. If your client is a national of one of the countries listed above, check the website of the U.S. Citizenship and Immigration Service—www.uscis.gov—to determine if the country is still designated. Also, if your client is not from a country listed above, but that country is now suffering from some dangerous condition, you can check the website to determine whether it has been designated for TPS.

E. Impact on Noncitizen without Immigration Status of a Conviction that Bars Deferred Action of Childhood Arrivals (DACA)

Some individuals without status might be eligible for Deferred Action for Childhood Arrivals (DACA) or may already have DACA. On June 15, 2012, the Obama Administration announced that it would not deport certain undocumented people who entered the U.S. as children. Deferred action means that even though the noncitizen is here without status and subject to deportation, the government agrees to "defer" any actions to remove them. Individuals granted DACA receive a two year deferral of deportation and are able to apply for work authorization and a social security number. While deferred action does not provide a pathway to getting LPR status or citizenship, it does allow noncitizens without status to work legally in the U.S. To qualify, the individual must:

- be younger than 31 years old as of June 15, 2012;
- have entered the U.S. when he or she was under age 16;
- have been physically present in the U.S. on June 15, 2012, and have continuously resided in the U.S. during the preceding five years (except for brief, casual, and innocent absences); and
- currently be in school or have graduated from high school or obtained a GED, or been honorably discharged from the coast guard or armed forces.

A broad array of criminal offenses, including any felony and certain misdemeanors, will bar eligibility unless a person can show "exceptional circumstances." For a chart of the DACA criminal bars, see *supra* § 3.7, Criminal Bars to Deferred Action for Childhood Arrivals. It is unclear whether the current administration will continue to grant DACA once individuals' grants expire, but it has thus far not eliminated the program.

F. Impact on Noncitizen without Immigration Status of a Conviction that Bars Voluntary Departure

If your client cannot avoid removal, he or she may be interested in "voluntary departure." Voluntary departure allows an individual to leave the U.S. voluntarily at his or her own expense in lieu of being removed by the government. Your client may prefer this alternative to deportation. For example, if deported by the government, your client will be barred from immigrating to the U.S. for a minimum statutory period of time (depending on the basis for the removal). *See supra* § 3.2C, Long-term Consequences of a Removal Order. If your client voluntarily departs, he or she may not be subject to these statutory bars to returning to the U.S. Also, your client may want to avoid any harassment or stigma in the country to which he or she returns as a result of forcible removal from the U.S. Last, the act of unlawfully reentering the U.S. after removal is a more serious and more commonly prosecuted offense than illegal reentry following a voluntary departure.

Clients interested in voluntary departure must avoid a conviction of an aggravated felony, which is a bar to voluntary departure. *See* INA §§ 240B(a)(1), (b)(1)(C), 8 U.S.C. §§ 1229c(a)(1), (b)(1)(C).

G. Enhanced Liability for Illegal Reentry after Removal

Many noncitizens removed from the United States subsequently reenter or attempt to reenter the country to join their families. If a noncitizen does so after a criminal conviction, he or she may face more criminal exposure than the sentence of two years otherwise possible. You should warn of enhanced prison penalties for a conviction of illegal reentry. Specifically:

- Removal after a conviction of any aggravated felony may result in a prison sentence of up to twenty years.
- Removal after a conviction of any felony may result in a prison sentence of up to ten years.
- Removal after a conviction of three or more misdemeanors involving drugs or crimes against the person, or both, may result in a prison sentence of up to ten years.

5.7   Summary of Priorities in Representing Noncitizen Clients by Status

The following is based on the likely priorities of noncitizen clients in criminal proceedings.

LPR's Immigration Priorities

1. Most importantly, an LPR should avoid an aggravated felony conviction, which bars most forms of relief from removal.
2. An LPR should also avoid other offenses triggering deportability, for which he or she can be removed.
3. If your client plans to travel abroad in the future, he or she should avoid a criminal disposition that triggers inadmissibility.
4. If your client cannot avoid deportability and wants to apply for relief from removal, he or she should avoid an aggravated felony or other offenses that bar relief from removal.
5. If your client is able to avoid a deportable offense, he or she may also want to avoid a disposition that bars naturalization.

Refugee's Immigration Priorities

1. Most importantly, a refugee should avoid an offense triggering deportability, as a refugee can be removed from the U.S. for such an offense.
2. A refugee should avoid an offense that triggers inadmissibility if he or she wants to adjust to LPR status.
3. If your refugee client cannot avoid an offense that triggers deportability and wants to apply for relief from removal, he or she should at least avoid a drug trafficking disposition, violent offenses, and particularly serious crimes.

Asylee's Immigration Priorities

1. An asylee should avoid a conviction of a particularly serious crime, specifically an aggravated felony, as he or she can lose his or her asylum status for such an offense.
2. Your asylee client should avoid an offense that triggers inadmissibility if he or she wants to adjust to LPR status.
3. If your asylee client cannot avoid an aggravated felony and wants to apply for relief from removal, he or she should at least avoid a drug trafficking disposition, violent offenses, and particularly serious crimes.

Immigration Priorities for Nonimmigrant Visa Holder

1. A nonimmigrant visa holder should avoid an offense that triggers deportability or otherwise results in loss of status.
2. A nonimmigrant visa holder should avoid an offense that triggers inadmissibility if he or she wants to adjust to LPR status.
3. If your nonimmigrant client cannot avoid a crime of inadmissibility and is otherwise able to adjust status, he or she should at least avoid a controlled substance offense, which precludes adjustment to LPR status through a 212(h) waiver.

Immigration Priorities for Noncitizen with Temporary Protected Status (TPS)

1. An individual with TPS should avoid any felony conviction or two or more misdemeanor convictions, which will result in a loss of status.
2. An individual with TPS should avoid a conviction of a particularly serious crime, specifically an aggravated felony, as he or she can lose his or her status for such an offense.
3. An individual with TPS should avoid a conviction of a crime involving moral turpitude, a drug offense, or evidence that supports a charge of drug trafficking, which will result in a loss of status.

Immigration Priorities for Noncitizen Client without Immigration Status

1. A noncitizen without immigration status should avoid an offense that triggers inadmissibility if he or she wants to acquire LPR status.
2. If a noncitizen client without immigration status cannot avoid a crime of inadmissibility, he or she should at least avoid a controlled substance offense, which permanently bars an individual from adjusting to LPR status.
3. If your client has a fear of persecution in the country of nationality, he or she should avoid any disposition that bars persecution-based relief.
4. If your client is eligible for or currently has DACA, he or she should avoid any disposition that would be a bar to the DACA program.
5. If your client is interested in voluntary departure, he or she should avoid an aggravated felony conviction.

Chapter 6
Options for Minimizing Adverse Immigration Consequences

6.1 General Rules   **6-2**
- A. Offenses That Do Not Carry Adverse Immigration Consequences
- B. Deferred Prosecution
- C. Categorical Approach and Record of Conviction
- D. Pleading Not Guilty
- E. Post-Conviction Relief

6.2 Cases Involving Aggravated Felonies   **6-4**
- A. Aggravated Felonies Triggered by a One Year Term of Imprisonment
- B. Theft Aggravated Felony
- C. Sexual Abuse of a Minor Aggravated Felony
- D. Aggravated Felonies Triggered by More than a $10,000 Loss
- E. Crime of Violence Aggravated Felony

6.3 Cases Involving Drugs   **6-8**
- A. Manufacture, Sale, or Delivery of a Schedule III Controlled Substance
- B. Simple Possession of a Controlled Substance
- C. Possession of 30 Grams or Less of Marijuana
- D. Drug Paraphernalia
- E. Delivery of Marijuana
- F. Possession by Trafficking
- G. Accessory after the Fact
- H. Non-Drug Charges

6.4 Cases Involving Crimes Involving Moral Turpitude   **6-12**
- A. Offense That Is Not a Crime Involving Moral Turpitude
- B. One Misdemeanor CMT
- C. One Felony CMT for Noncitizen Admitted to the U.S. for More Than Five Years

6.5 Cases Involving Firearms   **6-13**
- A. Weapons Offenses That Do Not Specifically Involve a Firearm
- B. Firearm Offenses That Do Not Come within the Federal Definition of Firearm

    C. Non-Aggravated Felony
    D. Accessory after the Fact

6.6   Cases Involving Domestic Violence   **6-15**
    A. Offense That Is Not a Crime of Violence
    B. Offense That Is Not Against a Person
    C. Offense That Is Not Against a Protected Person

6.7   Cases Involving Child Abuse   **6-16**

The immigration consequences of conviction can be severe and can extend to a large number of criminal dispositions. In some cases, however, your client may be able to avoid these adverse immigration consequences or at least minimize them so that he or she remains eligible for immigration relief from removal.

This chapter presents options for minimizing adverse immigration consequences in the criminal case. Section 6.1 describes approaches that are generally applicable regardless of the specific type of case. Whether that approach is feasible will depend, of course, on the circumstances of the case. The remaining sections are broken down by specific categories of offenses and discuss potential options applicable to that offense type. Bear in mind that the following options are not case-specific—they are not a substitute for individualized research or consultation with an immigration attorney.

6.1   General Rules

A. Offenses That Do Not Carry Adverse Immigration Consequences

If your client pleads guilty or is found guilty, the most favorable result for the client from an immigration standpoint is a plea and sentence to an offense that does not fall within a crime-based ground of removal (deportability or inadmissibility) or that does not bar immigration relief from removal. For example, if a number of different offenses are charged, it may be possible to identify a charge with less serious immigration consequences. In other cases, it may be possible to negotiate a plea to a lesser included offense, or a related offense, that does not contain an element triggering deportability or inadmissibility.

For example, the offense of indecent liberties with a child is a sexual abuse of a minor aggravated felony. A conviction of sexual battery, however, should not qualify as sexual abuse of a minor because the minor age of the victim is not an element of the offense.

To determine whether an offense and its lesser included and related offenses carry adverse immigration consequences, see *infra* Appendix A, Selected Immigration

Consequences of North Carolina Offenses. You should also contact an immigration attorney if you need assistance in a particular case.

B. Deferred Prosecution

A deferred prosecution may or may not constitute a conviction depending on the structure of the agreement. *See supra* 4.2A, Deferred Prosecution. Certain deferrals may be a favorable option from an immigration standpoint.

C. Categorical Approach and Record of Conviction

To determine whether an individual is removable based on a conviction, the immigration court examines the elements of the statute violated, not the individual's conduct. If the statute is divisible and proscribes both offenses that carry an immigration penalty and offenses that do not, then the immigration court is allowed to examine the record of conviction to determine the offense for which the defendant was convicted. *See supra* § 3.3A, Categorical Approach and Variations. If the record of conviction does not establish all of the elements necessary for a deportable offense, the noncitizen should not be found deportable.

The plea proceedings are considered a part of the record of conviction. In North Carolina, there is generally no transcription of the plea proceedings in district court. The record of conviction in district court is generally composed of the charging document (e.g., warrant), any judgment, and any other documents in the shuck. In superior court, plea proceedings are recorded and, thus, are part of the record of conviction in felony cases and misdemeanors appealed for trial de novo. There is also usually a written transcript of plea in superior court.

There may be steps counsel can take. For example, if your client is pleading guilty under a statute that is divisible, take care to avoid references in the record of conviction—including dismissed counts or during the plea colloquy—to the specific facts listed in the statute of conviction that would establish conviction under the prong of the divisible statute that comes within the removal ground.

Crafting an *Alford* plea where the statute is divisible may be another option. The Fourth Circuit Court of Appeals has held that the State's proffer of a factual basis for an *Alford* plea cannot establish with the requisite certainty that the conviction triggers a federal sentencing enhancement. *See United States v. Alston*, 611 F.3d 219, 227 (4th Cir. 2010). The same rationale may apply to removal consequences based on a conviction. Thus, should your client take an *Alford* plea, he or she may have a solid argument that the government cannot meets its burden of establishing under which prong of a divisible statute your client was convicted (at least in the Fourth Circuit).

Alternatively, where your client is pleading guilty to the non-deportable crime under a divisible statute, and there is no transcription of proceedings, you should try to have the court or prosecutor note this on the shuck or charging document. This will be particularly important if your client will be applying for relief from removal, where the burden is on the noncitizen.

In limited situations, the immigration court may look beyond the record of conviction to determine certain aspects of the crime that go beyond the elements of the offense. For example, decisions have allowed the immigration court to look beyond the record of conviction at the amount of loss to determine whether the offense was an aggravated felony triggered by a loss exceeding $10,000 and at the relationship between the parties in assault or other violent offense cases to determine whether the offense was a crime of domestic violence. *See supra* § 3.3A, Categorical Approach and Variations. Where the immigration court can look beyond the record of conviction, if possible defense counsel should try to plead affirmatively to an immigration-safe circumstance. For example, if the defendant is pleading guilty to a fraud offense, counsel could try to craft a plea for a sum certain that is $10,000 or less if appropriate. In other words, defense counsel should work to create a record of conviction that protects the client and negates the need to consider evidence outside the record of conviction.

D. Pleading Not Guilty

If the proposed plea carries adverse immigration consequences, your client may decide to plead not guilty. Even if a plea offer appears favorable in terms of the criminal consequences, the client may decide that the immigration consequences are a more important consideration. In those cases, you need to consider litigating possible suppression issues and other pretrial motions as appropriate. The client may want to take the case to trial to seek acquittal of all charges or at least of charges that carry immigration penalties.

E. Post-Conviction Relief

If a defendant has a final judgment of conviction that carries adverse immigration consequences, he or she may consider filing a motion to vacate the conviction or sentence, if warranted. For example, if trial counsel failed to advise the defendant of the immigration consequences of the conviction and the defendant relied on that information in deciding to plead guilty, the defendant may have grounds to file a post-conviction motion based on ineffective assistance of counsel under *Padilla v. Kentucky. See infra* Ch. 8, State Post-Conviction Relief.

6.2   Cases Involving Aggravated Felonies

A conviction of an aggravated felony carries the most severe immigration consequences, including mandatory deportation in most cases, mandatory detention during removal proceedings, a permanent bar from future immigration to the U.S., and a jail sentence of up to twenty years if the individual illegally reenters the U.S. after deportation.

The following options may not eliminate all the grounds of deportability or inadmissibility, but they may avoid the more severe immigration consequences of an aggravated felony conviction.

A. Aggravated Felonies Triggered by a One Year Term of Imprisonment

To constitute an aggravated felony, many offenses must be accompanied by a one year sentence of imprisonment (actual or suspended) or more. The principal offenses in this category are:

- Theft offenses
- Burglary and felony breaking and entering
- "Crimes of violence" as defined under immigration law, such as certain intentional violent assault offenses
- Forgery and counterfeiting offenses
- Obstruction of justice offenses

For a complete description of those offenses, see *supra* § 3.4A, Aggravated Felonies Generally.

Community Punishment. A judge may impose a fine, without a sentence of imprisonment, for felonies that authorize a community or "C" punishment under structured sentencing. A judge also may enter a prayer for judgment continued or PJC, without a sentence of imprisonment. Even though a sentence of imprisonment of one year or more is authorized, a fine or PJC would be the sentence imposed in those circumstances and therefore would not make the offense an aggravated felony under the one-year rule.

Consecutive Sentences with Individual Counts of Less Than 12 months. As long as no individual count results in a maximum sentence of 12 months or longer, a total term of imprisonment (active or suspended) of 12 months or more will not trigger these aggravated felony grounds. This concept does not come into play often in North Carolina because all felony sentences of imprisonment now exceed one year.[1]

---

1. There may be an argument that a person convicted of multiple felony offenses and sentenced to consecutive terms has not received a sentence of one year or more *for the second and subsequent offense*. For the second and subsequent offense, North Carolina law reduces the maximum sentence to be served by the period of post-release supervision for that offense. *See* G.S. 15A-1354(b). This argument may be helpful only where a non-aggravated felony is the first in the string of consecutive judgments (because the maximum sentence for the first-sentenced offense *will* include post-release supervision), followed by the potential aggravated felony offense (so that the reduction rule of G.S. 15A-1354(b) is applied to the potential aggravated felony). This argument may not succeed, as the maximum sentence "imposed" by the judge on the second and subsequent offense still includes the extra time for post-release supervision even though the defendant will never serve it.

B. Theft Aggravated Felony

A theft offense, plus a maximum sentence of imprisonment (active or suspended) of one year or longer, will be considered an aggravated felony offense. The U.S. Supreme Court has defined theft as the "taking of property or an exercise of control over property *without consent* with the criminal intent to deprive the owner of rights and benefits of ownership, even if such deprivation is less than total or permanent." *Gonzales v. Duenas-Alvarez*, 549 U.S. 183, 189 (2007) (emphasis added).

A crime that covers theft by trickery or deception is not considered a theft aggravated felony by the Board of Immigration Appeals, and Fourth and Eleventh Circuits. *See Matter of Garcia-Madruga*, 24 I&N Dec. 436 (BIA 2008); *Soliman v. Gonzales*, 419 F.3d 276 (4th Cir. 2005) (holding that Virginia credit care fraud did not come within theft aggravated felony); *Vassell v. U.S. Att'y Gen.,* 839 F.3d 1352 (11th Cir. 2016) (holding that Georgia theft statute does not qualify as theft aggravated felony). Consequently, if your client pleads to a fraud offense, it should not be considered a theft aggravated felony even if the defendant receives a sentence of imprisonment of twelve months or more (though it may come under a different aggravated felony ground if the loss is more than $10,000). Similarly, there is a good argument that a conviction under the North Carolina larceny statute should not come within the theft aggravated felony ground because it appears to cover larceny by trick. More specifically, the element of trespass—that is, a taking without consent—can be satisfied by a "constructive trespass" where property is fraudulently obtained by trick or artifice. *State v. Jones*, 177 N.C. App. 269 (2006). Because larceny by trick is not a separate crime from common-law larceny, no convictions under the larceny statute may qualify as an aggravated felony. *See supra* § 3.3A, Categorical Approach and Variations.

C. Sexual Abuse of a Minor Aggravated Felony

A conviction for an offense considered sexual abuse of a minor is an aggravated felony offense. The Board of Immigration Appeals has not defined sexual abuse of a minor, and the federal circuit court definitions vary. Under the categorical approach, a crime that lacks an element of age of minority of the victim should not qualify as sexual abuse of a minor. For example, a conviction for sexual battery under G.S. 14-27.33 should not qualify as sexual abuse of a minor because the minor age of the victim (under age 18) is not an element of the offense.

In the context of statutory rape-type offenses (where sexual intercourse is abusive solely because of the ages of the participants), the U.S. Supreme Court has held that the statute must require the victim to be less than age 16 for the offense to qualify as a "sexual abuse of a minor" aggravated felony. *See Esquivel-Quintana v. Sessions*, ___ U.S.___, 137 S. Ct. 1562 (2017) (holding that conviction under California statutory rape statute criminalizing unlawful sexual intercourse with a minor (defined as under age 18) who is more than three years younger than the offender is not categorically "sexual abuse of a minor").

D. Aggravated Felonies Triggered by More Than a $10,000 Loss

The convictions listed below will be considered an aggravated felony if the amount of loss is more than $10,000:

- Crimes involving fraud or deceit with a loss to the victim of more than $10,000
- Money laundering involving more than $10,000
- Tax evasion with a loss to the government of more than $10,000

The U.S. Supreme Court has held that the amount of loss is generally not an element of the fraud-related offenses listed above and, thus, may be proven by evidence outside the record of conviction. *Nijhawan v. Holder*, 557 U.S. 29, 42 (2009). *See supra* § 3.3A, Categorical Approach and Variations. If defense counsel is able to negotiate a loss of $10,000 or less, as indicated by the plea agreement, this category of aggravated felony should probably not apply.

There is a good argument that conviction of multiple counts of fraud, each carrying a loss of less than $10,000 but with an aggregate loss of more than $10,000, should not qualify as an aggravated felony. At least one conviction must be tethered to more than a $10,000 loss. *See Nijhawan v. Holder*, 557 U.S. at 42 (indicating that there must be a tether between the evidence of loss and the particular "conviction" and that the amount cannot be based on acquitted or dismissed counts or general conduct).

E. Crime of Violence Aggravated Felony

A crime of violence as defined in 18 U.S.C. § 16, plus a maximum sentence of imprisonment (active or suspended) of one year or longer, will be considered an aggravated felony offense. For a discussion of the definition of crime of violence, see *supra* § 3.4B, Specific Types of Aggravated Felonies.

A crime that penalizes negligent or accidental conduct is not considered a crime of violence under immigration law and therefore is not an aggravated felony. Consequently, negotiating a plea to an offense such as felony serious injury by vehicle under G.S. 20-141.4(a3) or felony death by vehicle under G.S. 20-141.4(a1) should not be considered a crime of violence aggravated felony even if the defendant receives a sentence of imprisonment of twelve months or more.

The U.S. Supreme Court has not resolved whether a state offense that requires proof of reckless use of force qualifies as a crime of violence, but both the Fourth and Eleventh Circuits have held that such an offense is not a crime of violence. *See, e.g., Garcia v. Gonzales*, 455 F.3d 465 (4th Cir. 2006); *United States v. Palomino Garcia*, 606 F.3d 1317, 1336 (11th Cir. 2010). For further discussion, see *supra* § 3.4B, Specific Types of Aggravated Felonies.

The second part of the crime of violence definition, which is in 18 U.S.C. § 16(b) and covers a felony offense that involves a substantial risk of use of force against person or property, could be struck down as void for vagueness. The U.S. Supreme Court will decide the issue by July 2018 in *Dimaya v. Lynch*. If that provision is found to be unconstitutionally vague, federal court and BIA cases finding that certain offenses are crimes of violence under § 16(b) will be overruled. For further discussion, see *supra* § 3.4B, Specific Types of Aggravated Felonies.

Also, the Board of Immigration Appeals has held that a crime committed by offensive touching does not require "violent" force and thus is not a crime of violence. *Matter of Velasquez*, 25 I&N Dec. 278, 282-83 (BIA 2010) (treating the rule in *Johnson v. United States,* 559 U.S. 133 (2010), which held that "physical force" in the context of the almost-identically defined Armed Career Criminal Act means violent force, as controlling authority in interpreting whether an offense is a "crime of violence" under § 16(a)). Under this case law, North Carolina common law robbery may not qualify as a crime of violence under § 16(a) because it can be committed using de minimis violence. The Fourth Circuit has made such a finding under a virtually identical crime of violence definition. *See United States of America v. Gardner,* 823 F.3d 793 (4th Cir. 2016) (holding that because the minimum conduct necessary to sustain a conviction for North Carolina common law robbery does not necessarily include the use, attempted use, or threatened use of "force capable of causing physical pain or injury to another person," as required under *Johnson v. United States*, it is not a violent felony under the force clause of the Armed Career Criminal Act).

Practice Note: A crime of violence aggravated felony does not cover any misdemeanor assault convictions because under North Carolina sentencing law the maximum sentence for a misdemeanor other than impaired driving is 150 days.

6.3   Cases Involving Drugs

Any violation of law relating to a federally controlled substance will subject your noncitizen client to removal based on controlled substance grounds (with the exceptions discussed below). Certain drug offenses may also be considered aggravated felonies and carry additional adverse immigration consequences.

In many cases, the consequences of a drug conviction are worse from a noncitizen client's perspective than other criminal-based grounds of removal (except for aggravated felonies). Specifically, drug offenses will likely render an LPR client deportable and ineligible for certain forms of relief. Drug offenses will likely render non-LPR clients inadmissible and permanently bar them from acquiring LPR status. If your client is charged with a drug offense, the following options may mitigate these immigration consequences or at least the additional consequences of an aggravated felony drug conviction.

"Controlled substance" is defined by federal law and refers to substances covered by the federal drug schedules. At the time of this revised edition of this manual, it appears that all of the drugs listed in the North Carolina state drug schedules are covered by the federal drug schedules, with one exception, chorionic gonadotropin in Schedule III, which steroid users employ to avoid testicular atrophy, a side-effect from steroids (which may be significant, as discussed in A., below).

A. Manufacture, Sale, or Delivery of a Schedule III Controlled Substance

A conviction of manufacture, sale, or delivery, or possession of a *federally* controlled substance with intent to manufacture, sell, or deliver constitutes a drug trafficking aggravated felony and triggers the severe consequences associated with aggravated felonies (with the exception for marijuana discussed in E., below).

It appears that the only North Carolina controlled substance that is not a controlled substance under federal law is chorionic gonadotropin in Schedule III, which steroid users employ to avoid testicular atrophy, a side-effect from steroids. A conviction for such an offense should not qualify as a drug trafficking aggravated felony. Also, if your client pleads guilty to a Schedule III drug and the record of conviction does not reveal the specific drug, there is a strong argument that your client is not deportable for a drug trafficking aggravated felony. *See Harbin v. Sessions*, 860 F.3d 58 (2d Cir. 2017); *see also supra* § 3.4D, Conviction of Any Controlled Substance Offense. However, if the charging document names a controlled substance other than chorionic gonadotropin, the client will be deportable.

B. Simple Possession of a Controlled Substance

A conviction of possession of a federally controlled substance with intent to manufacture, sell, or deliver constitutes a drug trafficking aggravated felony and triggers the severe consequences associated with aggravated felonies.

If a defendant has no prior drug convictions, a conviction of simple possession of a federally controlled substance (with the exception of possession of more than five grams of crack cocaine and any amount of flunitrazepam, commonly known as the date rape drug) is not considered a drug-trafficking aggravated felony. *See supra* § 3.4B, Specific Types of Aggravated Felonies.

While such a possession conviction will still have adverse immigration consequences as a conviction related to a controlled substance, it will not have the more severe consequences associated with an aggravated felony conviction. The difference in consequences may be particularly significant to an LPR client. *See supra* § 5.1B, Impact on LPR of an Aggravated Felony.

C. Possession of 30 Grams or Less of Marijuana

A conviction of possession of 30 grams or less of marijuana, although a drug offense, is exempt from many immigration consequences if the defendant has no prior drug convictions. An LPR will avoid deportability (but not inadmissibility after traveling abroad). A non-LPR will be inadmissible, but he or she will not necessarily be barred from adjusting to LPR status in the future because this ground of inadmissibility can be waived by the immigration court. Regarding this exception, the immigration court is *not* limited to the elements of the offense and to the record of conviction; instead, the 30 grams exception calls for a circumstance-specific inquiry into the noncitizen's actual conduct. Thus, to meet its burden of proof, the government can look to court documents outside of the record of conviction to establish that more than 30 grams of marijuana were in fact involved. *See supra* § 3.3A, Categorical Approach and Variations.

If your client is pleading guilty to a Class 1 misdemeanor possession of marijuana (which covers quantities of more and less than 30 grams), you should document in the record of conviction that the quantity involved is 30 grams or less, if applicable. It is important to do so in case your client is deemed inadmissible and needs to apply for a waiver of the conviction. *See supra* § 3.3C, Burden of Proof on Noncitizen in Applying for Relief and Demonstrating Admissibility.

The 30 grams exception also covers the possession of drug paraphernalia where the paraphernalia was merely an adjunct to the noncitizen's simple possession or use of 30 grams or less of marijuana. Thus, a client who pleads guilty to marijuana paraphernalia related to less than 30 grams of marijuana should not be deportable (assuming she has no other drug convictions). If a defendant is convicted under G.S. 90-113.22A (possession of marijuana drug paraphernalia) in a case involving 30 grams or less of marijuana, defenders should ensure that the record reflects the amount of marijuana. (There is also an argument that other drug paraphernalia convictions may not be controlled substance convictions, discussed in D., below.)

D. Drug Paraphernalia

A conviction for paraphernalia related to an unnamed Schedule III drug should not be a deportable offense for the same reason that conviction of manufacture, sale, or delivery, or possession with that intent, of an unnamed Schedule III drug possession is not a deportable offense, discussed in A., above. For that reason defenders may want to negotiate such language where appropriate. *See supra* § 3.4D, Conviction of Any Controlled Substance Offense.

Additionally, there is an argument that no North Carolina conviction for possession of drug paraphernalia under G.S. 90-113.22 is a deportable offense. Under *United States v. Mathis,* ___ U.S. ___, 136 S. Ct. 2243 (2016), the identity of the controlled substance is arguably not an element of the North Carolina paraphernalia statute (except when the paraphernalia involves marijuana under G.S. 90-113.22A). Because the state schedules are broader than the federal ones (because North Carolina's covers chorionic gonadotropin, discussed in A., above), a state paraphernalia conviction is arguably never a controlled substance offense. *See supra* § 3.4D, Conviction of Any Controlled Substance Offense. That analysis would appear to apply to the manufacture or delivery of paraphernalia under G.S. 90-113.23.

E. Delivery of Marijuana

The U.S. Supreme Court has held that a statute that punishes conduct that includes the transfer of small amounts of marijuana for no remuneration is not a "drug trafficking" aggravated felony. Under this law, there is a good argument that a conviction for delivery of marijuana or possession of marijuana with intent to manufacture, sell, or deliver under G.S. 90-95(a)(1) is not a drug trafficking aggravated felony. The reason is that a defendant can be convicted of delivery or possession with intent to manufacture, sell, or deliver without any evidence of remuneration and without the State establishing the amount of the marijuana. The Board of Immigration Appeals adopted this argument in an unpublished decision. *See infra* Appendix B, Relevant Immigration Decisions. For further discussion, *see supra* § 3.4B, Specific Types of Aggravated Felonies.

F. Possession by Trafficking

There is a strong argument, as evidenced by an unpublished administrative decision, that North Carolina possession by trafficking should not qualify as an aggravated felony. *See infra* Appendix B, Relevant Immigration Decisions. Federal law punishes possession as a misdemeanor, regardless of quantity. Thus, where the state offense, like North Carolina possession by trafficking, proscribes mere possession (even where the quantity is large), the offense would not constitute a felony under federal criminal law and thus should not qualify as drug trafficking aggravated felony. *See Lopez v. Gonzales*, 549 U.S. 47, 60 (2006).

G. Accessory after the Fact

The offense of accessory after the fact to a drug offense (under G.S. 14-7) is not considered a drug offense and thus does not trigger the immigration consequences associated with a drug offense. *See Matter of Batista-Hernandez*, 21 I&N Dec. 955 (BIA 1997). An accessory after the fact conviction is considered an "obstruction of justice offense," however. *See id.* Thus, if accompanied by a one-year term of imprisonment (active or suspended) or more, an accessory after the fact conviction will constitute an aggravated felony. An accessory after the fact offense is generally punishable two classes lower than the principal offense under North Carolina's structured sentencing scheme.

This rule does not apply to the offenses of attempt, conspiracy, and accessory before the fact to a drug offense, which probably *are* drug offenses.

H. Non-Drug Charges

Accompanying non-drug charges may have less serious or no adverse immigration consequences and may be an appropriate basis for a plea agreement. For assistance in determining whether accompanying charges may carry adverse immigration consequences, see Appendix A, Selected Immigration Consequences of North Carolina Offenses, or contact an immigration attorney.

6.4   Cases Involving Crimes Involving Moral Turpitude

There is no statutory definition for the immigration term "crime involving moral turpitude" (CMT). CMT determinations have generally been based on case law and are thus subject to the interpretation of an immigration judge.

A conviction for a CMT may render your client deportable or inadmissible. The following options may mitigate the immigration consequences that stem from a CMT offense.

A. Offense That Is Not a Crime Involving Moral Turpitude

Some of the offenses charged, their lesser included offenses, or related offenses may not be CMT offenses and may not have immigration consequences. For example, the offense of assault with a deadly weapon may be a CMT, but the offense of simple assault is not. Other examples of crimes not involving moral turpitude include misdemeanor breaking and entering, carrying a concealed weapon, trespass, unauthorized use of a vehicle, drunk and disruptive, and disorderly conduct.

An impaired driving conviction under North Carolina law may constitute a CMT offense depending on the presence of aggravating factors. An impaired driving offense with no aggravating factors is not a CMT. An impaired driving conviction with an aggravating factor of driving with a revoked license is possibly a CMT offense. An impaired driving conviction with other aggravating factors is probably not a CMT. For a further discussion, see *supra* § 3.4C, Conviction of a Crime Involving Moral Turpitude.

For assistance in determining whether an offense is considered a CMT, see Appendix A, Selected Immigration Consequences of North Carolina Offenses, or contact an immigration attorney.

B. One Misdemeanor CMT

If a noncitizen defendant has no prior CMT convictions and is convicted of only one non-DWI misdemeanor CMT, he or she avoids all adverse immigration consequences (including inadmissibility, deportability, and bar to naturalization), as long as the offense does not fall within another ground of removal (such as a domestic violence offense). *See supra* § 3.4C, Conviction of a Crime Involving Moral Turpitude (CMT deportation grounds for noncitizen admitted for less than five years); § 3.5B, Crime Involving Moral Turpitude; § 5.1E, Impact on LPR of a Criminal Disposition Barring Naturalization (petty offense exception for naturalization purposes). This approach is specific to North Carolina because under North Carolina's structured sentencing law the maximum sentence for a misdemeanor other than a DWI is 150 days. It is not clear whether a DWI, if a CMT, would satisfy the exceptions based on sentence length. *See supra* § 4.3D, Comparison to Potential Sentence.

C. One Felony CMT for Noncitizen Admitted to the U.S. for More Than Five Years

If your client was lawfully admitted to the U.S. more than five years ago and has no prior CMT convictions, he or she is not deportable if convicted of only one felony CMT or multiple CMTs arising out of the same transaction. *See supra* § 3.4C, Conviction of a Crime Involving Moral Turpitude (discussion of CMT deportation grounds for noncitizen admitted for more than five years). However, the felony CMT must not fall within another ground of removal, such as a crime of violence with a sentence of imprisonment of one year or more, which constitutes an aggravated felony conviction.

6.5 Cases Involving Firearms

Offenses in which the use of a firearm (as defined under federal law) is an essential element will render your lawfully-admitted client deportable based on the firearm ground of deportability. Certain firearm offenses may also be considered aggravated felonies and carry additional adverse immigration consequences.

There is no firearm ground of inadmissibility. If, however, the firearm-related offense constitutes a crime involving moral turpitude, which is one of the crimes of inadmissibility, the offense would render the person inadmissible. For example, an offense involving the sale of a firearm is probably a crime involving moral turpitude.

If your client is charged with a firearm offense, the following options may eliminate the immigration consequences or at least the added consequences of an aggravated felony firearm conviction.

A. Weapons Offenses That Do Not Specifically Involve a Firearm

If a noncitizen is convicted of an offense containing a general weapon element, and the elements of the offense do not establish that the weapon is a firearm, the offense does not qualify as a firearm offense for immigration purposes.

B. Firearm Offenses That Do Not Come within the Federal Definition of Firearm

The federal definition of firearm includes explosive-powered firearms and destructive devices (as defined in 18 U.S.C. § 921(a)(4)). The federal definition does not cover air-powered weapons like BB or pellet guns. There is also a federal exception for antique firearms. *See* 18 U.S.C. § 921(a)(3).

There is not a single definition of firearm under the North Carolina criminal law statutes. Some of the firearm definitions may be broader than the federal law, while others seem to match. For example, with regard to carrying a concealed pistol or gun under G.S. 14-269(a1), neither the statute nor the pattern jury instructions define "pistol" or "gun." Case law suggests that a gun or pistol must be a "firearm," *see, e.g., State v. Best*, 214 N.C. App. 39, 45 (2011), which other North Carolina statutes have defined as a weapon that "expels a projectile by action of an explosive." *See* G.S. 14-415.1(a) (possession of firearm by felon); *see also In re N.T.*, 214 N.C. App. 136 (2011) (so defining gun for assault by pointing gun). Because there is no stated exception under G.S. 14-269(a1) for an antique firearm as under federal law (and under G.S. 14-415.1), there is an argument that this state offense is broader than the federal firearm ground of removal. *See Moncrieffe v. Holder*, 569 U.S. 184, 133 S. Ct. 1678, 1693 (2013); *see supra* § 3.3A, Categorical Approach and Variations.

For assistance in determining whether a firearm-related offense may come within the firearm ground of removal, see Appendix A, Selected Immigration Consequences of North Carolina Offenses, or contact an immigration attorney.

C. Non-Aggravated Felony

A firearm offense can be considered an aggravated felony on two different grounds. First, certain offenses involving sale or delivery of firearms may be deemed a firearm trafficking offense. Second, specific firearm offenses, such as possession of a machine gun and possession of a firearm by a felon, are considered aggravated felonies because similar federal offenses have been designated as aggravated felonies in the immigration statute.

A non-aggravated felony firearm conviction will still have adverse immigration consequences as a firearm-related offense, but it will not have the more severe consequences associated with an aggravated felony conviction.

For assistance in determining whether a firearm-related offense may be considered an aggravated felony, *see* Appendix A, Selected Immigration Consequences of North Carolina Offenses, or contact an immigration attorney.

D. Accessory after the Fact

The offense of accessory after the fact to a firearm offense (under G.S. 14-7) is probably not a firearm offense and thus probably does not trigger the immigration consequences associated with a firearm offense. *Cf. Matter of Batista-Hernandez*, 21 I&N Dec. 955 (BIA 1997) (holding that federal accessory after the fact offense under 18 U.S.C. § 3 insufficiently relates to a controlled substance offense because it is not an inchoate crime, but a crime separate and apart from the underlying crime). An accessory after the fact conviction is considered an "obstruction of justice offense," however, and is considered an aggravated felony offense if accompanied by a one-year term of imprisonment (active or suspended) or more. An accessory after the fact offense is generally punishable two classes lower than the principal offense under structured sentencing.

This rule does not apply to the offenses of attempt, conspiracy, and accessory before the fact to a firearm offense, which probably *are* firearm offenses.

6.6   Cases Involving Domestic Violence

Domestic violence offenses may make your lawfully admitted client deportable based on the domestic violence ground of deportability. The elements of the offense must establish that the offense is a "crime of violence" as defined in 18 U.S.C. § 16. *See supra* § 3.4B, Specific Types of Aggravated Felonies. The offense also must be against a person in a domestic relationship with the defendant. *See supra* § 3.4F, Conviction of a Crime of Domestic Violence, Stalking, Child Abuse, Child Neglect, or Child Abandonment, or a Violation of a Protective Order. Actual or potential length of sentence of imprisonment is irrelevant for the domestic violence ground of deportability.

There is no domestic violence ground of inadmissibility. If, however, the domestic violence offense constitutes a crime involving moral turpitude, which is one of the grounds of inadmissibility, the offense would render the person inadmissible.

If your client is charged with a domestic violence offense, the following options may mitigate the adverse immigration consequences.

A.   Offense That Is Not a Crime of Violence

Some of the offenses charged, their lesser included offenses, or related offenses may not be considered a "crime of violence." For example, a conviction of domestic criminal trespass is generally not considered a "crime of violence" and therefore is not a crime of domestic violence for immigration purposes. However, the same sort of conduct may result in adverse immigration consequences if the defendant is convicted of violating a protective order based on that conduct. *See supra* § 3.4F, Conviction of a Crime of Domestic Violence, Stalking, Child Abuse, Child Neglect, or Child Abandonment, or a Violation of a Protective Order.

Under Fourth Circuit law, assault on a female does not satisfy the "crime of violence" definition. The Board of Immigration Appeals in an unpublished case has also found that assault on a female is not a crime of domestic violence for immigration purposes. *See infra* Appendix B, Relevant Immigration Decisions; *see also supra* § 3.4F, Conviction of a Crime of Domestic Violence, Stalking, Child Abuse, Child Neglect, or Child Abandonment, or a Violation of a Protective Order.

For assistance in determining whether an offense is considered a crime of domestic violence, see Appendix A, Selected Immigration Consequences of North Carolina Offenses, or contact an immigration attorney.

B.   Offense That Is Not Against a Person

A crime of domestic violence must be against a *person*, not property. Thus, a conviction of an offense involving the destruction of property should not be considered a crime of domestic violence (although if the court finds a violation of certain portions of a protective order in the process, the conduct would be a ground of deportability, as discussed *supra* in § 3.4F, Conviction of a Crime of Domestic Violence, Stalking, Child Abuse, Child Neglect, or Child Abandonment, or a Violation of a Protective Order.

C. Offense That Is Not Against a Protected Person

A crime of domestic violence must be against a protected person. Thus, a conviction of an offense involving a neighbor or a former spouse's current partner should not be considered a crime of domestic violence.

6.7. Cases Involving Child Abuse

Offenses of child abuse and neglect may make your lawfully admitted client deportable. The elements of the offense must establish that the offense is against a "minor" or a "child," defined as anyone under age 18. Therefore, convictions for offenses that do not contain as an element "minor" or "child" should not come within this ground of removal. *See supra* § 3.4F, Conviction of a Crime of Domestic Violence, Stalking, Child Abuse, Child Neglect, or Child Abandonment, or a Violation of a Protective Order.

Chapter 7
Procedures Related to Removal

7.1 Summary of Procedures Related to Removal   **7-1**

7.2 Identification of In-Custody Persons Subject to Removal   **7-2**

7.3 Immigration Detainer   **7-3**
A. Purpose of Detainer
B. Definition
C. Detention During and Beyond the 48-Hour Hold
D. Bond Considerations for a Client with an Immigration Detainer

7.4 What Happens after Your Client is Released into the   **7-5**
Custody of ICE
A. Mandatory Detention
B. Removal Proceedings
C. Order of Removal

This chapter reviews procedures and practices related to the identification of noncitizens subject to removal, immigration detainers, and removal proceedings. Defense counsel should have a general understanding of procedures related to removal to advise clients, particularly those in custody, about what they are likely to encounter. The chapter begins with a general description of the removal process. It then focuses on removal-related procedures with respect to clients who are in custody on state criminal charges.

7.1   Summary of Procedures Related to Removal

U.S. Immigration and Customs Enforcement (ICE) is responsible for the detention and removal of noncitizens. One of the agency's priorities is removing certain noncitizens in jails and prisons. Currently, five counties in North Carolina—Wake, Mecklenburg, Gaston, Cabarrus, and Henderson—have also prioritized the removal of noncitizens in the criminal justice system by entering into agreements with the federal government to enforce federal immigration law. ICE and cooperating law enforcement agents generally identify such individuals for removal by submitting their fingerprints through various federal databases.

If an individual may be removable based on a lack of status or a prior criminal conviction, ICE takes the position that it can issue a detainer pretrial to assume custody of the individual. *See infra* § 7.3A, Purpose of Detainer. If an individual with lawful status becomes removable upon conviction, ICE will likely assume custody of the individual upon completion of any jail or prison sentence. Even if ICE does not take any immediate action against someone who has become removable due to a conviction, such an individual may still be placed into removal proceedings upon a future contact with immigration officials. For example, noncitizens have been placed in removal proceedings when returning to the U.S. after traveling abroad, when applying for a green card, or when applying to naturalize. There is no statute of limitations on how long after a conviction ICE can initiate removal proceedings against a noncitizen.

Once an individual has been formally charged as removable, ICE has broad discretion to detain the person pending removal. Some noncitizens are eligible for immigration bond, but many noncitizens with criminal convictions are not eligible for release on bond and are therefore detained pending the completion of removal proceedings. *See infra* § 7.4A, Mandatory Detention.

There are different types of removal procedures. Many noncitizens receive a hearing in immigration court. At a removal hearing, the immigration court determines whether the noncitizen is removable under the charged grounds of inadmissibility or deportability and eligible for any relief from removal. *See infra* § 7.4B, Removal Proceedings.

7.2   Identification of In-Custody Persons Subject to Removal

The federal government currently uses existing information-sharing programs between local, state, and federal law enforcement agencies to determine the immigration status of arrested individuals. Local law enforcement officers send the fingerprints of all individuals arrested and taken into custody to the FBI, which are automatically forwarded to ICE to be checked against federal immigration databases to determine whether noncitizen arrestees may be removable.

In addition, North Carolina law requires administrators of jails and correctional facilities to determine the immigration status of any person charged with a felony or impaired driving offense by questioning such individuals and submitting a query to ICE. *See* G.S. 162-62; *see also* John Rubin, *2007 Legislation Affecting Criminal Law and Procedure,* Administration of Justice Bulletin 2008/01 at 33–34 (Jan. 2008).

Noncitizens interviewed or questioned by federal immigration agents or local law enforcement do not have to discuss their immigration status or manner of entry into the U.S. The Fifth Amendment privilege against self-incrimination covers immigration status if that information could lead to a criminal prosecution. Certain immigration violations are federal crimes, including entering the U.S. without inspection. *See supra* § 2.3D, Advise Your Clients of Their Rights.

Noncitizens have also been identified as subject to removal when serving a sentence of imprisonment in a Division of Adult Correction facility or serving a sentence of probation. Community Corrections, now a part of the Department of Public Safety, has issued a policy guidance regarding undocumented immigrants. *See* North Carolina Department of Public Safety, Division of Adult Correction and Juvenile Justice, Community Corrections Policy & Procedures, Chapter C Offender Supervision § .0624 Undocumented Immigrants and Deportation (Aug. 2016). It states that the division will assist ICE with the identification and possible removal of undocumented immigrants placed on probation. It directs probation officers to notify ICE of any information regarding a probationer's undocumented status.

7.3   Immigration Detainer

A. Purpose of Detainer

An ICE detainer—or "immigration hold"—is one of the key tools ICE uses to apprehend individuals who come in contact with local and state law enforcement agencies and to place them in removal proceedings.

B. Definition

An immigration detainer is a written request to a local law enforcement agency to detain a named individual for up to 48 hours after that person would otherwise be released (excluding Saturdays, Sundays, and holidays), in order to provide ICE an opportunity to assume custody of that individual for removal purposes. *See* 8 C.F.R. § 287.7. The 48-hour period begins to run when the named individual is no longer subject to detention by the local law enforcement agency—that is, after the individual has posted bond or completed a jail or prison sentence. Law enforcement agencies include jails and prisons that have custody of the named individual.

The detainer is neither a warrant nor an order by a judge. It is a request and is not mandatory, *see, e.g., Galarza v. Szalczyk*, 745 F.3d 634 (3rd Cir. 2014), though most law enforcement agencies in North Carolina honor ICE detainers. Hundreds of jurisdictions across the country—including many in Washington, Illinois, California, Oregon, and Vermont—no longer comply with ICE detainer requests, or they comply with them in limited circumstances only. Further, several federal courts have held that holding an individual on an ICE detainer is an illegal arrest in violation of the Fourth Amendment where it is not based on a judicial determination of probable cause. *See, e.g., Morales v. Chadbourne*, 793 F.3d 208, 217 (1st Cir. 2015). Thus, a court could find that where a local jail holds an individual on a detainer that is not based on probable cause, when the individual has posted bail or is otherwise entitled to release, the jail may be liable for money damages based on an unconstitutional detention. *See, e.g., Miranda-Olivares v. Clackamas County*, 2014 WL 1414305, No. 3:12-cv-02317-ST (D. Or. Apr. 11, 2014).

In addition, the highest court in Massachusetts has ruled that Massachusetts courts and law enforcement officials—including sheriffs and police officers—are not authorized to hold people based solely on immigration detainers. *Lunn v. Commonwealth*, 78 N.E.3d 1143 (Mass. 2017). Specifically, the Court found that detention based on an immigration detainer constitutes an arrest, which must be authorized under state law. *Id*. at 1153–54. It further found that there was no authority under state law—either statutory or common law—for an arrest for civil immigration purposes. *Id*. at 1154–56.

ICE no longer uses Form I-247 (Immigration Detainer-Notice of Action), which has been deemed problematic by courts for the reasons mentioned above. It uses the following new form:

- *Form 1-247A, Notice of Action*: Form 1-247A requests that the law enforcement agency (LEA) notify ICE as early as practicable (at least 48 hours, if possible) of the pending release from custody of the named individual and maintain custody of the named individual for a period not to exceed 48 hours *beyond* the time when he or she would have otherwise been released from custody. On this form, ICE must identify the basis for ICE's determination of probable cause. (The form does *not* represent a judge's determination of probable cause.) The LEA must serve a copy of the request on the individual for it to take effect.

Effective April 2, 2017, ICE issued a new policy directing that all ICE detainers be accompanied by an immigration warrant signed by an authorized ICE officer. *See* Immigration and Customs Enforcement Policy Number 10074.2, Issuance of Immigration Detainers by ICE Immigration Officers (Mar. 24, 2017). ICE warrants direct authorized federal immigration officers to arrest an individual for civil violations of immigration law, not criminal charges. *See* 8 C.F.R. § 287.5. Because these warrants are not reviewed by a judge or any neutral party, they do not appear to satisfy the probable cause requirement. *See e.g.*, *El Badrawi v. Dep't of Homeland Security*, 579 F. Supp. 2d. 249, 275 (D. Conn. 2008) (finding that an arrest based on an immigration warrant is considered "warrantless" for federal constitutional law purposes) Immigration warrants also do not provide authority for local law enforcement to arrest or detain someone for a crime.

C. Detention During and Beyond the 48-Hour Hold

If a detainer is lodged pretrial against an individual and he or she posts bail, the cases discussed in B., above, indicate that the local jail or correctional facility may not have the authority to detain an individual during the 48-hour period without a judicial finding of probable cause. The law is certainly clear that if the jail holds the person for the 48-hour period and ICE fails to assume custody of the individual during that period, the individual should be immediately released. Even assuming the initial 48-hour detention is permissible, the local jail or correctional facility has no authority to detain an individual once the detainer has expired. Any additional detention is unlawful and in violation of state pretrial release laws and could subject the facility to suit for false imprisonment. Similarly, the state lacks authority to hold someone who has served his or her maximum sentence for the offense. In practice, however, jails and correctional facilities may be reluctant to release the detained individual.

When clients have been detained pursuant to an ICE hold without a judicial finding of probable cause or beyond the 48-hour hold, some defense attorneys have contacted counsel for the sheriff or the jail and pressed them to release their clients. If the client is not released, a writ of habeas corpus can be filed to secure release under G.S. 17-1 et seq. The filing of a writ of habeas corpus could prompt ICE to pick up the detained individual, making the action moot.

D. Bond Considerations for a Client with an Immigration Detainer

An immigration detainer is often lodged against a client before he or she has an opportunity to post bond. In those circumstances, if the client posts bond, the jail may transfer immediate custody of him or her to ICE. If ICE takes your client into custody and detains him or her, he or she will likely be sent to an out-of-state immigration detention facility for the institution of removal proceedings. To date, immigration authorities generally have not transported clients so that they can attend state court proceedings, but it is unclear whether prosecutors have made that request. As a result, the client may be called and failed in the state criminal case, be the subject of an order for arrest, and have the bond forfeited (though defense counsel should argue against the issuance of a failure to appear). *See* 1 NORTH CAROLINA DEFENDER MANUAL § 1.9H, Post-Release Issues Affecting Noncitizen Clients (2d ed. 2013). The time spent in a detention center will not count toward jail credit if your client is later convicted and sentenced in the criminal case.

Another possibility is that ICE will deport your client before resolution of the criminal case.

7.4   What Happens after Your Client is Released into the Custody of ICE

Once your client has been picked up by ICE officers, he or she will likely be taken to an immigration detention facility in South Carolina or Georgia.

A. Mandatory Detention

If your client is eligible for and able to post an immigration bond, he or she will be released during the removal proceedings. Many clients with criminal convictions, however, are not eligible for release on immigration bond and therefore will be detained pending completion of removal proceedings. The U.S. Supreme Court is considering the constitutionality of mandatory detention. *Jennings v. Rodriguez*, 136 S. Ct. 2489 (2016), *granting cert.,* 804 F.3d 1060 (9th Cir. 2015).

Mandatory detention provisions apply to the following people who are released from physical custody after October 9, 1998 (as set forth in INA § 236(c)(1), 8 U.S.C. § 1226(c)(1)). They apply to people who are:

- inadmissible by reason of having committed any offense covered in the criminal grounds of inadmissibility
- deportable for having committed two or more crimes involving moral turpitude (CMT)
- deportable for an aggravated felony
- deportable for a drug offense
- deportable for a firearm offense
- deportable for security-related crimes
- deportable for having committed a CMT for which the actual sentence of imprisonment is one year or more; and
- involved in terrorist activity.

The mandatory detention provisions do not apply to people who are:

- deportable for having committed one CMT for which the actual sentence of imprisonment is less than one year; and
- deportable for a domestic violence-related offense.

B. Removal Proceedings

There are several procedures for removing noncitizens. Your clients are likely to encounter one of the proceedings described below.

Removal Proceedings in Immigration Court. Many of your clients will have a hearing in immigration court. Removal proceedings for a detained client are to take place expeditiously. At this time, most removal proceedings for detained clients take place in Georgia, where they are detained, and for non-detained clients in the immigration court in Charlotte.

Removal proceedings in immigration court commence when the government files a charging document known as a Notice to Appear (NTA) with the immigration court. The NTA specifies the formal charges, the statutory provisions allegedly violated, and the individual's acts or conduct that allegedly violate the law. *See* INA § 239(a), 8 U.S.C. § 1229(a). A noncitizen has a right to an attorney at his or her own expense in the removal proceedings. A noncitizen does not have a right to a court-appointed attorney because such proceedings are considered civil in nature and not criminal.

The immigration court first determines whether a noncitizen is removable under the grounds of inadmissibility or deportability alleged in the NTA. If the noncitizen is found removable, the court can consider and grant an application for some form of relief from removal, if he or she qualifies, allowing the noncitizen to remain in the U.S. Generally, after the completion of the hearing there will be one of three outcomes: (1) the immigration judge orders the noncitizen removed from the U.S.; (2) the immigration judge grants some form of relief from removal; or (3) the immigration judge terminates the proceedings because removability has not been established by the government. In some cases, the immigration judge may administratively close the case, which means the case is removed from the docket with the possibility of it being re-calendared later by the government. Either party can appeal the decision of the immigration judge to the Board of Immigration Appeals (BIA).

Immigration authorities may remove a person from the U.S. without a formal removal hearing. Those circumstances are discussed below.

Administrative Removal. Administrative removal applies to noncitizens who are not lawful permanent residents of the U.S. and are charged with having been convicted of an aggravated felony. INA § 238(b), 8 U.S.C. § 1228(b). This summary removal process is essentially a paper process without a formal hearing and provides the noncitizen with ten days to rebut the government's charge. There is no opportunity to apply for discretionary relief from removal, though individuals may be able to apply for withholding of removal if they express a credible fear of persecution. A designated immigration officer decides whether the noncitizen's conviction qualifies as an aggravated felony.

Reinstatement. Reinstatement generally applies to noncitizens who return to the U. S. without authorization after having removed under a prior removal order. The government simply "reinstates" the prior order of removal. Reinstatements generally account for more deportations than any other procedure.

Expedited Removal. Expedited removal currently applies to people who arrive at a port-of-entry or within 100 miles of the border with fraudulent or insufficient documents. Immigration officers patrolling the border are authorized to issue the removal orders in this context. There is limited process and opportunities for appeal, though individuals may be able to apply for asylum if they express a credible fear of persecution.

Stipulation of Removal. A stipulated removal order involves a noncitizen who agrees to accept a removal order and waives his or her right to an immigration court hearing. The immigration court enters the order based on a review of the written stipulation and charging document, often in the absence of the parties. In practice, some clients sign such a stipulation when initially interviewed by an immigration officer, agreeing to removal and waiving their right to a hearing before an immigration judge (sometimes unknowingly). These individuals are processed for immediate removal. You should advise your clients not to waive their rights to a hearing until all of their options are fully evaluated.

C. Order of Removal

If your client is ordered removed, ICE is generally required to physically remove your client from the U.S. within a period of 90 days from the date of a final order of removal. *See* INA § 241(a)(1)(A), 8 U.S.C. § 1231(a)(1)(A). ICE is required to detain your client, without bond or other pre-removal condition of release, during the 90-day period. *See* INA § 241(a)(2), 8 U.S.C. § 1231(a)(2). Not all noncitizens, however, are removed during the 90-day period, particularly those who have meritorious arguments and continue to litigate their cases in the Courts of Appeal.

Chapter 8
State Post-Conviction Relief

8.1 Authority for State Post-Conviction Relief   8-1

8.2 Challenges under *Padilla v. Kentucky*   8-2
  A. Standard of Proof
  B. Retroactivity
  C. Deficient Advice
  D. Material Misrepresentation
  E. Duty to Negotiate

8.3 Judge's Failure to Provide Immigration Advisement   8-5

8.4 Other Errors   8-6

8.5 Immigration Effect of Motion for Appropriate Relief   8-7

Post-conviction relief generally seeks to correct a legal error in the underlying criminal proceedings. Post-conviction relief, if warranted, may also provide an avenue to mitigate the adverse immigration consequences that flow from the criminal disposition. This chapter is intended to provide guidance, but it is not a comprehensive treatment of post-conviction challenges.

8.1 Authority for State Post-Conviction Relief

In North Carolina, the primary vehicle to collaterally challenge a conviction is a motion for appropriate relief (MAR), authorized by G.S. 15A-1411 through G.S. 15A-1422. An MAR is a post-trial motion, usually made at the trial level, to correct errors occurring before, during, or after a criminal trial. *See State v. Handy*, 326 N.C. 532 (1990). If filed within ten days of entry of judgment, an MAR can be used to address "any error committed during or prior to the trial." *See* G.S. 15A-1414(a). After ten days of entry of judgment, an MAR can be used to address specified errors, such as a violation of a defendant's constitutional rights. For possible grounds for relief, see G.S. 15A-1415(b).

8.2   Challenges under *Padilla v. Kentucky*

In *Padilla v. Kentucky*, 559 U.S. 356 (2010), the U.S. Supreme Court established that criminal defense attorneys have an obligation, as part of the Sixth Amendment guarantee of effective assistance of counsel, to advise noncitizen clients about the immigration consequences of the criminal charges against them. Chapter 1 of this manual focuses on the impact of the *Padilla* decision from the perspective of trial counsel—that is, the steps trial counsel should take to represent noncitizen clients effectively. The discussion below addresses *Padilla* and other decisions from the perspective of how they may support a post-conviction challenge to trial counsel's performance.

A. Standard of Proof

In North Carolina, the standard of proof for an ineffective assistance of counsel claim is governed by the two-prong test set out by the United States Supreme Court in *Strickland v. Washington*, 466 U.S. 688 (1984). *See State v. Braswell*, 312 N.C. 553 (1985) (adopting the *Strickland* test as the standard for evaluating ineffective assistance of counsel claims under the North Carolina constitution). To establish ineffective assistance of counsel, a defendant must show that counsel's representation fell below an objective standard of reasonableness under prevailing professional norms and that counsel's deficient performance was prejudicial.

The same two-pronged test applies to an ineffectiveness claim based on *Padilla*. *See State v. Nkiam*, ___ N.C. App. ___, 778 S.E.2d 863, 866 (2015).

B. Retroactivity

The North Carolina Court of Appeals has held that *Padilla* does not apply retroactively and does not afford relief to a person whose conviction was final before *Padilla* was decided on March 31, 2010. *State v. Alshaif*, 219 N.C. App. 162 (2012); *accord Chaidez v. United States*, 568 U.S. 342 (2013) (holding that *Padilla* does not apply retroactively to federal convictions).

Ineffective assistance of counsel claims based on other grounds may still be available to noncitizens whose convictions became final before March 31, 2010. These possibilities are discussed in section D., Material Misrepresentation, and section E., Duty to Negotiate below.

C. Deficient Advice

Counsel's Performance. Counsel has a bifurcated duty to advise under *Padilla*. The nature of the advice required varies according to the clarity of the immigration consequences. *Padilla*, 559 U.S. 356, 368–69. Where the immigration consequences are clear, defense counsel must provide specific and correct advice. *Id.* at 369; *Nkiam*, 778 S.E.2d 863, 868–69. For example, counsel's performance would be deficient if he advises his permanent resident client that a plea to cocaine sale *might* result in removal because such a conviction constitutes a drug trafficking aggravated felony resulting in virtually certain removal. Where the immigration consequences are unclear or uncertain, defense counsel at a minimum must still advise clients about immigration consequences, but the advice need only be that the criminal charges may carry adverse immigration consequences. *Padilla*, 559 U.S. 356, 369. For example, defense counsel's performance may be deficient where he or she fails to provide any immigration advice or simply refers the client to an immigration lawyer. *Id.* at 369 n.10.

Prejudice. In cases in which the defendant pled guilty, he must show that there is a reasonable probability that, but for counsel's errors, he or she would not have pled guilty but instead would have insisted on going to trial. *Hill v. Lockhart*, 474 U.S. 52, 59 (1985); *see also Lee v. United States*, ___ U.S. ___, 137 S. Ct. 1958, 1965 (2017) (applying *Hill* test to *Padilla* claim).

In applying this standard to a *Padilla* claim, the North Carolina Court of Appeals held that a defendant adequately demonstrates prejudice "by showing that rejection of the plea offer would have been a rational choice, even if not the best choice, when taking into account the importance the defendant places upon preserving his right to remain in this country." *Nkiam*, 778 S.E.2d 863, 874. The Court of Appeals found prejudice even though the defendant was likely to be convicted at trial. *Id.*

The U.S. Supreme Court has similarly held that it is not "irrational" for a noncitizen with substantial ties to the United States to take his chances at trial and risk additional prison time in exchange for whatever small chance there might be of an acquittal that would let him remain in the United States. *Lee v. United States*, 137 S. Ct. 1958, 1968–69 (finding that the noncitizen established that he was prejudiced by his attorney's misadvice regarding the immigration consequences). To demonstrate prejudice under *Lee*, a practitioner should submit contemporaneous evidence of a probability that the client would not have pled guilty if properly advised of the immigration consequences, including evidence of expressed concern regarding the immigration consequences and evidence of any strong connections to the United States. *Id.* at 1967–68.

Can prejudice be shown alternatively by the possibility that a different, immigration safe plea was available? In *Nkiam,* the Court of Appeals noted that had the immigration consequences of the plea been factored into the plea bargaining process, "trial counsel may have obtained an alternative plea that would not have the consequence of mandatory deportation." *Nkiam*, 778 S.E.2d 863, 875. This observation may support an argument that prejudice can be established or at least bolstered by showing that an alternative, immigration-safe plea was available. *See, e.g., United States v. Swaby*, 855 F.3d 233, 241 (4th Cir. 2017) (holding that a defendant establishes prejudice if there is a reasonable probability that the defendant could have negotiated a plea agreement that did not affect his immigration status) In *Lee*, the Supreme Court expressly reserved the question. *Lee*, 137 S. Ct. 1958, 1966 n.2.

Can prejudice caused by counsel's error be cured by an immigration warning or advisement by the trial court? In *Nkiam*, the Court of Appeals specifically addressed this question. It found that where defense counsel is required to provide specific advice, a boilerplate court warning merely advising of the risk of deportation is inadequate and does not cure any possible prejudice. *Nkiam*, 778 S.E.2d 863, 872.

D. Material Misrepresentation

Although *Padilla* does not apply retroactively (discussed in B., Retroactivity, above), noncitizen clients whose convictions were final before the issuance of *Padilla* may have an alternative Sixth Amendment challenge based on erroneous immigration advice. The U.S. Supreme Court and North Court of Appeals decisions holding that *Padilla* is not retroactive did not foreclose this alternative basis for relief.

In *Chaidez v. United States*, 568 U.S. 342 (2013)*,* the U.S. Supreme Court explicitly distinguished *erroneous advice* claims from the *failure to advise* claim at issue in that case (in other words, wrong advice vs. no advice). The Court described a "separate rule for material misrepresentations," which is not particular to the type of misrepresentation. *Id.* at 356 (recognizing that "a lawyer may not affirmatively misrepresent[s] his expertise or otherwise actively mislead[s] his client on any important matter, however related to a criminal prosecution.") In *State v. Alshaif*, 219 N.C. App. 162 (2012), the court did not specifically address the issue.

North Carolina courts have recognized in other contexts that a conviction may be set aside where defense counsel erroneously advises the defendant about a collateral consequence and the defendant relies on that advice in pleading guilty. *See State v. Goforth*, 130 N.C. App. 603 (1998) (finding that lawyer who misadvised defendant about collateral consequences of plea was deficient in his performance; in this case, attorney misadvised defendant about appealability of sentence). Before *Padilla*, some noncitizens successfully argued under *Goforth* that counsel was ineffective when he or she provided incorrect advice about the immigration consequences of the plea. Because North Carolina courts have recognized erroneous advice claims with respect to collateral consequences at least since 1998, a defendant may be able to prevail on such a claim even for a conviction that became final before *Padilla* was decided.

For example, a noncitizen may be able to argue ineffective assistance based on erroneous advice for a pre-2010 conviction where the defense attorney advised that a deferred prosecution involving an admission of guilt is not a conviction for immigration purposes and does not result in adverse immigration consequences. For immigration law purposes an admission of guilt coupled with court imposed conditions or punishment constitutes a conviction. *See supra* § 4.1, Conviction for Immigration Purposes

---

Practice Note: In framing material misrepresentation claims for noncitizen clients with pre-*Padilla* convictions, the focus should be on "affirmative misrepresentations," "erroneous advice," and "misleading the client," not on *Padilla*.

E. Duty to Negotiate

Recent U.S. Supreme Court cases and practice standards support a Sixth Amendment duty to negotiate effectively to avoid or minimize immigration consequences. *See supra* § 1.2D, Impact on Duty to Negotiate (discussing *Missouri v. Frye*, 566 U.S. 134 (2012), and *Lafler v. Cooper*, 566 U.S. 156 (2012)). Thus, if investigation of the immigration consequences reveals that the proposed plea will result in adverse immigration consequences, defense counsel should assist the client in seeking to obtain an alternative disposition that would avoid or mitigate those consequences, particularly where the client has conveyed that the immigration consequences are a priority.

Where trial counsel failed to negotiate effectively for potentially available safe pleas, you may consider investigating a claim for deficient plea bargaining under *Missouri v. Frye* and *Lafler v. Cooper. See also State v. Redman*, 224 N.C. App. 363, 369 (2012) ("During plea negotiations defendants are entitled to the effective assistance of competent counsel.") (quoting *Lafler*, 566 U.S. 156, 162). For example, counsel's performance may be deficient if his or her LPR client is charged with discharging a firearm in violation of a local ordinance and counsel does not explore the possibility of a plea to disorderly conduct or other immigration-safe offense. Although only a Class 3 misdemeanor under North Carolina law, a plea to an ordinance violation involving discharge of a firearm (as that term is defined under federal law) will make an LPR client deportable (even if he or she has a gun permit), but a plea to disorderly conduct or even simple assault is a safe plea.

In making a claim that defense counsel did not secure a reasonably negotiable alternative plea or sentence to limit the adverse immigration consequences, practitioners should document the following: alternative safe pleas that would have been available for the charged offense in the respective jurisdiction; that local defense counsel seek such alternative safe pleas; and existing resources available to assist trial counsel to develop safe immigration pleas.

Such a claim may be available to noncitizens whose convictions predate *Padilla. Lafler* and *Frye* are not "new rules" and therefore should apply retroactively to pre-*Padilla* convictions. *See In re Graham*, 714 F.3d 1181, 1182 (10th Cir. 2013); *Gallagher v. United States,* 711 F.3d 315, 315–16 (2d Cir. 2013); *Williams v. United States*, 705 F.3d 293, 294 (8th Cir. 2013); *Buenrostro v. United States,* 697 F.3d 1137, 1140 (9th Cir. 2012); *In re King,* 697 F.3d 1189, 1189 (5th Cir. 2012); *Hare v. United States,* 688 F.3d 878, 879, 881 (7th Cir. 2012); *In re Perez,* 682 F.3d 930, 932–34 (11th Cir. 2012).

8.3   Judge's Failure to Provide Immigration Advisement

G.S. 15A-1022(a)(7) requires judges to provide a general advisement to a defendant before accepting a guilty plea, warning the defendant that if he or she is a noncitizen the conviction may result in adverse immigration consequences. A failure to provide the general advisement is a violation of the statute.

There is an argument that a trial court's failure to provide the advisement also affects the voluntariness of the plea and thus constitutes a violation of constitutional law as well. In *Padilla*, the Supreme Court recognized that immigration consequences of a criminal conviction are "uniquely difficult to classify as either a direct or a collateral consequence" of a guilty plea. *Padilla*, 559 U.S. 356, 366. The court further recognized that because deportation has such a "close connection to the criminal process" and is so significant for noncitizen defendants, the Sixth Amendment requires defense counsel to advise defendants about the immigration consequences of a conviction. *Id*. at 366–74. A similar argument can be made about a judicial advisement: that because deportation constitutes such a substantial and unique consequence of a plea, fundamental fairness requires the trial court to advise the defendant of that possibility. *See, e.g., People v. Peque*, 3 N.E.3d 617, 621 (N.Y. 2013) ("We therefore hold that due process compels a trial court to apprise a defendant that, if the defendant is not an American citizen, he or she may be deported as a consequence of a guilty plea to a felony."). Under this rationale, a court's failure to give a noncitizen defendant at least a general advisement about immigration consequences may violate the constitutional requirement that the plea be knowing and voluntary.

Such an error may be present in some cases. From a practical standpoint, however, it may be easier to demonstrate a Sixth Amendment violation under *Padilla* than establish a Fifth Amendment violation that the plea was not knowing and voluntary.

8.4   Other Errors

Other procedural defects or substantive violations that may form a basis for an MAR for noncitizen defendants include:

- The defendant's failure to understand the nature of the proceedings.
- The failure of the court to explain sufficiently the nature and right to a jury trial. (This requirement is particularly important for noncitizens who may have no previous experience with the U.S. legal system and may be unfamiliar with jury trials and other aspects of criminal justice and procedure in the U.S.).
- Violations in the use or conduct of interpreters.
- Other due process violations.

There should not be a retroactivity problem for these types of errors; therefore, they may provide relief for clients who are unable to seek relief under *Padilla* because of the date of their convictions. For a list of other established claims for post-conviction relief, see *generally* NORTON TOOBY & J.J. ROLLIN, POST-CONVICTION RELIEF FOR IMMIGRANTS (2004).

8.5   Immigration Effect of Motion for Appropriate Relief

A conviction vacated on the basis of a procedural or legal defect will eliminate the conviction for immigration purposes. *See Matter of Rodriguez-Ruiz*, 22 I&N Dec.1378 (BIA 2000). The immigration court may look to see if the vacating court had subject matter jurisdiction to vacate the judgment, but it may not look beyond the order to determine if such relief was proper under North Carolina law. *Id.* A conviction is not eliminated for immigration purposes, however, if it was vacated for reasons "solely related to rehabilitation or immigration hardships. . . ." *Matter of Pickering*, 23 I&N Dec. 621 (BIA 2003)), *rev'd on other grounds*, 465 F.3d 263 (6th Cir. 2006); *cf. Yanez-Popp v. I.N.S.*, 998 F.2d 231, 235 (4th Cir.1993) ("[U]nless a conviction is vacated on its merits, a revoked state conviction is still a 'conviction' for federal immigration purposes.").

Thus, a conviction vacated through an MAR based on the grounds of ineffective assistance, involuntariness of a guilty plea, or other constitutional or statutory violations will be accorded full faith and credit by immigration authorities and eliminate the conviction for immigration purposes. However, even though an MAR is used to correct legal error, an order of relief that refers primarily to the petitioner's equities or immigration hardships might not be honored and may not eliminate the conviction for immigration purposes. The record of the proceedings—the motion papers, hearing, and order—should therefore reflect the legal errors justifying relief and should refer to immigration issues only as necessary to explain those errors (for example, prior counsel was ineffective for misadvising the petitioner about the possibility of removal and, but for counsel's deficient performance, the petitioner would not have pled guilty). If the MAR is by consent of the prosecutor (*see* G.S. 15A-1420(e) ("[n]othing in this section shall prevent the parties to the action from entering into an agreement for appropriate relief"), the record and judge's order granting the MAR should still reflect the legal errors justifying relief.

Appendix A
Selected Immigration Consequences of North Carolina Offenses

The chart analyzes the potential likelihood of removal based on conviction of selected North Carolina offenses. Additional immigration consequences not listed here may arise from these offenses, such as the denial of naturalization or denial of discretionary relief. Because the immigration consequences of crime are a complex and constantly changing area of law, practitioners should use this chart as a starting point; it is not a substitute for individualized legal research. Additionally, the actual impact of an offense will vary depending on the client's immigration status and criminal history.

The chart is organized by subject area of offense—e.g., homicides, assaults, etc. Within each subject area, the chart is organized numerically by statute. Following each offense is the applicable state statute and then whether the offense constitutes an aggravated felony (AF) or crime involving moral turpitude (CMT). If the offense may trigger other grounds of removal, that possibility is noted in the next column, Other Grounds of Removal. The last column includes additional information relevant to the offense, including information about related offenses that would not constitute grounds for removal. The chart is intended for criminal defense attorneys and thus takes a conservative approach to assessing the immigration consequences of selected offenses.

Key Immigration Concepts

Aggravated Felony Conviction. A noncitizen should avoid an aggravated felony (AF) conviction if at all possible. A noncitizen with an AF conviction, even a long time lawful permanent resident, will be held in mandatory detention, has virtually no relief or defense to deportation, and will be barred from returning to the U.S. for life. Crimes of violence, theft offenses, and certain other categories of offenses require a conviction *and* a sentence of imprisonment (active or suspended) of one year or more to constitute an AF. If a defendant receives a PJC or fine only in this category of offenses, the person would not have a sentence of one year or more and that possibility is noted in the chart. Other categories of offenses, such as "drug trafficking," murder, rape, and sexual abuse of a minor require only a conviction to constitute an AF, regardless of sentence length. For a detailed definition and discussion of AFs, see *supra* § 3.4A, Aggravated Felonies Generally and §3.4B, Specific Types of Aggravated Felonies.

Crime Involving Moral Turpitude (CMT). This category has no statutory definition and covers a broad category of criminal offenses, including offenses containing an element to steal or defraud, sex offenses, and certain assault offenses. CMT offenses are both a ground of deportability and inadmissibility, but there are technical rules governing each ground. Thus, an offense may by a CMT but still not be a removable offense if the offense is a misdemeanor and the client has no prior CMT convictions. For a detailed discussion of CMTs, see *supra* § 3.4C, Conviction of a Crime Involving Moral Turpitude.

Conviction. The definition of a "conviction" for immigration purposes is determined by federal law. State law does not determine whether a state disposition will be considered a conviction for immigration law purposes. For a discussion of state court dispositions that constitute a conviction for immigration law purposes, see Chapter 4, Conviction and Sentence for Immigration Purposes.

Sentence. Under federal immigration law, a "sentence" includes any period of incarceration ordered by the court, whether active or suspended. Therefore, any references in the chart to "a one-year sentence or longer" means an active or suspended sentence of imprisonment of one year or more. Also, a sentence is considered to be a sentence for the maximum term imposed even if the defendant was released before serving the maximum term. Thus, a defendant who is sentenced to 3 months minimum and 13 months maximum in a felony case will be treated as having been sentenced to 13 months in jail for immigration purposes, even if he or she ultimately serves only 3 months in jail and nine months on post-release supervision. The term of probation does not count towards the sentence. For a discussion of the impact of sentence length, see *supra* § 4.3, Sentence to a Term of Imprisonment.

Offense	Statute	Aggravated Felony (AF)?	Crime Involving Moral Turpitude (CMT)?	Other Grounds of Removal?	Comments and Related Offenses
Homicide Offenses					
Murder – 1st & 2d degree	14-17 Class A or B1 felony	Yes	Yes		
Manslaughter (voluntary)	14-18 Class D felony	Probably, as a crime of violence under 8 U.S.C. § 1101(a)(43)(F)	Yes		Involuntary manslaughter may not be considered an AF
Manslaughter (involuntary)	14-18 Class F felony	Possibly, as a crime of violence under 8 U.S.C. § 1101(a)(43)(F)[1]	Possibly[2]		Felony death by vehicle is not a removable offense There is an argument that involuntary manslaughter through culpable negligence should not qualify as an aggravated felony or CMT
Felony death by vehicle	20-141.4(a1) Class D felony	No		No	
Misdemeanor death by vehicle	20-141.4(a2) Misdemeanor	No		No	

---

1. The elements of involuntary manslaughter are: (1) unintentional killing; (2) proximately caused by either (a) an unlawful act not amounting to a felony and not ordinarily dangerous to human life, or (b) culpable negligence. *State v. Hudson*, 345 N.C. 729 (1997). If 2(a) and 2(b) are alternative elements there is a strong argument that a killing by culpable negligence should not qualify as a crime of violence (COV). *See Leocal v. Ashcroft*, 543 U.S. 1 (2004) (holding that an offense requiring proof of negligent conduct, even when involving death, is not purposeful enough to qualify as an aggravated felony crime of violence); *United States v. Vinson*, 805 F.3d 120, 126 (4th Cir. 2015) (culpable negligence as defined in North Carolina is a lesser standard of culpability than recklessness, which requires at least "a conscious disregard of risk"). If the two are means, then no conviction of involuntary manslaughter should qualify as a COV. *See* § 3.3A, Categorical Approach and Variations.

2. There is an argument that a conviction based on culpable negligence does not rise to a CMT. *See* § 3.4C, Conviction of a Crime Involving Moral Turpitude.

Offense	Statute	Aggravated Felony (AF)?	Crime Involving Moral Turpitude (CMT)?	Other Grounds of Removal?	Comments and Related Offenses
Rape and Other Sex Offenses (see also infra Prostitution)					
Rape – 1st degree	14-27.21 Class B1 felony	Yes, as a rape offense under 8 U.S.C. § 1101(a)(43)(A)	Yes		Crime against nature may not qualify as an AF (where there is no finding of lack of consent). See infra n.3.
Rape – 2d degree	14-27.22 Class C felony	(a)(1) as a rape offense and (a)(2) probably as a rape offense under 8 U.S.C. § 1101(a)(43)(A)	Yes		Crime against nature may not qualify as an AF (where there is no finding of lack of consent). See infra n.3.
Sexual offense - 1st & 2d degree	14-27.26, 14-27.27 Class B1, C felony	Probably, as a crime of violence under 8 U.S.C. § 1101(a)(43)(F)	Yes		Crime against nature may not qualify as an AF (where there is no finding of lack of consent). See infra n.3.
Sexual battery	14-27.33 Misdemeanor	Should not be sexual abuse of a minor under 8 U.S.C. § 1101(a)(43)(A)	Yes	May fall within the domestic violence ground of deportability if the evidence establishes that the victim is a protected family member	Sexual battery should not constitute sexual abuse of a minor under the categorical approach because the minor age of the complainant is not an element of the offense
Statutory rape/sex offense of a person 15 years old or younger/1st degree statutory rape	14-27.25, 14-27.30, 14-27.24 Class B1 or C felony	Yes, as sexual abuse of a minor under 8 U.S.C. § 1101(a)(43)(A)	Yes	Yes, under child abuse ground of deportability	Sexual battery should not qualify as an AF
Statutory rape of a child by an adult	14-27.23 Class B1 felony	Yes, as sexual abuse of a minor under 8 U.S.C. § 1101(a)(43)(A)	Yes	Yes, under child abuse ground of deportability	Sexual battery should not qualify as an AF

App. A: Selected Immigration Consequences (Sept. 2017)

Offense	Statute	Aggravated Felony (AF)?	Crime Involving Moral Turpitude (CMT)?	Other Grounds of Removal?	Comments and Related Offenses
Crime against nature[3]	14-177 Class I felony	Should not be sexual abuse of a minor under 8 U.S.C. § 1101(a)(43)(A)[4] Possibly, as crime of violence under 8 U.S.C. § 1101(a)(43)(F) if the sentence is one year or more. See n.3.	Possibly. See n.3.		There is an argument that a conviction of a crime against nature based on an *Alford* plea is not a deportable offense. *See* § 6.1C, Categorical Approach and Record of Conviction. A PJC or fine-only-sentence would be a sentence of less than one year
Indecent liberties with a child	14-202.1 Class F felony	Probably,[5] as sexual abuse of a minor	Probably	Yes, under child abuse ground of deportability	Sexual battery should not qualify as an AF

3. Although North Carolina courts have upheld the crime against nature statute on its face (*see, e.g., State v. Pope,* 168 N.C. App. 592 (2005)), there is an argument that prosecution under this statute is unconstitutional under Fourth Circuit law. *See MacDonald v. Moose,* 710 F.3d 154 (4th Cir. 2013) (finding similar Virginia crime against nature statute unconstitutional as applied to minors, prostitution, public places, or non-consent). If constitutional, the offense may not be an aggravated felony depending on how courts interpret the elements of the offense. North Carolina courts have narrowed the offense to acts that are non-consensual, with minors, commercial, or public. *See, e.g., State v. Pope.* It is unclear what the elements are under the narrowed statute. It may be that the statute now defines four different offenses (non-consensual sex acts, sex acts with minors, sex acts for payment, and public sex acts), which would allow the immigration court to look to the record of conviction, as non-consensual acts might be an aggravated felony crime of violence. Or, it may be that these four acts are alternative means and do not have to be found unanimously by a jury. In that case the minimum conduct is a public sex act, which should not qualify as an aggravated felony or CMT.

4. In the context of a sex offense that criminalizes sexual conduct based solely on the ages of the participants, the state statute must contain an element that the victim be less than age 16 for the offense to qualify as "sexual abuse of a minor." *See Esquivel-Quintana v. Sessions,* ___ U.S. ___, 137 S. Ct. 1562 (2017). Even if acting with a minor is a possible element of the offense, crime against nature should not constitute sexual abuse of a minor because it appears to cover consensual sex acts committed against a 16- or 17-year old. *See State v. Hunt,* 221 N.C. App. 489, 496–97 n.3 (2012). It is possible the Department of Homeland Security (DHS) would still charge the offense as a deportable one.

5. *See United States v. Perez-Perez,* 737 F.3d 950 (4th Cir. 2013) (finding that North Carolina offense of indecent liberties was sexual abuse of a minor as defined by the U.S. Sentencing Guidelines).

Immigration Consequences of a Criminal Conviction in North Carolina

Offense	Statute	Aggravated Felony (AF)?	Crime Involving Moral Turpitude (CMT)?	Other Grounds of Removal?	Comments and Related Offenses
Violation of sex-offender registration requirements	14-208.11(a)(1)-(3) Class F felony	No	Possibly[6]		
Assaults, Threats, and Related Offenses					
Assault with deadly weapon with intent to kill, inflicting serious injury	14-32(a) Class C felony	Probably, as a crime of violence under 8 U.S.C. § 1101(a)(43)(F)	Yes	Probably, under the domestic violence ground of deportability if the evidence establishes that the victim is a protected family member	There is an argument that assault with deadly weapon, inflicting serious injury under G.S. 14-32(b) is not a deportable offense
Assault with deadly weapon, inflicting serious injury	14-32(b) Class E felony	Possibly, as a crime of violence under 8 U.S.C. § 1101(a)(43)(F)[7]	Possibly[8]	May fall within the domestic violence ground of deportability if the evidence establishes that the	

---

6. DHS may charge this offense as a CMT. While the Fourth Circuit has held a failure to register as a sex offender statute is not a CMT because it is a regulatory provision, *see Mohamed v. Holder*, 769 F.3d 885 (4th Cir. 2014), the Board of Immigration Appeals (BIA) has held that failure to register is a CMT. *Matter of Tobar-Lobo*, 24 I&N Dec. 143 (BIA 2007). This is the law that applies in other circuits including the Eleventh Circuit, where many North Carolina immigrants are detained and have their removal hearings.

7. There is a strong argument that this offense does not qualify as a crime of violence. The U.S. Supreme Court has held that an offense requiring only proof of negligent conduct, even when involving serious physical injury or death, is not purposeful enough to qualify as an aggravated felony crime of violence. *Leocal v. Ashcroft*, 543 U.S. 1 (2004). Because this offense, at its minimum, can be committed through culpable negligence, it arguably does not qualify as a crime of violence. *See State v. Jones*, 353 N.C. 159 (2000) (upholding conviction for assault with a deadly weapon inflicting serious injury for DWI-related deaths where defendant operated his automobile in a culpably or criminally negligent manner); *United States v. Vinson*, 805 F.3d 120, 126 (4th Cir. 2015) (culpable negligence as defined in North Carolina is a lesser standard of culpability than recklessness, which requires at least "a conscious disregard of risk").

8. Because the minimum conduct under this statute involves culpable negligence, there is an argument that it should not rise to a CMT. *See* § 3.4C, Conviction of a Crime Involving Moral Turpitude.

Offense	Statute	Aggravated Felony (AF)?	Crime Involving Moral Turpitude (CMT)?	Other Grounds of Removal?	Comments and Related Offenses
Assault with deadly weapon with intent to kill	14-32(c) Class E felony	Probably, as a crime of violence under 8 U.S.C. § 1101(a)(43)(F)	Yes	victim is a protected family member[9] Probably, under the domestic violence ground of deportability if the evidence establishes that the victim is a protected family member	There is an argument that assault with deadly weapon, inflicting serious injury under G.S. 14-32(b) is not a deportable offense
Assault inflicting serious bodily injury	14-32.4(a) Class F felony	Possibly, as a crime of violence under 8 U.S.C. § 1101(a)(43)(F) if sentence is one year or more	Possibly	Possibly, under the domestic violence ground of deportability if the evidence establishes that the victim is a protected family member	A PJC would be a sentence of less than one year
Simple assault	14-33(a) Misdemeanor	No	No		
Assault inflicting serious injury	14-33(c)(1) Misdemeanor	No	Possibly[10]	Possibly, within the domestic violence ground of deportability if the evidence establishes that the victim is a protected family member	Simple assault is not a CMT

9. The same argument in n.7, *supra*, applies here.

10. Because the minimum conduct under this statute involves culpable negligence, there is an argument that it should not rise to a CMT. *See* § 3.4C, Conviction of a Crime Involving Moral Turpitude.

Offense	Statute	Aggravated Felony (AF)?	Crime Involving Moral Turpitude (CMT)?	Other Grounds of Removal?	Comments and Related Offenses
Assault with a deadly weapon	14-33(c)(1) Misdemeanor	No	Possibly[11]	Possibly, under the domestic violence ground of deportability if the evidence establishes that the victim is a protected family member	Simple assault is not a CMT
Assault on a female	14-33(c)(2) Misdemeanor	No	Should not[12]	Should not fall within the domestic violence ground of deportability[13]	Simple assault is not a CMT
Assault on a child under 12	14-33(c)(3) Misdemeanor	No	Possibly[14]	Probably, under the child abuse ground of deportability	Simple assault is not a CMT

---

11. Because the minimum conduct under this statute involves culpable negligence, there is an argument that it should not rise to a CMT. *See State v. Jones*, 353 N.C. 159 (2000) (upholding conviction for assault with a deadly weapon for DWI-related deaths where defendant operated his automobile in a culpably or criminally negligent manner); *see also* § 3.4C, Conviction of a Crime Involving Moral Turpitude.

12. Because the minimum conduct under this statute involves culpable negligence, the BIA has found in an unpublished decision that it does not rise to a CMT. *See* § 3.4C, Conviction of a Crime Involving Moral Turpitude. DHS may still charge the noncitizen with a CMT.

13. Under Fourth Circuit law, assault on a female does not satisfy the "crime of violence" definition. The BIA in an unpublished case has also found that assault on a female is not a crime of domestic violence for immigration purposes. *See* § 3.4F, Conviction of a Crime of Domestic Violence, Stalking, Child Abuse, Child Neglect, or Child Abandonment, or a Violation of a Protective Order.

14. Because the minimum conduct under this statute involves culpable negligence, there is an argument that it should not rise to a CMT. *See supra* § 3.4C, Conviction of a Crime Involving Moral Turpitude.

Offense	Statute	Aggravated Felony (AF)?	Crime Involving Moral Turpitude (CMT)?	Other Grounds of Removal?	Comments and Related Offenses
Assault on a government official	14-33(c)(4) Misdemeanor	No	Possibly[15]		Simple assault is not a CMT Disorderly conduct is not a removable offense
Assault in presence of minor on a personal relation	14-33(d) Misdemeanor	No	Possibly	Possibly, under the domestic violence ground of deportability	Simple assault is not a CMT Assault on a female should not be a CMT
Assault by pointing a gun	14-34 Misdemeanor	No	Probably[16]	Probably, under the firearm ground of deportability[17]	Simple assault is not a CMT
Discharging a barreled weapon or firearm into occupied property	14-34.1 Class E felony	Possibly, as a crime of violence under 8 U.S.C. § 1101(a)(43)(F)	Possibly	Should not, under the firearm ground of deportability for a conviction of a barreled weapon Possibly, under the firearm ground of deportability for a	A discharge of a barreled-weapon under the statute should not come within the firearm ground There is an argument that a conviction of this offense based on an *Alford* plea is not a firearms offense. *See* § 6.1C, Categorical

---

15. Because the minimum conduct under this statute involves spitting, there is a good argument that it should not rise to a CMT. *See* § 3.4C, Conviction of a Crime Involving Moral Turpitude.

16. *See supra* n.14, though DHS will charge it as a CMT.

17. Neither the statute nor the pattern jury instructions define "gun" for the purposes of this statute. The North Carolina Court of Appeals has found that the definition of "gun" for the purposes of the statute is synonymous with "firearm," a weapon that uses "explosive force." *In re N.T.*, 214 N.C. App. 136 (2011). Because there is no stated exception here for an antique firearm as under federal law, there is an argument that this state offense is broader than the federal firearm ground of removal. *See Moncrieffe v. Holder*, 569 U.S. 184, 133 S. Ct. 1678, 1693 (2013); *see also* § 3.4E, Conviction of a Firearm or Destructive Device Offense.

App. A: Selected Immigration Consequences (Sept. 2017)

Offense	Statute	Aggravated Felony (AF)?	Crime Involving Moral Turpitude (CMT)?	Other Grounds of Removal?[18]	Comments and Related Offenses
				conviction of a firearm[18]	Approach and Record of Conviction.
Domestic criminal trespass	14-134.3(a) Misdemeanor	No	No	Possibly, as a violation of protective order ground of deportability under 8 U.S.C. § 1227(a)(2)(E) if a protective order was violated in the course of the domestic trespass	
Communicating threats	14-277.1 Misdemeanor	No	Possibly	May fall within the domestic violence ground of deportability if directed against a protected family member[19]	A conviction for a threat to damage property would not come within the domestic violence ground
Stalking	14-277.3A Misdemeanor	No	Probably	Probably, under the stalking ground of deportability	Assault on a female should not be a deportable offense

18. A person can be convicted for discharging a firearm or barreled weapon, which includes pellet guns. The statute may be divisible and define two different crimes. A conviction for a barreled gun should *not* qualify as a firearm offense because it does not expel a projectile by action of an explosion as required under federal law. There is also an argument that a conviction for a firearm does not qualify as a firearms offense. Neither the statute nor the pattern jury instructions define "firearm" for the purposes of this statute. Because there is no stated exception here for an antique firearm as under federal law, there is an argument that this state offense is broader than the federal firearm ground of removal. See *Moncrieffe v. Holder*, 569 U.S. 184, 133 S. Ct. 1678, 1693 (2013); *State v. Thomas*, 132 N.C. App. 515 (1999) (upholding discharging conviction for a black powder muzzle loader shotgun, which would appear to come within federal antique exception); *see also* § 3.4E, Conviction of a Firearm or Destructive Device.

19. This offense (or at least the portion of the statute punishing a threat to damage *property*, assuming that is a separate element) should not qualify as a crime of domestic violence, which requires a threat of use of force to a protected *person*.

App. A: Selected Immigration Consequences (Sept. 2017)

Offense	Statute	Aggravated Felony (AF)?	Crime Involving Moral Turpitude (CMT)?	Other Grounds of Removal?	Comments and Related Offenses
Misdemeanor child abuse	14-318.2 Misdemeanor	No	Possibly	Probably, under the child abuse ground of deportability	Simple assault is not a deportable offense
Felony child abuse	14-318.4(a) Class D felony	Probably, as a crime of violence under 8 U.S.C. § 1101(a)(43)(F)	Probably	Yes, under the child abuse ground of deportability	There is an argument that conviction under subsection (a4) or (a5) should not qualify as an aggravated felony or CMT. *See infra* nn. 20–21.
Felony child abuse - serious bodily injury or impairment	14-318.4(a5) Class G felony	Possibly, as a crime of violence under 8 U.S.C. § 1101(a)(43)(F) if the sentence is one year or more[20]	Possibly[21]	Yes, under the child abuse ground of deportability	Where applicable, ensure that the record reflects that the defendant was convicted for a grossly negligent act There is an argument that a conviction of this offense based on an *Alford* plea is not a deportable AF or CMT. *See* § 6.1C, Categorical

20. There is an argument that this offense (or at least the portion of the statute punishing grossly negligent act or omission, assuming that is a separate element) should not qualify as a crime of violence because it covers grossly negligent conduct. *See infra* n.21; *Leocal v. Ashcroft*, 543 U.S. 1 (2004) (holding that an offense requiring only proof of negligent conduct, even when involving serious physical injury or death, is not purposeful enough to qualify as an aggravated felony "crime of violence," as defined in 18 U.S.C. § 16).

21. Because the statute covers grossly negligent conduct (defined as a "reckless disregard for the rights and safety of others," *see* N.C.P.I.—CRIM. 239.55C), there is an argument that it does not constitute a CMT. The BIA generally requires a scienter of at least recklessness for an offense to qualify as a CMT, which the BIA defines as a "conscious[] disregard[] [of] a substantial and unjustifiable risk that circumstances exist or that a result will follow, and such disregard constitutes a gross deviation from the standard of care which a reasonable person would exercise in the situation." *See Matter of Franklin*, 20 I&N Dec. 867 (BIA 1994).

Offense	Statute	Aggravated Felony (AF)?	Crime Involving Moral Turpitude (CMT)?	Other Grounds of Removal?	Comments and Related Offenses
					Approach and Record of Conviction. A PJC would be a sentence of less than one year
Violation of valid protective order	50B-4.1(a) Misdemeanor	No	Possibly	Yes, as a violation of protective order ground of deportability under 8 U.S.C. § 1227(a)(2)(E), if finding of violation of portion of order that involves protection against credible threats of violence, repeated harassment, or bodily injury in domestic violence context[22]	Simple assault is not a deportable offense
Kidnapping and Abduction Offenses					
Kidnapping - 1st & 2d degree	14-39 Class C, E felony	Probably, as a crime of violence under 8 U.S.C. § 1101(a)(43)(F)	Probably		False imprisonment is not an AF
False imprisonment	Common law Misdemeanor	No	Possibly		

22. Thus, a violation of the child visitation portion (and certain other portions) of a protective order should not render a noncitizen deportable under this ground.

Immigration Consequences of a Criminal Conviction in North Carolina

App. A: Selected Immigration Consequences (Sept. 2017)

Offense	Statute	Aggravated Felony (AF)?	Crime Involving Moral Turpitude (CMT)?	Other Grounds of Removal?	Comments and Related Offenses
Abduction of minor	14-41 Class F felony	Possibly, as a crime of violence under 8 U.S.C. § 1101(a)(43)(F) if the sentence is one year or more	Possibly	Possibly, under the child abuse ground of deportability	False imprisonment is not an AF / A PJC would be a sentence of less than one year
Felonious restraint	14-43.3 Class F felony	Possibly, as a crime of violence under 8 U.S.C. § 1101(a)(43)(F) if the sentence is one year or more	Possibly	May fall within the domestic violence ground of deportability if the evidence establishes that the victim is a protected family member	False imprisonment is not an AF / A PJC would be a sentence of less than one year
Robbery Offenses					
Common-law robbery	14-87.1 Class G felony	Yes, as a theft offense under 8 U.S.C. § 1101(a)(43)(G) if the sentence is one year or more	Yes		A PJC would be a sentence of less than one year
Armed robbery	14-87 Class D felony	Yes, as theft or attempted theft offense under 8 U.S.C. § 1101(a)(43)(G)	Yes	Probably, under the firearm ground of deportability if the defendant was convicted under firearm element[23]	Common-law robbery will not constitute an AF if the sentence is less than 1 year through a PJC

23. Neither the statute nor the pattern jury instructions define "firearm" for the purposes of this statute. Other North Carolina statutes have defined "firearm" as a weapon that "expels a projectile by action of an explosion." Because there is no stated exception here for an antique firearm as under federal law, there is an argument that this state offense is broader than the federal firearm ground of removal. *See Moncrieffe v. Holder*, 569 U.S. 184, 133 S. Ct. 1678, 1693 (2013); *see also* § 3.4E, Conviction of a Firearm or Destructive Device Offense.

Offense	Statute	Aggravated Felony (AF)?	Crime Involving Moral Turpitude (CMT)?	Other Grounds of Removal?	Comments and Related Offenses
Burglary, Trespass, and Related Offenses					
Burglary - 1st & 2d degree	14-51 Class D, G felony	Yes, as a burglary offense under 8 U.S.C. § 1101(a)(43)(G) if the sentence is 1 year or more	Yes[24]		Burglary in the second degree will not constitute an AF if the sentence is less than 1 year through a PJC
					Misdemeanor breaking or entering is not a removable offense
Felony breaking or entering building	14-54(a) Class H felony	Yes, as a burglary offense under 8 U.S.C. § 1101(a)(43)(G) if the sentence is 1 year or more[25]	Probably, if the record of conviction reveals an intent to commit a larceny or other offense that is a CMT[26]		Felony breaking or entering will not constitute an AF if the sentence is less than 1 year through a PJC or fine only
					Misdemeanor breaking or entering is not a removable offense

---

24. *See, e.g., Uribe v. Sessions*, 855 F.3d 622 (4th Cir. 2017).

25. *See United States v. Mungro*, 754 F.3d 267 (4th Cir. 2014) (holding that "breaking or entering" under G.S. 14–54(a) is categorically a burglary offense because state law makes clear that state statute, despite its ambiguous language, requires a breaking or entry without consent, which corresponds to the "unlawful" entry requirements of the generic definition of burglary).

26. In North Carolina, at common law the State was required to allege the specific intended crime (whether a felony or any larceny) and the jury had to unanimously find that the defendant intended to commit that specific crime after breaking and entering. *State v. Silas*, 360 N.C. 377 (2006). However, the enactment of G.S. 15A-924(a)(5) liberalized the common law rule so burglary and felony breaking and entering indictments no longer have to specify the specific intended felony. *Id.* A jury now is not required to unanimously decide between "larceny" versus "any felony" or to unanimously agree as to the "felony." Thus, the statute is not divisible with regard to the intended offense, and the immigration court should not be able to look to the record of conviction to identify the intended offense. As the minimum conduct to commit burglary in North Carolina does not involve an intent to commit a larceny or other CMT, it arguably should not qualify as a CMT. See § 3.3A, Categorical Approach and Variations.

Offense	Statute	Aggravated Felony (AF)?	Crime Involving Moral Turpitude (CMT)?	Other Grounds of Removal?	Comments and Related Offenses
Misdemeanor breaking or entering building	14-54(b) Misdemeanor	No	No		
Breaking or entering a car with intent to commit felony or larceny	14-56 Class I felony	Possibly, as a crime of violence under 8 U.S.C. § 1101(a)(43)(F) if the sentence is 1 year or more Probably, as an attempted theft offense under 8 U.S.C. § 1101(a)(43)(U) if the sentence is 1 year or more	Probably		Breaking or entering a car will not constitute an AF if the sentence is less than 1 year through a PJC or fine only Misdemeanor breaking or entering is not a removable offense
Breaking into coin/currency-operated machine	14-56.1 Misdemeanor	No	Yes		
Injury to real property	14-127 Misdemeanor	No	Possibly		Disorderly conduct in a public building is not a removable offense
Trespass - 1st degree	14-159.12(a)-(c) Misdemeanor	No	No		
Trespass - 2nd degree	14-159.13 Misdemeanor	No	No		
Domestic criminal trespass	14-134.3(a) Misdemeanor	No	No	Possibly, under the domestic violence ground of deportability if a protective order was violated in the	

Immigration Consequences of a Criminal Conviction in North Carolina

App. A: Selected Immigration Consequences (Sept. 2017)

Offense	Statute	Aggravated Felony (AF)?	Crime Involving Moral Turpitude (CMT)?	Other Grounds of Removal?	Comments and Related Offenses
Injury to personal property	14-160 Misdemeanor	No	Possibly	course of the domestic trespass	
Arson and Burning Offenses					
Arson - 1st & 2d degree	14-58 Class D, G felony	Probably, as an arson offense under 8 U.S.C. § 1101(a)(43)(E)(i)	Probably		Injury to real or personal property is not an AF
Burning building under construction	14-62.1 Class H felony	Possibly, as an arson offense under 8 U.S.C. § 1101(a)(43)(E)(i)	Probably		Injury to real or personal property is not an AF
Burning personal property	14-66 Class H felony	Probably, as an arson offense under 8 U.S.C. § 1101(a)(43)(E)(i)	Probably		Injury to personal property is not an AF
Larceny, Embezzlement, and Related Offenses					
Misdemeanor larceny	14-72(a) Misdemeanor	No	Yes		
Felonious larceny	14-72 Class H felony	Possibly as a theft offense under 8 U.S.C. § 1101(a)(43)(G)[27] if the sentence is 1 year or more	Yes		Felonious possession/receiving of stolen goods may not constitute an AF Larceny will not constitute an AF if the sentence is less

27. There is an argument that a conviction under the North Carolina larceny statute should not come within the theft aggravated felony ground because it appears to cover larceny by trick. See § 6.2B, Theft Aggravated Felony.

Offense	Statute	Aggravated Felony (AF)?	Crime Involving Moral Turpitude (CMT)?	Other Grounds of Removal?	Comments and Related Offenses
					than 1 year through a PJC or fine only
Misdemeanor possession/receiving of stolen goods	14-72(a) Misdemeanor	No	Possibly[28]		
Felonious possession/receiving of stolen goods	14-71, 14-71.1, 14-72 Class H felony	Should not,[29] as a theft offense under 8 U.S.C. § 1101(a)(43)(G) even if the sentence is 1 year or more	Possibly[30]		
Unauthorized use of a motor-propelled conveyance	14-72.2 Misdemeanor	No	No		
Concealment of merchandise	14-72.1(a) Misdemeanor	No	Possibly not, because there is no intent to deprive or even a taking of property as under the larceny statute, though DHS may still charge this as such		

28. The BIA has held that the crime of receiving stolen property is a CMT where the offense includes an element of knowing that the property is stolen. *See Matter of Salvail*, 17 I&N Dec. 19 (BIA 1979); *Matter of Patel*, 15 I&N Dec. 212, 213 (BIA 1975). The North Carolina statute appears to be broader than such statutes because a conviction can be obtained for knowingly receiving/possessing property *or* having reasonable grounds to believe it is stolen. Because knowing or having reasonable grounds to believe appear to be alternate means to satisfy the knowledge element, there is an argument that no conviction under the statute is a CMT. *See* § 3.3A, Categorical Approach and Variations.

29. *Matter of Deang*, 27 I&N Dec. 57 (BIA 2017) holds that a receiving/possession offense does not satisfy the aggravated felony theft definition where it only requires a mental state of "reasonable grounds to believe" that the property was stolen. Because knowing or having reasonable grounds to believe appear to be alternate means to satisfy the knowledge element under the North Carolina statute, no conviction under the statute should qualify as an AF. *See* § 3.3A, Categorical Approach and Variations. It is possible that DHS will still charge this as a deportable offense.

30. *See supra* n.28.

Immigration Consequences of a Criminal Conviction in North Carolina

App. A: Selected Immigration Consequences (Sept. 2017)

Offense	Statute	Aggravated Felony (AF)?	Crime Involving Moral Turpitude (CMT)?	Other Grounds of Removal?	Comments and Related Offenses
Embezzlement	14-90 Class C, H felony	Probably, as a fraud offense under 8 U.S.C. § 1101(a)(43)(M)(i) if the loss to the victim exceeds $10,000	Possibly		Embezzlement will not constitute an AF if record indicates that the loss is $10,000 or less
Offenses Involving Fraud					
Obtaining property by false pretenses	14-100 Class C, H felony	Yes, as a fraud offense under 8 U.S.C. § 1101(a)(43)(M)(i) if the loss to the victim exceeds $10,000	Yes		Obtaining property by false pretenses will not constitute an AF if the record indicates that the loss is $10,000 or less
Obtaining property by worthless check	14-106 Misdemeanor	Yes, as a fraud offense under 8 U.S.C. § 1101(a)(43)(M)(i) if the loss to the victim exceeds $10,000	Yes		Obtaining property by worthless check will not constitute an AF if the record indicates that the loss is $10,000 or less Writing a worthless check may not be a removable offense
Writing worthless check	14-107 Misdemeanor	Possibly, if the loss to the victim exceeds $10,000	Probably not[31]		

31. The Board has held that, absent an intent to defraud, convictions for drawing worthless checks are not crimes involving moral turpitude. *Matter of Balao*, 20 I&N Dec. 440, 443 (BIA 1992) (finding that knowing issuance of bad checks where there is no intent to defraud is not a CMT); *Matter of Zangwill*, 18 I&N Dec. 22 (BIA 1981); *Matter of Colbourne*, 13 I&N Dec. 319 (BIA 1969); *Matter of Stasinski*, 11 I&N Dec. 202 (BIA 1965). There is no intent to defraud explicit in G.S. 14-107 or added through case law. *See State v. Levy*, 220 N.C. 812 (1942) (gravamen of offense is putting worthless commercial paper into circulation); *Nunn v. Smith*, 270 N.C. 374 (1967) (same). Though a number of immigration judges have found this offense not to be a CMT, DHS has initiated removal proceedings based on a conviction for this offense.

Offense	Statute	Aggravated Felony (AF)?	Crime Involving Moral Turpitude (CMT)?	Other Grounds of Removal?	Comments and Related Offenses
Financial transaction card forgery	14-113.11 Class I felony	Yes, as a fraud offense under 8 U.S.C. § 1101(a)(43)(M)(i) if the loss to the victim exceeds $10,000 Probably, as a forgery offense under 8 U.S.C. § 1101(a)(43)(R)[32] if the sentence is 1 year or more	Probably		Financial transaction card forgery will not constitute an AF fraud offense if the record indicates that the loss is $10,000 or less Financial transaction card forgery will not constitute an AF forgery if the sentence is less than 1 year through a PJC or fine only
Financial transaction card fraud	14-113.13 Misdemeanor, Class I felony	Yes, as a fraud offense under 8 U.S.C. § 1101(a)(43)(M)(i) if the loss to the victim exceeds $10,000 under subsections (a), (b), (c1), or (d) Possibly, as a fraud offense under 8 U.S.C. § 1101(a)(43)(M)(i) if the loss to the victim exceeds $10,000 under subsection (c)	Yes, under subsections (a), (b), (c1), or (d) Possibly, under subsection (c)		Financial transaction card fraud will not constitute an AF if the record indicates that the loss is $10,000 or less
Identity theft	14-113.20 Class F, G felony	Yes, as a fraud offense under 8 U.S.C. § 1101(a)(43)(M)(i) if the	Probably		Identity theft will not constitute an AF if record

32. See infra n.34.

Offense	Statute	Aggravated Felony (AF)?	Crime Involving Moral Turpitude (CMT)?	Other Grounds of Removal?	Comments and Related Offenses
		loss to the victim exceeds $10,000			indicates that the loss is $10,000 or less
Extortion	14-118.4 Class F felony	Possibly, as a crime of violence under 8 U.S.C. § 1101(a)(43)(F) if the sentence is 1 year or more Possibly as theft offense under 8 U.S.C. § 1101(a)(43)(G) if the sentence is one year or more [33]	Possibly		A PJC or fine-only-sentence would be a sentence of less than one year
Common law forgery	Common law Misdemeanor	Possibly, as a fraud offense under 8 U.S.C. § 1101(a)(43)(M)(i) if the loss to the victim exceeds $10,000	Yes		

33. There is an argument that this offense is not a theft aggravated felony because it covers a threat to obtain anything of value or any acquittance, advantage, or immunity, Because the minimum conduct does not require a taking of property, there is an argument that it is not a theft aggravated felony. *State v. Wright*, 240 N.C. App. 270 (2015).

Offense	Statute	Aggravated Felony (AF)?	Crime Involving Moral Turpitude (CMT)?	Other Grounds of Removal?	Comments and Related Offenses
Forgery of bank notes, checks, and securities Uttering forged instrument or forging endorsement	14-119, 14-120 Class I felony	Possibly,[34] as a forgery offense under 8 U.S.C. § 1101(a)(43)(R) if the sentence is 1 year or more Possibly, as a counterfeiting offense under 8 U.S.C. § 1101(a)(43)(R) if the sentence is 1 year or more Probably, as a fraud offense under 8 U.S.C. § 1101(a)(43)(M)(i) if the loss to the victim exceeds $10,000[35]	Probably		A plea to misdemeanor common law forgery is not an AF if the loss to the victim is $10,000 or less Forgery of bank notes will not constitute an AF if the sentence is less than 1 year through a PJC or fine

Prostitution and Related Offenses

Offense	Statute	Aggravated Felony (AF)?	Crime Involving Moral Turpitude (CMT)?	Other Grounds of Removal?	Comments and Related Offenses
Prostitution	14-204 Misdemeanor	No	Yes	Possibly triggers the prostitution ground of inadmissibility	Disorderly conduct in a public building is not a removable offense

34. There is an argument that North Carolina forgery of banknotes is broader than the generic definition of forgery. Generic forgery lies where document is falsely executed, rather than a document that is genuinely executed but merely contains false information, *see Alvarez v. Lynch*, 828 F.3d 288 (4th Cir. 2016), but the North Carolina offenses appears to cover a document that has been falsely copied, reproduced, forged, manufactured, embossed, encoded, duplicated, or altered. *See* N.C.P.I.—CRIM. 221.10. It is unclear whether G.S. 14-119 is divisible into separate crimes or defines only one offense.

35. There may be an argument that forgery or uttering is not a fraud offense because it can be committed with an intent to injure. *See e.g., Akinsade v. Holder*, 678 F.3d 138 (2d Cir. 2012) (finding that offense of embezzlement committed with an intent to injure, as opposed to defraud, may not be a fraud aggravated felony offense).

Offense	Statute	Aggravated Felony (AF)?	Crime Involving Moral Turpitude (CMT)?	Other Grounds of Removal?	Comments and Related Offenses
Solicitation of prostitution Patronizing prostitution	14-205.1, 14-205.2 Misdemeanor	No	Yes	May trigger the prostitution ground of inadmissibility	
Weapons Offenses					
Carrying a concealed weapon other than a pistol or gun	14-269(a) Misdemeanor	No	No		
Carrying a concealed pistol or gun	14-269(a1) Misdemeanor	No	No	Probably, under the firearm/destructive device ground of deportability[36]	Carrying a concealed weapon other than a pistol or gun under 14-269(a) is not a removable offense
Manufacture, sale, possession, etc. of weapon of mass death and destruction	14-288.8 Class F felony	Possibly, under 8 U.S.C. 1101(a)(43)(C) if the conviction is for selling/offering to sell[37] a weapon	Possibly[38]	Yes, under the firearm/destructive device ground of deportability	Where appropriate, the record should reflect that the conviction was for possession, which is not an AF There is an argument that a conviction of this offense

36. Neither the statute nor the pattern jury instructions define "pistol" or "gun" for the purposes of this statute. Case law suggests that a gun or pistol must be a "firearm," *see, e.g., State v. Best*, 214 N.C. App. 39 (2011), which other North Carolina statutes have defined as a weapon that "expels a projectile by action of an explosion." *See* G.S. 14-415.1(a) (possession of firearm by felon). Because there is no stated exception here for an antique firearm as under federal law (and under G.S. 14-415.1), there is an argument that this state offense is broader than the federal firearm ground of removal. *See Moncrieffe v. Holder*, 569 U.S. 184, 133 S. Ct. 1678, 1693 (2013). *See* § 3.4E, Conviction of a Firearm or Destructive Device Offense.

37. This assumes that sale of such a weapon is a distinct crime from possessing, etc. such a weapon. If they are alternative means, then a conviction under the statute would not come within 8 U.S.C. 1101(a)(43)(C), which covers the trafficking of weapons.

38. If the statute is divisible by the actus reus (sell vs. possess, etc.), it may be a CMT to sell, manufacture, deliver, or offer to sell.

App. A: Selected Immigration Consequences (Sept. 2017)

Offense	Statute	Aggravated Felony (AF)?	Crime Involving Moral Turpitude (CMT)?	Other Grounds of Removal?	Comments and Related Offenses
					based on an *Alford* plea is not a deportable AF or CMT. *See* § 6.1C, Categorical Approach and Record of Conviction.
Possession of a firearm or weapon of mass death and destruction by felon	14-415.1 Class G felony	Yes, under 8 U.S.C. 1101(a)(43)(E)(ii)	No	Yes, under the firearm/destructive device ground of deportability	Carrying a concealed pistol or gun is not an AF
Obstruction of Justice, Disorderly Conduct, and Related Offenses					
Disorderly conduct in a public building	14-132 Misdemeanor	No	No		
Resisting, delaying, or obstructing officer	14-223 Misdemeanor	No	Possibly[39]		Simple assault is not a CMT
Making false report to law enforcement agency or officer	14-225 Misdemeanor	No	Possibly		Disorderly conduct is not a CMT
Disorderly conduct	14-288.4 Misdemeanor	No	No		

39. There is an argument that this offense should not qualify as a CMT because the BIA has previously found that an element of actual injury is required for an assault-type crime to be a CMT. *See Matter of Danesh*, 19 I&N Dec. 669 (BIA 1988) (finding that an aggravated assault against a peace officer, which results in bodily harm to the victim and which involves knowledge by the offender that his force is directed to an officer who is performing an official duty, constitutes a CMT); *see also Matter of Solon*, 24 I&N Dec. 239, 245 (BIA 2007) (finding that the offense of assault in the third degree in violation of section 120.00(1) of the New York Penal Law is a CMT, as such an offense requires both a specific intent to cause injury and physical injury to the victim); *see also Cano v. U.S. Atty. Gen.*, 709 F.3d 1052 (11th Cir. 2013) (holding that Florida resisting arrest is a CMT because the statute "requires intentional violence against an officer"). No such element is present in G.S. 14-223.

Offense	Statute	Aggravated Felony (AF)?	Crime Involving Moral Turpitude (CMT)?	Other Grounds of Removal?	Comments and Related Offenses
Drunk and disruptive in public	14-444 Misdemeanor	No	No		
Motor Vehicle Offenses					
Driving while license suspended or revoked	20-28(a) Misdemeanor	No	No		
Receiving, transferring, or possessing stolen vehicle	20-106 Misdemeanor	Should not, as a theft offense[40]	Possibly[41]		Unauthorized use of a motor-propelled conveyance is not an AF or CMT
Impaired Driving	20-138.1 Misdemeanor	No	Possibly; a simple DWI with no aggravating factors is not a CMT, but a DWI with an aggravating factor of driving with revoked license is possibly a CMT	Probably, under the controlled substance ground of deportability or inadmissibility for a violation under (a)(3)[42]	A simple DWI (no aggravating factors) is not a CMT
Habitual Impaired Driving	20-138.5 Misdemeanor	No	Probably not	Probably, under the controlled substance ground of deportability or inadmissibility for a violation under (a)(3)[43]	

40. See supra n.29.
41. See supra n.28.
42. But, there may be an argument that G.S. 20-138.1 defines only one crime and that the various subsections are all alternative means (theories). See State v. Oliver, 343 N.C. 202, 215 (1996). If that is so, the offense would not qualify as a controlled substance offense, as the minimum conduct involved is impairment based on alcohol. See § 3.3A, Categorical Approach and Variations.
43. See supra n.42.

Offense	Statute	Aggravated Felony (AF)?	Crime Involving Moral Turpitude (CMT)?	Other Grounds of Removal?	Comments and Related Offenses
Reckless driving	20-140 Misdemeanor	No	Probably not		
Felony speeding to elude arrest	20-141.5(b) Class H felony	Possibly, as a crime of violence under 8 U.S.C. § 1101(a)(43)(F) if the sentence is 1 year or more	Possibly		Felony speeding to elude arrest is not an AF if the sentence is less than 1 year through a PJC or fine only Reckless driving may not be a removable offense
Misdemeanor speeding to elude arrest	20-141.5(a) Misdemeanor	No	Possibly		Reckless driving may not be a removable offense
Failure to stop or remain at scene when personal injury or death occurs	20-166(a) Class F felony	Probably not	Possibly		
Failure to give information or assistance when injury or death occurs	20-166(b) Misdemeanor	No	Possibly		
Failure to stop or give information when injury not apparent or property damage occurs	20-166(c) Misdemeanor	No	Possibly		
Drug Offenses					
Sale, manufacture, delivery, or possession	90-95(a)(1)	Yes, as a drug trafficking offense under 8 U.S.C. §	Yes	Yes, under the controlled substance	Simple possession of a controlled substance (other

Immigration Consequences of a Criminal Conviction in North Carolina

App. A: Selected Immigration Consequences (Sept. 2017)

Offense	Statute	Aggravated Felony (AF)?	Crime Involving Moral Turpitude (CMT)?	Other Grounds of Removal?	Comments and Related Offenses
with intent to manufacture, sell, or deliver any controlled substance	Felony (various)	1101(a)(43)(B), except for a conviction for delivery of marijuana or possession of marijuana with intent to deliver, or for a conviction of chorionic gonadotropin[44]		ground of deportability and the controlled substance ground of inadmissibility, except involving chorionic gonadotropin[45]	than any amount of flunitrazepam) is not an AF if no prior drug convictions There is an argument that a conviction for a Schedule III drug where the record of conviction does not reveal the specific drug does not make a person deportable for a drug trafficking aggravated felony. *See* § 6.3A, Manufacture, Sale, or Delivery of a Schedule III Controlled Substance
Sale or delivery of counterfeit controlled substance	90-95(a)(2) Class I felony	Yes, under 8 U.S.C. § 1101(a)(43)(B) for a substance defined in G.S. 90-87(6)a. (actual controlled substance)[46] Probably not, under 8 U.S.C. § 1101(a)(43)(B) for	Possibly	Yes, under the controlled substance ground of deportability and the controlled substance ground of inadmissibility for a substance defined in	There is an argument that conviction for a substance defined in G.S. 90-87(6)b. (not a controlled substance) is not a drug trafficking AF or controlled substance offense

---

44. *See* § 3.4B, Drug Trafficking Aggravated Felony; § 6.3A, Manufacture, Sale, or Delivery of a Schedule III Controlled Substance.

45. *See* § 3.4D, Conviction of any Controlled Substance Offense.

46. It is unclear whether the definition of "counterfeit controlled substance" is divisible, setting forth two alternative elements that a jury would have to unanimously find. If it is divisible, conviction under G.S. 90-87(6)a. for an actual controlled substance comes within the drug trafficking AF. *See Matter of Sanchez-Cornejo*, 25 I&N Dec. 273, 274–75 (BIA 2010). But conviction under G.S. 90-87(6)b. should not. *Id.* If the definitional provision contains alternate means, not elements, then there is an argument that no conviction qualifies as an AF.

Offense	Statute	Aggravated Felony (AF)?	Crime Involving Moral Turpitude (CMT)?	Other Grounds of Removal?	Comments and Related Offenses
		a substance defined in G.S. 90-87(6)b. (not a controlled substance)		G.S. 90-87(6)a. (actual controlled substance) Possibly, under the controlled substance ground of deportability and inadmissibility for a substance defined in G.S. 90-87(6)b. (not a controlled substance)[47]	
Possession of controlled substance	90-95(a)(3) Misdemeanor, Felony	No, if first offense Possibly, under 8 U.S.C. § 1101(a)(43)(B) if prosecuted as a recidivist offense	No	Yes, under the controlled substance ground of deportability and the controlled substance ground of inadmissibility, except involving chorionic gonadotropin[48] There is an exception to deportability for a single conviction of possession of 30 grams or less of marijuana if	Class 3 or Class 1 misdemeanor possession of marijuana (if 30 grams or less of marijuana) is not a deportable offense if no prior drug convictions. Such a conviction will make a noncitizen inadmissible, but can be waived by an immigration judge under certain circumstances. If less than 30 grams of marijuana involved, counsel

47. There is an argument that an offense that does not contain an element of an actual controlled substance cannot trigger the controlled substance ground of removal. See Mellouli v. Lynch, 135 S. Ct. 1980, 1991 (2015) (holding that an offense cannot trigger the controlled substance ground of removability where "[no] controlled substance (as defined in [§ 802]) figures as an element of the offense"). But see Matter of Sanchez-Cornejo, 25 I&N Dec. 273 (BIA 2010). For how the analysis is affected by whether the definition of "counterfeit controlled substance" contains alternate means vs. elements, see supra n.46.

48. See § 6.3A, Manufacture, Sale, or Delivery of a Schedule III Controlled Substance.

App. A: Selected Immigration Consequences (Sept. 2017)

Offense	Statute	Aggravated Felony (AF)?	Crime Involving Moral Turpitude (CMT)?	Other Grounds of Removal?	Comments and Related Offenses
				no prior drug convictions	should ensure the record reflects that There is an argument that a conviction for a Schedule III drug where the record of conviction does not reveal the specific drug does not make a person deportable for a controlled substance offense
Trafficking in any controlled substance	90-95(h) Felony (various)	Yes under 8 U.S.C. § 1101(a)(43)(B), except involving chorionic gonadotropin[49] Also, trafficking by possession may not be an AF[50]	Yes	Yes, under the controlled substance ground of deportability and the controlled substance ground of inadmissibility, except involving chorionic gonadotropin[51]	Simple possession of a controlled substance (other than any amount of flunitrazepam) is not an AF if no prior drug convictions
Maintaining store, dwelling, boat, or other place for use,	90-108(a)(7) Misdemeanor, Class I felony	Possibly, under 8 U.S.C. § 1101(a)(43)(B)[52]	Possibly	Possibly, under the controlled substance ground of deportability and the controlled	

---

49. *See* § 6.3A, Manufacture, Sale, or Delivery of a Schedule III Controlled Substance.

50. *See* "Drug Trafficking Aggravated Felony" in § 3.4B, Specific Types of Aggravated Felonies.

51. *See* § 3.4D, Conviction of any Controlled Substance Offense.

52. In an unpublished case, the BIA found that the misdemeanor version was not an aggravated felony because it was broader than the analogous federal offense (as the minimum conduct punished under the state offense requires only the knowing conduct of keeping a controlled substance). *See In re of Sanchez-Vazquez,* 2013 WL 4925089 (BIA Aug. 30, 2013) (unpublished).

Immigration Consequences of a Criminal Conviction in North Carolina

App. A: Selected Immigration Consequences (Sept. 2017)

A-29

Offense	Statute	Aggravated Felony (AF)?	Crime Involving Moral Turpitude (CMT)?	Other Grounds of Removal?	Comments and Related Offenses
storage, or sale of controlled substance				substance ground of inadmissibility	
Possession of drug paraphernalia	90-113.22 Misdemeanor	No	No	Possibly, under the controlled substance ground of deportability and the controlled substance ground of inadmissibility[53]	
Possession of marijuana drug paraphernalia	90-113.22A Misdemeanor	No	No	Yes, under the controlled substance ground of deportability or inadmissibility There is an exception to deportability for a single conviction of paraphernalia related to 30 grams or less of marijuana if no prior drug convictions. Such a conviction will make a noncitizen inadmissible, but can be waived by an immigration judge under certain circumstances.	If less than 30 grams of marijuana involved, counsel should ensure the record reflects that Class 3 misdemeanor possession of marijuana is not a deportable offense if no prior drug convictions. Such a conviction will make a noncitizen inadmissible, but can be waived by an immigration judge under certain circumstances.

53. There is a strong argument that such a conviction is not a controlled substance conviction. *See* § 3.4D, Conviction of any Controlled Substance Offense, § 6.3D, Drug Paraphernalia.

Immigration Consequences of a Criminal Conviction in North Carolina

Offense	Statute	Aggravated Felony (AF)?	Crime Involving Moral Turpitude (CMT)?	Other Grounds of Removal?	Comments and Related Offenses
Inchoate Offenses					
Attempt	Common-law	Probably, if the underlying offense is an AF	Probably, if the underlying offense is a CMT	Probably, if the underlying offense is a removable offense	
Solicitation	Common-law	Possibly, if the underlying offense is an AF	Probably, if the underlying offense is a CMT	Possibly, if the underlying offense is a controlled substance or firearm offense	
Conspiracy	Common-law	Probably, if the underlying offense is an AF[54]	Probably, if the underlying offense is a CMT	Probably, if the underlying offense is a removable offense	
Accessory after the fact	14-7	Probably, as an obstruction of justice offense under 8 U.S.C. § 1101(a)(43)(S) if the sentence is 1 year or more	Probably, if the underlying offense is a CMT	Accessory after the fact to a controlled substance or firearm offense is probably not a removable offense under the controlled substance or firearm ground of deportability or inadmissibility	

54. There is an argument that conspiracy as defined in North Carolina, which does not require an overt act (*State v. Gallimore*, 272 N.C. 528, 532 (1968)), is broader than and not a categorical match to the federal generic definition of conspiracy, which the Ninth Circuit has held requires an overt act. *See United States v. Garcia-Santana*, 774 F.3d 528, 535 & n.4 (9th Cir. 2014). *But see Matter of Richardson*, 25 I&N Dec. 226, 228 (BIA 2010) (adopting common law definition of conspiracy as generic definition, which does not require an overt act).

Appendix B
Relevant Immigration Decisions

This appendix contains the following unpublished decisions by the Board of Immigration Appeals concerning immigration consequences of North Carolina criminal convictions.

Matter of X-X-X-, A 090 764 102 (BIA Mar. 28, 2014)   **B-2**
(holding that assault on a female is not a crime of domestic violence
or a crime involving moral turpitude)

Matter of Garcia Olvera (BIA Mar. 25, 2015)   **B-7**
(holding that a conviction under G.S. 90-95(a)(1) for delivery or
possession with intent to deliver marijuana is not a drug trafficking
aggravated felony)

Matter of V-M-B-B-, A XXX XXX 723 (BIA Mar. 27, 2015)   **B-14**
(holding that a conviction under G.S. 90-95(h)(3) for trafficking by
possession is not a drug trafficking aggravated felony)

U.S. Department of Justice

Executive Office for Immigration Review

Board of Immigration Appeals
Office of the Clerk

5107 Leesburg Pike, Suite 2000
Falls Church, Virginia 20530

Jama Ibrahim
6065 Roswell Rd. N.E., Suite 950
Atlanta, GA 30328

DHS/ICE Office of Chief Counsel - ATL
180 Spring Street, Suite 332
Atlanta, GA 30303

Name: ████████████████   ██████████

Date of this notice: 3/28/2014

Enclosed is a copy of the Board's decision and order in the above-referenced case.

Sincerely,

Donna Carr

Donna Carr
Chief Clerk

Enclosure

Panel Members:
Pauley, Roger

schwarzA
Userteam: Docket

U.S. Department of Justice
Executive Office for Immigration Review

Decision of the Board of Immigration Appeals

Falls Church, Virginia 20530

File: ▓▓▓▓▓▓ – Atlanta, GA   Date: MAR 2 8 2014

In re: ▓▓▓▓▓▓▓▓▓▓▓▓▓▓▓▓▓▓▓

IN REMOVAL PROCEEDINGS

APPEAL

ON BEHALF OF RESPONDENT: Jama A. Ibrahim, Esquire

ON BEHALF OF DHS: Gene Hamilton
                      Assistant Chief Counsel

CHARGE:

    Notice: Sec. 237(a)(2)(A)(ii), I&N Act [8 U.S.C. § 1227(a)(2)(A)(ii)] -
    Convicted of two or more crimes involving moral turpitude

         Sec. 237(a)(2)(E)(i), I&N Act [8 U.S.C. § 1227(a)(2)(E)(i)] -
    Convicted of crime of domestic violence, stalking, or child abuse, child neglect, or child abandonment

APPLICATION: Termination

The Department of Homeland Security ("DHS") appeals from an Immigration Judge's March 4, 2013, decision terminating proceedings. The respondent has filed a brief in opposition to the appeal. For the reasons that follow, the appeal will be dismissed.

At issue on appeal is whether the DHS met its burden of proving that the respondent's August 2010 conviction for assault on a female in violation of North Carolina law is a crime involving moral turpitude, which would combine with a 1996 conviction for felony theft under Florida law to satisfy the charge of removal arising under section 237(a)(2)(A)(ii) of the Immigration and Nationality Act. In addition, the DHS argues on appeal that the assault on a female conviction under section 14-33(c)(2) of the North Carolina statute is also a crime of domestic violence, satisfying the removal charge under section 237(a)(2)(E)(i) of the Act.[1] We

---

[1] In its Notice of Appeal, the DHS also raised the question whether the Immigration Judge erred in finding that it had failed to prove that the respondent's March 2012 conviction for cyberstalking in violation of section 14-196.3 constituted a crime involving moral turpitude. However, in its appeal brief, the DHS does not elaborate on this argument, nor support it with pertinent legal authority. We therefore deem this argument abandoned. Nevertheless, to the extent that the DHS challenges the Immigration Judge's findings with regard to whether the cyberstalking conviction can go towards satisfying the charge of removal under section 237(a)(2)(A)(ii) of the Act, we affirm the Immigration Judge's finding in this regard (Tr. at 85-86). *See Cano v. U.S. Att'y Gen.*, 709 F.3d 1052, 1053 n. 3 (11th Cir. 2013) (analysis must

(Continued . . . .)

A090 764 102

review these legal questions de novo. *See* 8 C.F.R. § 1003.1(d)(3)(ii). We also note that there are no contested questions of fact arising in this appeal that would trigger clear error review. *See* 8 C.F.R. § 1003.1(d)(3)(i).

The question whether the assault conviction under the above-referenced section of North Carolina law constitutes a crime involving moral turpitude is informed by the Supreme Court's decision in *Descamps v. United States*, 133 S. Ct. 2276 (2013), which was issued after the Immigration Judge rendered his decision in this case. In *Descamps*, the Supreme Court explained that the modified categorical approach operates narrowly, and applies only if: (1) the statute of conviction is divisible in the sense that it lists multiple discrete offenses as enumerated alternatives or defines a single offense by reference to disjunctive sets of "elements,"[2] more than one combination of which could support a conviction, and (2) some (but not all) of those listed offenses or combinations of disjunctive elements are a categorical match to the relevant generic standard. *Id.* at 2281, 2283. Thus, after *Descamps* the modified categorical approach does not apply merely because the elements of a crime can sometimes be proved by reference to conduct that fits a generic federal standard; according to the *Descamps* Court, such crimes are "overbroad" but not "divisible." *Id.* at 2285-86, 2290-92.[3]

The state statute under which the respondent was convicted for misdemeanor assault provides in relevant part that ". . . any person who commits any assault, assault and battery, or affray, is guilty of a Class A1 misdemeanor if, in the course of the assault, assault and battery, or affray, he or she. . . (2) [a]ssaults a female, he being a male person at least 18 years of age." *See* N.C. Gen. Stat. 14-33(c)(2). The Immigration Judge found that this statute did not categorically define a crime involving moral turpitude, but pursuant to the parties' agreement, conducted a modified categorical analysis of the conviction record, to determine if the conviction would support the charge under section 237(a)(2)(A)(ii) of the Act (I.J. at 2-3).

We disagree that under *Descamps v. United States*, *supra*, the statute lends itself to a modified categorical inquiry into whether the respondent's conviction thereunder is for a crime involving moral turpitude. While the language referencing the commission of "any assault,

---

determine if least culpable conduct necessary to sustain a conviction under the statute meets the standard of a crime involving moral turpitude). The cyberstalking conviction was not alleged as a factual predicate for the charge under section 237(a)(2)(E)(i) of the Act, and the DHS does not allege on appeal that this conviction would support removal under section 237(a)(2)(E)(i) of the Act. *See* DHS's Brief at 3, n. 2 and Exh. 5.

[2] By "elements," we understand the *Descamps* Court to mean those facts about a crime which must be proved to a jury beyond a reasonable doubt *and* about which the jury must agree by whatever margin is required to convict in the relevant jurisdiction. *Id.* at 2288 (citing *Richardson v. United States*, 526 U.S. 813, 817 (1999)).

[3] The Eleventh Circuit has held that the requirements of the categorical and modified categorical approaches may not be relaxed in CIMT cases. *Fajardo v. U.S. Att'y Gen.*, 659 F.3d 1303, 1305 (11th Cir. 2011).

2

assault and battery, or affray," describes alternative means of committing the crime, we do not read the Supreme Court's opinion to support a conclusion that these are disparate "elements" of the crime, supporting a modified categorical approach. Moreover, the balance of the statute relating to the perpetrator being "a male person at least 18 years of age" who "assaults a female" suggests no alternative *elements* of assault—certainly no question about a domestic relationship—about which North Carolina jurors must agree in order to convict. *See Descamps v. United States, supra*, at 2285 n. 2. We therefore find the modified categorical approach undertaken here to be unwarranted under intervening precedent.[4]

Even if the modified categorical approach was appropriate here, we affirm the Immigration Judge's determination that under noticeable documents, the DHS did not meet its burden to prove that the respondent's assault on a female conviction involved moral turpitude. *Fajardo v. U.S. Att'y Gen., supra*. As the Immigration Judge found, the documents indicate that the respondent was convicted after trial by the district court acting as the trier of fact (I.J. at 2-3). The record of conviction, which included the warrant of arrest and the judgment (Exh. 3), does not reflect the factual basis for the finding of guilty, insofar as the warrant, even assuming that it is equivalent to an indictment, was not shown on this record to be the basis for a plea or finding of guilty (I.J. at 3; Tr. at 52-57). Accordingly, assuming that a modified categorical approach was appropriate, we find that the Immigration Judge properly found that the DHS did not prove that this record reflected the type of "willful" "infliction of bodily harm upon a person with whom one has . . . a familial relationship" that would indicate that the respondent's assault conviction involves moral turpitude. *Matter of Tran*, 21 I&N Dec. 291, 294 (BIA 1996).

Furthermore, we affirm the Immigration Judge's finding that the record does not support a finding that the conviction for assault on a female was for a crime of domestic violence. First, the North Carolina statute at issue does not set forth a categorical crime of violence as described under 18 U.S.C. § 16(a),[5] which would be necessary to a finding of a "domestic violence" crime. *See Matter of Velasquez*, 25 I&N Dec. 278, 279-80 (BIA 2010). That is because an "assault" for purposes of this statute is defined according to common law to include a battery, which requires a showing of *any* level of force, either direct or indirect, to the person of another. *See United States v. Kelly*, 917 F.Supp.2d 553, 559 (W.D.N.C. 2013) (*citing State v. Britt*, 154 S.E.2d 519 (N.C. 1967)). Battery under North Carolina law does not require the application of violent force or force capable of causing injury, and indeed has been described as requiring only "offensive touching." *See City of Greenville v. Haywood*, 502 S.E.2d 430, 433 (N.C. Ct. App. 1998). We

---

[4] We note that the parties conceded that the respondent's 1996 conviction for grand theft under section 812.014 of the Florida statutes was categorically a crime involving moral turpitude (Tr. at 82). However, *Descamps v. United States, supra*, may undermine any such finding, since we read the Florida theft statute to permit conviction for temporary or permanent takings, raising the question whether these would constitute alternative elements to the offense, so as to invite a modified categorical approach under relevant precedent.

[5] Because the respondent's conviction under section 14-33(c)(2) of the North Carolina statute was for a misdemeanor, it can only constitute a crime of violence if it is "an offense that has as an element the use, attempted use, or threatened use of physical force against the person or property of another." *See Matter of Velasquez*, 25 I&N Dec. 278, 280 (BIA 2010).

3

A090 764 102

have held that this conduct does not equate to an element of "physical force" that is required to qualify an offense as a crime of violence under 18 U.S.C. § 16(a). *See Matter of Velasquez, supra*, at 281-82; *Johnson v. United States*, 559 U.S.133 (2010). Even if we assume that the underlying assault conviction would not include a battery, it does not appear that violent force is always a requisite element of the crime of assault under North Carolina, since common law does not consistently require the showing of "force and violence" to convict under the statute. *See United States v. Kelly, supra*, at 557-58 (noting cases wherein conviction for assault predicated on showing of "force *or* violence" or a show of force).

We do not find that a modified categorical inquiry into the crime of violence question is viable in light of *Descamps v. United States, supra*. Furthermore, even if it were, the record does not contain the requisite judicially noticeable documents to reveal the manner in which the "assault" conviction occurred, since the record does not reflect that the facts in the "warrant" were considered and found by the trier of fact. These findings make unnecessary our consideration of evidence outside of the record of conviction to determine that the victim and the respondent were in a requisite "domestic" relationship, as urged by the DHS on appeal. *See Bianco v. Holder*, 624 F.3d 265 (5th Cir. 2010); DHS's Brief at 12-13.

Accordingly, we find no cause to disturb the Immigration Judge's decision to terminate proceedings. The following order will therefore be entered.

ORDER: The appeal is dismissed.

FOR THE BOARD

4

U.S. Department of Justice

Executive Office for Immigration Review

Board of Immigration Appeals
Office of the Clerk

5107 Leesburg Pike, Suite 2000
Falls Church, Virginia 20530

Michael Christian Urbina-Pabon, Esquire
The Urbina Law Firm, LLC
P.O. BOX 70
Acworth, GA 30101

DHS/ICE Office of Chief Counsel - SDC
146 CCA Road, P.O.Box 248
Lumpkin, GA 31815

Name: ▉▉▉▉▉▉▉▉▉▉▉▉   ▉▉▉▉▉▉▉▉

Date of this notice: 3/25/2015

Enclosed is a copy of the Board's decision and order in the above-referenced case.

Sincerely,

Donna Carr

Donna Carr
Chief Clerk

Enclosure

Panel Members:
Greer, Anne J.
Pauley, Roger
Geller, Joan B

Userteam: Docket

For more unpublished BIA decisions, visit
www.irac.net/unpublished/index

Cite as: Miguel Garcia Olvera, ▉▉▉▉▉▉ (BIA March 25, 2015)

U.S. Department of Justice

Executive Office for Immigration Review

Board of Immigration Appeals
Office of the Clerk

5107 Leesburg Pike, Suite 2000
Falls Church, Virginia 20530

GARCIA OLVERA, MIGUEL

████████

STEWART DETENTION CENTER
146 CCA ROAD
P.O. BOX 248
LUMPKIN, GA 31815

DHS/ICE Office of Chief Counsel - SDC
146 CCA Road, P.O.Box 248
Lumpkin, GA 31815

Name: **GARCIA OLVERA, MIGUEL**   ████████

Date of this notice: 3/25/2015

Enclosed is a copy of the Board's decision in the above-referenced case. This copy is being provided to you as a courtesy. Your attorney or representative has been served with this decision pursuant to 8 C.F.R. § 1292.5(a). If the attached decision orders that you be removed from the United States or affirms an Immigration Judge's decision ordering that you be removed, any petition for review of the attached decision must be filed with and received by the appropriate court of appeals within 30 days of the date of the decision.

Sincerely,

Donna Carr

Donna Carr
Chief Clerk

Enclosure

Panel Members:
Greer, Anne J.
Pauley, Roger
Geller, Joan B

Userteam:

U.S. Department of Justice
Executive Office for Immigration Review

Decision of the Board of Immigration Appeals

Falls Church, Virginia 20530

File: ▓▓▓▓▓▓▓ – Lumpkin, GA

Date:

In re: MIGUEL GARCIA OLVERA

MAR 2 5 2015

IN REMOVAL PROCEEDINGS

APPEAL

ON BEHALF OF RESPONDENT: Michael Christian Urbina-Pabon, Esquire

ON BEHALF OF DHS: Fayaz Habib
                         Assistant Chief Counsel

CHARGE:

Notice: Sec.   237(a)(2)(A)(iii), I&N Act [8 U.S.C. § 1227(a)(2)(A)(iii)] -
                 Convicted of aggravated felony

APPLICATION: Termination

    The respondent appeals from an Immigration Judge's December 3, 2014, decision ordering him removed from the United States. The Department of Homeland Security ("DHS") opposes the appeal. The appeal will be sustained and the removal proceedings will be terminated.

    The respondent is a native and citizen of Mexico and a lawful permanent resident of the United States. In 1999 the respondent was convicted in North Carolina of possessing marijuana with intent to manufacture, sell, or deliver, a felony violation of section 90-95(a)(1) of the North Carolina General Statutes (hereinafter "§ 90-95(a)(1)") for which he was sentenced to an indeterminate term of imprisonment of 4-6 months. The question on appeal is whether that conviction renders the respondent removable under section 237(a)(2)(A)(iii) of the Immigration and Nationality Act, 8 U.S.C. § 1227(a)(2)(A)(iii), as an alien convicted of an "aggravated felony." Upon de novo review, we conclude that it does not.

    The term "aggravated felony" is defined to include "illicit trafficking in a controlled substance (as defined in section 802 of Title 21), including a drug trafficking crime (as defined in section 924(c) of Title 18)." Section 101(a)(43)(B) of the Act, 8 U.S.C. § 1101(a)(43)(B). The phrase "illicit trafficking" refers to "any state, federal, or qualified foreign felony conviction involving the unlawful trading or dealing" in a controlled substance as defined by Federal law. *Matter of L-G-H-*, 26 I&N Dec. 365, 368 (BIA 2014) (citations omitted). However, an offense that does not involve unlawful "trading or dealing" within the meaning of the "illicit trafficking" concept may nonetheless qualify as an aggravated felony if it is a "drug trafficking crime" under 18 U.S.C. § 924(c); that is, a felony punishable under the Federal Controlled Substances Act ("CSA"), 21 U.S.C. § 802 et seq. A state drug offense qualifies as a "drug trafficking crime" only if it corresponds categorically to an offense punishable by a maximum term of imprisonment of more than 1 year under the CSA. *Moncrieffe v. Holder*, 133 S. Ct. 1678, 1683 (2013).

In 1999, when the respondent committed his offense and sustained his conviction, § 90-95(a)(1) provided that "it is unlawful for any person … [t]o manufacture, sell or deliver, or possess with intent to manufacture, sell or deliver, a controlled substance." According to the North Carolina Supreme Court, § 90-95(a)(1) establishes three distinct offenses: "(1) manufacture of a controlled substance, (2) transfer of a controlled substance by sale or delivery, and (3) possession with intent to manufacture, sell or deliver a controlled substance." *State v. Moore*, 395 S.E.2d 124, 126 (N.C. 1990). A "sale" is defined as "a transfer of property for a specified price payable in money" while a delivery is "the actual [sic] constructive, or attempted transfer from one person to another of a controlled substance[.]" *Id.* at 382, 395 S.E.2d at 127 (citations and quotations omitted).

In 1999, violations of § 90-95(a)(1) carried different maximum sentences depending upon the identity of the substance involved and the nature of the underlying offense conduct. A violation of § 90-95(a)(1) involving a remunerative "sale" of marijuana (a schedule VI controlled substance under North Carolina law) was punishable as a class H felony while a violation involving manufacture or non-remunerative "delivery" of marijuana was punishable as a class I felony, *unless* the violation involved "[t]he transfer of less than 5 grams of marijuana for no remuneration," in which case it was not to be treated as a "delivery" at all. N.C. Gen. Stat. § 90-95(b)(2) (1999). Finally, offenses involving the manufacture, sale, delivery, or possession of more than 10 pounds of marijuana were chargeable as discrete offenses under § 90-95(h) and were punished more severely than violations of § 90-95(a)(1).

To determine whether a violation of § 90-95(a)(1) qualifies as a categorical aggravated felony under section 101(a)(43)(B), we ask whether the "minimum conduct" that has a "realistic probability" of being successfully prosecuted under the statute corresponds to the "illicit trafficking" or "drug trafficking crime" definitions. *See Moncrieffe v. Holder, supra*, at 1684-85. The "minimum conduct" punishable under § 90-95(a) is possession of 5 grams of marijuana with intent to "deliver" without remuneration. The Immigration Judge found that § 90-95(a)(1) defines a categorical "drug trafficking crime" under 18 U.S.C. § 924(c) because possession of 5 grams of marijuana with the intent to deliver corresponds to conduct punishable by up to 5 years in prison under 21 U.S.C. §§ 841(a)(1) and 841(b)(1)(D). We respectfully disagree.

As the *Moncrieffe* Court determined, and as the Immigration Judge acknowledged, possession of a "small amount" of marijuana for "no remuneration" is punishable as a federal misdemeanor under 21 U.S.C. § 841(b)(4). In *Matter of Castro Rodriguez*, 25 I&N Dec. 698, 703 (BIA 2012), we noted that the phrase "small amount" was not statutorily defined but concluded that 30 grams was a "useful guidepost" for immigration cases because Congress has employed that quantity throughout the Act as a threshold for identifying which marijuana offenses should give rise to immigration consequences and which should not. According to the Immigration Judge, the 30-gram guidepost discussed in *Matter of Castro Rodriguez* was merely advisory rather than "dispositive," and thus he elected to invoke North Carolina's 5-gram threshold instead. We reverse.

It is true that the 30-gram threshold described in *Castro Rodriguez* is a guidepost rather than an inflexible standard. As federal courts interpreting 21 U.S.C. § 841(b)(4) have recognized, whether a quantity of marijuana is "small" can depend upon context—i.e., 5 grams of marijuana may not be a "small amount" if it is delivered in a prison or to a child. *See, e.g., United States v. Carmichael*, 155 F.3d 561 (4th Cir. 1998) (Table) (upholding district court's determination that 1.256 grams of marijuana is not a "small amount" under 21 U.S.C. § 841(b)(4) when distributed in a prison). Thus, we do not discount the possibility that some cases may present principled reasons for departing from *Castro Rodriguez*'s 30-gram threshold. However, the Immigration Judge identified no such principled reasons here, and thus we disagree with his decision to treat 5 grams of marijuana as a non-"small" amount.[1]

The language of § 90-95(a)(1) leaves open the possibility that defendants may be convicted for possessing 30 grams or less of marijuana with the intent to deliver without remuneration. That possibility is not dispositive of the aggravated felony question, however, because the categorical approach is concerned *not* with the minimum conduct that could theoretically be prosecuted under the statute of conviction, but rather with the minimum conduct that has a "realistic probability" of actually being successfully prosecuted thereunder. *See Moncrieffe v. Holder, supra*, at 1684-85 (explaining that "our focus on the minimum conduct criminalized by the state statute is not an invitation to apply 'legal imagination' to the state offense; there must be 'a realistic probability, not a theoretical possibility, that the State would apply its statute to conduct that falls outside the generic definition of a crime.'") (citing *Gonzales v. Duenas-Alvarez*, 549 U.S. 183, 193 (2007)).

To demonstrate the requisite "realistic probability" here, the evidence must reflect that North Carolina actually prosecutes defendants under § 90-95(a)(1) for possessing 30 grams or less of marijuana with intent to deliver. *Accord Moncrieffe v. Holder, supra*, at 1693; *Gonzales v. Duenas-Alvarez, supra*, at 193. The respondent has carried his burden of proof in that regard because in *State v. Blackburn*, 239 S.E.2d 626, 629-30 (N.C. Ct. App. 1977), the North Carolina Court of Appeals upheld a § 90-95(a)(1) conviction in which the jury found that the defendant possessed 14 grams of marijuana with intent to deliver. As the minimum conduct that has a realistic probability of being successfully prosecuted under § 90-95(a)(1) is possession of less than 30 grams of marijuana with the intent to deliver without remuneration, that offense corresponds categorically to the federal misdemeanor offense described in 21 U.S.C. § 841(b)(4),

---

[1] Although *Moncrieffe* did not adopt a test for evaluating whether or not a particular amount of marijuana is "small" within the meaning of 21 U.S.C. § 841(b)(4), the Supreme Court's decision does provide some guidance on the question. Specifically, in support of its determination that Mr. Moncrieffe's statute of conviction—Ga. Code § 16-13-30(j)(1)—encompassed the distribution of "small amounts" of marijuana, the Court relied upon *Taylor v. State*, 581 S.E.2d 386, 388 (Ga. App. Ct. 2003), in which a defendant was convicted for possessing 6.6 grams of marijuana with intent to distribute. *See Moncrieffe v. Holder, supra*, at 1686. The *Moncrieffe* Court's determination that 6.6 grams of marijuana is a "small amount" is irreconcilable with the Immigration Judge's determination that 5 grams is not.

3

which in turn means that it is not a categorical aggravated felony.[2] The Immigration Judge's contrary determination will be reversed.

Having determined that § 90-95(a)(1) does not define a categorical aggravated felony under section 101(a)(43)(B) of the Act, we now turn to the separate question whether § 90-95(a)(1) is "divisible" vis-à-vis the aggravated felony definition, such that the Immigration Judge may conduct a "modified categorical" inquiry into the respondent's conviction records to determine whether his particular conviction was for possession of more than 30 grams of marijuana with intent to deliver. According to the United States Court of Appeals for the Eleventh Circuit, in whose jurisdiction this case arises, "a divisible statute is one that 'sets out one or more elements of the offense in the alternative'" and in which at least one (but not all) of those alternative elements (or sets of elements) categorically matches the "generic" federal offense to which it must correspond. *United States v. Estrella*, 758 F.3d 1239, 1244-45 (11th Cir. 2014) (quoting in part *Descamps v. United States*, 133 S. Ct. 2276, 2281, 2283 (2013)).

Section 90-95(a)(1) is phrased in the disjunctive, defining three discrete offenses: (1) manufacture of a controlled substance, (2) transfer of a controlled substance by sale or delivery, and (3) possession with intent to manufacture, sell or deliver a controlled substance. *State v. Moore*, 395 S.E.2d 124, 126 (N.C. 1990). The first alternative defined by § 90-95(a)(1), i.e., "manufacturing" a controlled substance, may well correspond categorically to the analogous federal felony offense defined under 21 U.S.C. § 841(a)(1). However, the second and third alternatives defined by § 90-95(a)(1) do not correspond categorically to federal felonies because of their potential applicability to offenses involving distribution (or possession with intent to distribute) small amounts of marijuana for no remuneration. Under the circumstances, we conclude that it would be permissible for the Immigration Judge to conduct a modified categorical inquiry in order to determine which of the three alternative offenses the respondent was convicted of committing. As it is undisputed that the respondent was convicted of possession of marijuana with intent to deliver rather than manufacturing, such a modified categorical inquiry would not establish the respondent's removability.

Section 90-95(b)(2) also contains language which arguably makes § 90-95(a)(1) divisible. Specifically, by establishing that a transfer of less than 5 grams of marijuana for no remuneration does not qualify as a "delivery," § 90-95(b)(2) could be viewed as effectively adding a minimum quantity "element" to any marijuana "delivery" charge; that is, a North Carolina prosecutor who charges a defendant with violating § 90-95(a)(1) on the basis of a non-remunerative "delivery" of marijuana would need to prove to the jury beyond a reasonable doubt that the transfer involved 5 grams or more of marijuana. *See State v. Land*, 733 S.E.2d 588, 592 (N.C. Ct. App. 2012), *aff'd*, 742 S.E.2d 803 (2013) (explaining that "the State can, under … § 90–95(b)(2), prove

_____

[2] As § 90-95(a) encompasses the non-remunerative delivery of marijuana, moreover, it is not an "illicit trafficking" offense under section 101(a)(43)(B). *See Matter of L-G-H-, supra*, at 371-72 & n. 9 (explaining that "to meet the definition of 'illicit trafficking under the Act, the offense must involve a commercial transaction," i.e., a "passing of goods from one person to another for money or other consideration.")

4

delivery of marijuana by presenting evidence *either* (1) of a transfer of five or more grams of marijuana, or (2) of a transfer of less than five grams of marijuana for remuneration.").

The existence of such a minimum quantity element would not make § 90-95(a)(1) divisible vis-à-vis section 101(a)(43)(B), however, because for the reasons stated in *Moncrieffe* not all offenses involving possession of 5 grams or more of marijuana with intent to deliver would correspond to federal felonies under the CSA. Although a North Carolina jury may sometimes need to agree that a defendant delivered 5 grams or more of marijuana, it would never need to agree about the extent to which the amount exceeded 5 grams, nor would it need to find that the amount exceeded 30 grams—the default "small amount" threshold for immigration cases.

In view of the foregoing, we conclude that § 90-95(a)(1) is neither a categorical aggravated felony under section 101(a)(43)(B) nor divisible in any manner which would serve to support the respondent's removability. Accordingly, the removal charge under section 237(a)(2)(A)(iii) of the Act will be dismissed. The DHS has not lodged any other removal charges against the respondent, moreover, and therefore the removal proceedings will be terminated.

ORDER: The appeal is sustained and the removal proceedings are terminated.

FOR THE BOARD

U.S. Department of Justice

Executive Office for Immigration Review

Board of Immigration Appeals
Office of the Clerk

5107 Leesburg Pike, Suite 2000
Falls Church, Virginia 20530

Winograd, Benjamin Ross
Immigrant & Refugee Appellate Center
3602 Forest Drive
Alexandria, VA 22302

DHS/ICE Office of Chief Counsel - ATL
180 Spring Street, Suite 332
Atlanta, GA 30303

Name: B█████-B████████, V█████ M█ ...   A█████████723

Date of this notice: 3/27/2015

Enclosed is a copy of the Board's decision and order in the above-referenced case.

Sincerely,

Donna Carr

Donna Carr
Chief Clerk

Enclosure

Panel Members:
Greer, Anne J.
Pauley, Roger
Guendelsberger, John

TranC
Userteam: Docket

For more unpublished BIA decisions, visit
www.irac.net/unpublished/index

U.S. Department of Justice
Executive Office for Immigration Review

Decision of the Board of Immigration Appeals

Falls Church, Virginia 20530

File: ████ ██ 723 – Atlanta, GA   Date: MAR 2 7 2015

In re: V██████ ██████████ B██████ -B████████

IN REMOVAL PROCEEDINGS

APPEAL

ON BEHALF OF RESPONDENT: Ben Winograd, Esquire[1]

ON BEHALF OF DHS: Gene P. Hamilton
                           Assistant Chief Counsel

CHARGE:

> Notice: Sec. 237(a)(2)(A)(iii), I&N Act [8 U.S.C. § 1227(a)(2)(A)(iii)] -
> Convicted of aggravated felony (illicit trafficking offense)
>
> Sec. 237(a)(2)(A)(iii), I&N Act [8 U.S.C. § 1227(a)(2)(A)(iii)] -
> Convicted of aggravated felony (attempt or conspiracy offense)
>
> Lodged: Sec. 237(a)(2)(B)(i), I&N Act [8 U.S.C. § 1227(a)(2)(B)(i)] -
> Convicted of controlled substance violation

APPLICATION: Cancellation of removal

The Department of Homeland Security (DHS) appeals from the decision of the Immigration Judge, dated March 5, 2014, finding the respondent removable on the lodged charge, and granting the respondent's application for cancellation of removal under section 240A(a) of the Immigration and Nationality Act, 8 U.S.C. § 1229b(a), in the exercise of discretion (I.J. at 4-7).[2] The respondent, a native and citizen of Venezuela, opposes the appeal, which will be dismissed. The record will be remanded to permit DHS to conduct the necessary background and security checks.

The Immigration Judge held that DHS carried its burden of proof to show that the respondent was removable under section 237(a)(2)(B)(i) of the Act, 8 U.S.C. § 1227(a)(2)(B)(i), but that it had not done so with respect to the charges under section 237(a)(2)(A)(iii) of the Act (I.J. at 1-4).

---

[1] We acknowledge and appreciate the pro bono representation of counsel before us in this case.

[2] The Immigration Judge also denied the respondent's applications for asylum, withholding of removal, and protection under the Convention Against Torture, which we need not address given our disposition of the case (I.J. at 7-8).

The Immigration Judge granted cancellation of removal, concluding the respondent was statutorily eligible for such relief, and that a grant was warranted in discretion (I.J. at 4-7).

On appeal, DHS argues that it established the respondent's removability under section 237(a)(2)(A)(iii) of the Act by clear and convincing evidence, asserting the respondent's conviction was for an aggravated felony as defined by section 101(a)(43)(B) or (U) of the Act, 8 U.S.C. §§ 1101(a)(43)(B), (U), and that the respondent is therefore statutorily ineligible for cancellation of removal (DHS Br. at 9-22). In the alternative, DHS argues the Immigration Judge should have denied cancellation of removal in the exercise of discretion (DHS Br. 22-27). DHS also argues the Immigration Judge erred in denying its motion to reconsider in which it asserted the "stop-time" rule at section 240A(d) of the Act rendered the respondent ineligible for cancellation of removal (DHS Br. at 27-37).[3]

In opposition, the respondent asserts the Immigration Judge's decision to grant cancellation of removal should be sustained. He argues the Immigration Judge correctly held that he was not convicted of an aggravated felony as defined in section 101(a)(43)(B) of the Act, asserting his conviction was not categorically for an aggravated felony, and that DHS did not show the statute is divisible. He further asserts that, even applying the modified categorical approach, the record of conviction does not establish the conviction was for an aggravated felony (Resp't Br. at 9-20). The respondent also argues the Immigration Judge correctly determined he merits a favorable exercise of discretion (Resp't Br. at 20-26).

On review, we agree with the Immigration Judge that DHS did not show that the respondent's 2011 conviction for trafficking in cocaine in violation of N.C. GEN. STAT. § 90-95(h)(3) was categorically for an aggravated felony as defined in section 101(a)(43)(B) or (U) of the Act, because the statute only requires that an individual possess cocaine, and that DHS did not show that the modified categorical approach was applicable to this determination, because the statute is overbroad rather than divisible (I.J. at 2-4).

With respect to the categorical approach, DHS asserts that the aggravated felony of "illicit trafficking in a controlled substance" defined in section 101(a)(43)(B) of the Act includes other subsets of crimes in addition to "drug trafficking crimes," and, citing *Matter of Davis*, 20 I&N Dec. 536 (BIA 1992), that the Board has stated that other crimes fall within the "illicit trafficking" definition if they are a felony under state law, involve "unlawful trading and dealing," and involve a federally controlled substance (DHS Br. at 9-22). DHS argues that all

---

[3] In its appeal brief, DHS asserts that it simultaneously filed two Notices of Appeal, one pertaining to an appeal from the Immigration Judge's March 5, 2014, merits decision, and one pertaining to the Immigration Judge's March 18, 2014, motion decision, but that the Board only issued one briefing schedule (DHS Br. at 1, 8). Upon review, however, we find the record does not reflect that an appeal was filed from the March 18, 2014, motion decision. Accordingly, we agree with the respondent that the March 18, 2014, denial of the DHS' motion for reconsideration is not properly before us because the DHS has not separately appealed from that decision (Resp't Br. at 26-27). *See Matter of G-A-*, 23 I&N Dec. 366, 367 n.1 (BIA 2002).

723

conduct that can be prosecuted under N.C. GEN. STAT. § 90-95(h)(3) satisfies all three requirements, including the requirement that the offense involve "unlawful trading and dealing," because the "statutory scheme infers an intent to traffic from the large quantity of cocaine" (DHS Br. at 14-15).

We agree with the Immigration Judge and the respondent that the statute of conviction is not categorically an aggravated felony. As the Immigration Judge held and as the respondent argues, N.C. GEN. STAT. § 90-95(h)(3) criminalizes simple possession of 28 grams or more of cocaine, which does not involve the element of illicit trafficking, and which is not a felony under the Controlled Substances Act (I.J. at 2-4; Resp't Br. at 9-11). As the respondent asserts, the relevant inquiry is not whether the statute "infers an intent to traffic" (DHS Br. at 14-15), but what the conviction necessarily entails. The United States Court of Appeals for the Fourth Circuit has held that not all violations of this statute involve such an "intent to distribute." *See United States v. Brandon*, 247 F.3d 186, 195 (4th Cir. 2001) ("[I]t cannot fairly be said that an intent to distribute is inherent in all violations of N.C. GEN. STAT. § 90–95(h)."). Moreover, DHS conceded below that the offense was not categorically an aggravated felony (Tr. at 17-18). Finally, as the respondent asserts, simple possession is a misdemeanor and not a felony under the Controlled Substances Act. *See Lopez v. Gonzales*, 549 U.S. 47, 60 (2006).

With respect to the modified categorical approach, DHS argues that, even if not all conduct covered under the statute satisfies *Matter of Davis*, the statute "is clearly divisible because it is drafted in the alternative" (DHS Br. at 15 n.9). DHS asserts that the modified categorical approach shows the respondent's offense involved at least 400 grams of cocaine, which "evinces an intent to distribute" under state law, notwithstanding *United States v. Brandon, supra* (DHS Br. at 16-19). Further, DHS argues the offense constitutes a "drug trafficking crime" as defined in 18 U.S.C. § 924(c) because the offense would have been penalized under the distribution rather than the simple possession provisions of the Controlled Substances Act, although the state statute does not have a mens rea element (DHS Br. at 20-22).

We also agree with the Immigration Judge and the respondent that the statute of conviction is overbroad and indivisible. As the respondent asserts, DHS did not produce authority establishing that the statute contains alternative elements upon which a jury must unanimously agree in order to convict, rather than alternative means of committing the offense (Resp't Br. at 11-12). *See Descamps v. United States*, 133 S.Ct. 2276 (2013); *Matter of Chairez (Chairez I)*, 26 I&N Dec. 349 (BIA 2014).[4] Further, to the extent DHS argues the amount of cocaine at issue

---

[4] The Board recently issued a new decision in *Matter of Chairez (Chairez II)*, 26 I&N Dec. 478 (BIA 2015), in which we observed that, because Immigration Judges must follow the law of the circuit court of appeals in whose jurisdiction they sit in evaluating issues of divisibility, the interpretation of *Descamps v. United States*, 133 S.Ct. 2276 (2013), reflected in *Matter of Chairez*, 26 I&N Dec. 349 (BIA 2014), applies only insofar as there is no controlling authority to the contrary in the relevant circuit. In *United States v. Estrella*, the Eleventh Circuit agreed with the Board's jury unanimity approach. 758 F.3d 1239, 1245-46 (11th Cir. 2014) ("[I]f the statutory scheme is not such that it would typically require the jury to agree to convict on the
(continued...)

"evinces an intent to distribute," we observe that such an inference would not satisfy the requirement that a jury unanimously "agree to convict on the basis of one alternative as opposed to the other." *See United States v. Estrella*, 758 F.3d 1239, 1245-46 (11th Cir. 2014). Accordingly, we agree with the Immigration Judge that the 2011 conviction did not render the respondent removable under section 237(a)(2)(A)(iii) of the Act or ineligible for cancellation of removal under section 240A(b)(1)(C) of the Act.

We are also not persuaded by DHS's appellate contention that the Immigration Judge should have denied the respondent's application for cancellation of removal under section 240A(a) of the Act in the exercise of discretion (DHS Br. 22-27). DHS argues the Immigration Judge did not properly balance the relevant factors, asserting that the Immigration Judge should have required additional corroboration, should have found that the respondent's conviction was for a "serious crime," and should not have found that the respondent demonstrated rehabilitation.

In exercising discretion, an Immigration Judge, upon review of the record as a whole, "must balance the adverse factors evidencing the alien's undesirability as a permanent resident with the social and humane considerations presented in his (or her) behalf to determine whether the granting of...relief appears in the best interest of this country." *Matter of C-V-T-*, 22 I&N Dec. 7, 11 (BIA 1998) (holding that the general standards developed in *Matter of Marin*, 16 I&N Dec. 581, 584-85 (BIA 1978), for the exercise of discretion under section 212(c) of the Act, 8 U.S.C. § 1182(c), are applicable to the exercise of discretion under section 240A(a) of the Act)).

Favorable considerations include such factors as family ties within the United States, residence of long duration in this country (particularly when the inception of residence occurred at a young age), evidence of hardship to the respondent and his family if removal occurs, service in this country's armed forces, a history of employment, the existence of property or business ties, evidence of value and service to the community, proof of genuine rehabilitation if a criminal record exists, and other evidence attesting to a respondent's good character. *Id.* Adverse factors include the nature and underlying circumstances of the grounds of removal that are at issue, the presence of additional significant violations of this country's immigration laws, the existence of a criminal record and, if so, its nature, recency, and seriousness, and the presence of other evidence indicative of a respondent's bad character or undesirability as a permanent resident of this country. *Id.*

The Immigration Judge weighed the respondent's criminal history against his positive equities and decided to grant cancellation of removal (I.J. at 4-7). The Immigration Judge found that the respondent's credible testimony demonstrated that his positive equities include the respondent's family ties (i.e., he lives with his mother, a United States citizen), his lengthy residence in the United States (i.e., he has been a lawful permanent resident for over 14 years), hardship his removal would cause his family (i.e., his mother who has had a kidney transplant

---

(...continued)

basis of one alternative as opposed to the other, then the statute is not divisible in the sense required to justify invocation of the modified categorical approach.").

4

and is unable to work), his positive work history and filing of income taxes, that he performs community service and attends a church on a regular basis, and that he does not have any family members in his home country of Venezuela.

We have no wish to minimize the seriousness of the respondent's criminal record. It includes convictions for obtaining property by false pretenses and for possessing cocaine. The respondent was sentenced to 44 to 62 months' imprisonment for the drug conviction. We agree, however, with the Immigration Judge's assessment that the respondent's serious criminal history is offset by his strong equities and rehabilitation, since he has taken responsibility for the offense and provided assistance to the government.[5]

We find this is a close case, but in balancing the respondent's adverse factors against his positive equities, we conclude that one final chance to remain with his family is warranted in this case. *See Matter of C-V-T-*, 22 I&N Dec. 7 (BIA 1988); *see also* section 240A(c)(6) of the Act (providing that cancellation of removal can only be granted once). The DHS's appeal will be dismissed, and the record will be remanded to allow DHS to perform the necessary background investigation. The following orders shall be issued.

ORDER: The DHS's appeal is dismissed.

FURTHER ORDER: Pursuant to 8 C.F.R. § 1003.1(d)(6), the record is remanded to the Immigration Judge for the purpose of allowing the Department of Homeland Security the opportunity to complete or update identity, law enforcement, or security investigations or examinations, and further proceedings, if necessary, and for the entry of an order as provided by 8 C.F.R. § 1003.47(h).

_____
FOR THE BOARD

Board Member Roger A. Pauley respectfully dissents and would deny cancellation of removal in the exercise of discretion in light of the respondent's serious criminal record.

---

[5] We are not persuaded by DHS's assertion that *Matter of Y-L-, A-G-, & R-S-R-*, 23 I&N Dec. 270 (A.G. 2002), informs the instant analysis, especially given that we agree with the Immigration Judge that the conviction was not an illicit trafficking aggravated felony and, moreover, that the respondent's eligibility for withholding of removal is not at issue.